PRAISE FOR
THE GLORY FIELD
BY WALTER DEAN MYERS:

"A stunning novel about the perseverance and courage of one African-American family from the author of the award-winning *Somewhere in the Darkness*. . . . In this fluid, simple book, Myers brings to life an entire history of a people, highlighting the Lewis family's commitment and strength. A must read for absolutely everyone."
— *Kirkus Reviews*, pointed review

"Spanning nearly 250 years of African-American history, this emotionally charged saga of the Lewis family traces an ongoing battle for freedom and equality. . . . Myers . . . illuminates shadowy corners of history and reveals the high cost — and the excruciatingly slow process — of justice. The obstacles facing the Lewis family will be remembered as clearly as their triumphs. . . ."
— *Publishers Weekly*, starred review

"This wonderful book takes the reader on a . . . journey, crossing miles and generations. . . . This is a lovely book about a strong family that overcomes incredible hardship." — *USA Today*

". . . a grand, impressive sweep of a book. . . ."
— *Detroit Free Press*

". . . worth every minute of reading. . . . a thorough and unforgettable story of one family that survives despite many obstacles."
— *Chicago Tribune*

THE GLORY FIELD

Walter Dean Myers

SCHOLASTIC INC.
New York Toronto London Auckland Sydney

No part of this publication may be reproduced in whole or in part, or stored in a retrieval system, or transmitted in any form or by any means, electronic, mechanical, photocopying, recording, or otherwise, without written permission of the publisher. For information regarding permission, write to Scholastic Inc., 555 Broadway, New York, NY 10012.

ISBN 0-590-45898-1

24 23 22 21 20 19 18 17 16 15 14   2/0

Printed in the U.S.A.   01

THE
GLORY FIELD

THE LEWIS FAMILY

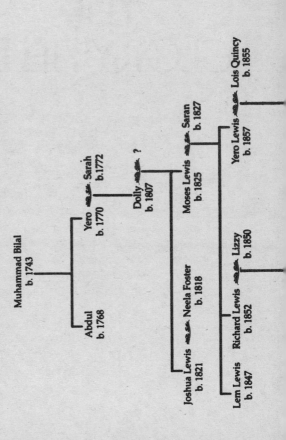

Muhammad Bilal
b. 1743

Abdul
b. 1768

Yero
b. 1770 ❤ Sarah
b.1772

Dolly ❤ ?
b. 1807

Joshua Lewis
b. 1821 ❤ Neela Foster
b. 1818

Moses Lewis
b. 1825 ❤ Saran
b. 1827

Lem Lewis
b. 1847

Richard Lewis
b. 1852 ❤ Lizzy
b. 1850

Yero Lewis
b. 1857 ❤ Lois Quincy
b. 1855

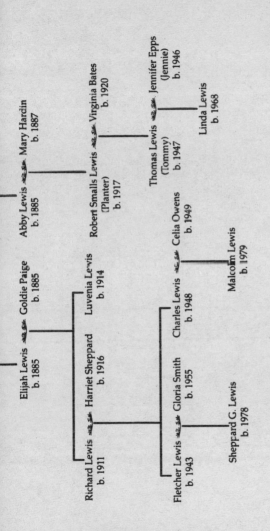

JULY 1753,
OFF THE COAST
OF SIERRA LEONE,
WEST AFRICA

Eleven-year-old Muhammad Bilal flinched. The sore on his ankle rubbed against the iron shackle that held him, sending shivers of pain up his thin leg. He pushed his foot closer to the wooden board to which he was fastened and tried to shift his body. The man chained next to him made a noise, it sounded almost like a hoarse bark, and Muhammad knew the man's throat must have pained from lack of water. He looked at the small square of light slanting through the grating a few feet from him. Particles of dust floated in the heavy air, as if suspended in the stifling heat that rose from the bowels of the ship, and from the bowels of the dark creatures within its hold. In the days when he had first been brought on the ship, a small knot of men had forced their way beneath the hatch opening so that they could suck in the occasional breeze. He remembered seeing how their black faces strained upward toward the deck of the rolling ship. He wondered if they were warriors, or traders, or like him, the sons of farmers. Their faces, like ebony masks edged in gold, were lit by the sun. Their arms, their bodies, their dreams, lay in the darkness below.

The ship rocked gently in its mooring for eighteen days, and for eighteen days more and more men and young boys were dragged down into the dark hold. There was no room to move, to stretch aching muscles, even to lift a sore hip or elbow from the hard wood of the ship. On the nineteenth day the ship moved. First it lurched, then it rolled, the boards creaking and groaning like the bellowing of some dying beast. By the twenty-third day the first man on board the ship had died.

Muhammad's thoughts kept going back to the day he was captured. They had been warned about the men without color who were taking people away. But it was the people from beyond the mountain who had attacked his village. He thought they spoke a Mande language, but it was a different accent than he knew. Others said that though they were black, they were dead men who had sold their souls.

Muhammad remembered having his arms wrenched behind him and tied and then being put into a line with other boys his age. A rope was put around his neck and tied to a long pole. His friend Abdul was with him, and Kwesi. He did not cry out or weep. If he was to die, it would be like a warrior, he told himself. He did not cry out, but his heart betrayed him, pounding in his chest when he was put into the pens and later when he was put into one of the small boats and taken out to the ship. He had heard of people who sacrificed their prisoners, using the blood to appease their gods.

He prayed.

The pale men on the ships were frightful, most of them thin and poorly built. Several of them looked sick. Kaiman, the son of a healer from Muhammad's village, refused to go into the hole they pushed him toward. With his arms still tied behind his back, the proud youth was beaten on the legs and shoulders with clubs until, bruised and bloody, he crawled into the hold. The seamen pointed their boomsticks toward the sky and made them boom. One by one the captives were pushed below deck where others were waiting to chain them down. When it came his turn, Muhammad felt the terror swell in his chest and fill his throat. It was all he could do not to scream out as he was pushed roughly against another man.

Men tore at their bindings, ripping the skin from their wrists as they pulled themselves toward the grating.

He had never been trapped like this before; never had anything hold him captive. He wondered about those who had already died, wondered if the long march to the ships had killed them, or the beatings, or if it had been something from within. As he wondered, the sea pounded against the rolling ship, and the boards of the ship groaned in complaint. He closed his eyes and looked into himself and tried to speak, but no sound came. He gathered what moisture he could from his parched throat, licked his lips, and whispered a vow to himself that he would live.

Sometimes the older men would cry out in their sleep as they tried to ease the sores that came from lying in one position too long. But there was no place to turn, no room to move in their prison.

There were men from many different peoples chained together. Those who, like himself, were followers of Islam often prayed. Some talked about what might become of them. Most of them thought they would be killed, and a foolish boy even thought he would be eaten by the white men. Muhammad did not think he would be eaten. He did not want to think of what would happen to him.

The second man and the third died on the same day.

Sometimes, if he held his knees high, the shackles would not rub against the raw spots on his ankles. And for this he thanked Allah.

They were fed once a day. And given water twice a day, in the mornings and just before sunset. A small, wide man with few teeth came down and gave each a drink from a cup he dipped into a bucket. Some men tried to bite him, and he would kick them and not give them water.

He thought of Saran, his mother, and of Odebe, his father. He did not know if they were alive or dead, if the screams he heard on that dark night had come from their sweet lips. At first they filled his mind each day. Now he saw their faces, their eyes, the hands that would say so much to him with a touch. He thought of his mother thinking of him, wondering where he was, and his eyes filled with tears.

In the ship's hold, he heard men from near his home and from far away. And, when he was taken on deck to jump around as he was told, he saw that there were women on the ship as well. The few moments each day on deck were a small joy that made the darkness of the hold even worse. From the deck of the ship there was nothing to be seen but water. Muhammad looked about, hoping to glimpse a tree or a mountain, or even some small piece of earth in the distance. But there were only clouds, drifting white beasts in the cold and distant sky, and the endless sea. He remembered stories of Abu Bakir, the king who had sailed from Mali, who had challenged the sea and was never heard from again. But if the sights from the deck were confusing, the hold was truly terrifying.

For it was Death itself that crowded into the hold with them. Death that nestled in the darkness next to them, his stench choking and crushing them, that mocked them, that gnawed at their feet so they could not sleep. And, in the darkness, that took them quietly away.

By the end of the first month all that filled Muhammad's mind was the effort to breathe. He fought against death from breath to breath, trying always to fill his lungs for the next minute of life, trying to ease the pain of the shackles around his legs, trying to think forward to an ending of his torment, trying to think of being free again.

MARCH 1864,
LIVE OAKS PLANTATION,
CURRY ISLAND,
SOUTH CAROLINA

THE LEWIS FAMILY. 1864

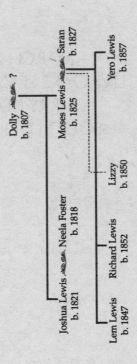

Dolly ❧❧ ?
b. 1807

Joshua Lewis ❧❧ Neela Foster
b. 1821   b. 1818

Moses Lewis ❧❧ Saran
b. 1825   b. 1827

Lem Lewis
b. 1847

Richard Lewis
b. 1852

Lizzy
b. 1850

Yero Lewis
b. 1857

They were up early. The sun had not yet burned the dew off the well-kept lawns of Live Oaks, and Lizzy's bare feet and ankles were wet as she headed toward the fields. Moses led them into the fields as usual, with Mister Joe Haynes, the overseer, a few feet behind him on his horse. Usually, when they went into the fields in the mornings, Moses or somebody would have started a song, something to get them going. But this morning was different. It was the first time that they had been taken into the field on a Sunday in over a year. But it wasn't the crops that were on their minds, or on Mister Joe Haynes's mind, either.

Mister Joe Haynes took them around the field, spitting on the ground where he wanted them to work. He had Moses and the other men in the middle of the field and the women and the children along the edges. Mister Joe Haynes sat under an oak, his dark hat slouched over his eyes, his rifle across his lap, watching them. Watching Moses in particular.

Lizzy didn't care about the work, or even about being in the field on a Sabbath day. Her mind was with Joshua and Lem. When she could, she looked over to where Moses bent over the crop, weeding, tending to the banks of sweet potatoes that were going to be for the use of old man Lewis and his family. Moses looked for all the world as if he didn't have a care in the world. But everybody knew that it was his son, Lem, and his brother, Joshua, who had run off. They had seen the riders gather the night before, tall men used to horses, used to hunting runaway Negroes.

The day went on forever. The sun stayed high. On the far edge of the field blackbirds sat on the top rail of the fence in small groups as if they, too, were waiting. It was hard for Lizzy to keep her head down. It was as if the road leading down toward the creek were drawing her eyes. Once in a while she looked back toward the twin rows of live oaks that formed a boulevard over the brick path leading to the front of the big house. She didn't think that if Joshua and Lem were caught they would bring them back that way. Old Master Lewis didn't allow any poor whites coming down the big road; they had to come around the back road the same as the black folks did. And that's who had come to Live Oaks, the poor white folks who made up the patrollers. There weren't but a few of them left; the rest had gone off to fight in the war.

Joshua was a full-grown man and strapping,

too. He was married to Neela, and they were a
fine-looking couple. Neela was from the Foster
place, a mile and a half down the road. She was
pretty, black as a berry, and with the prettiest
smile that Lizzy had ever seen. Joshua had met
her at a corn-shucking at the Foster place and
had gone sweet on her. She had gone sweet on
him, too, and after a year he had asked Old
Master Lewis if he could marry her. Master
Lewis went over to the Foster place and asked
Mister Foster, who had said yes if they could
split up the children.

Old Master Lewis didn't want to do that and
knew that Joshua wouldn't want to, either. The
thing was that Mister Foster wanted to sell Neela
and wanted a good piece of money for her.
That's what Master Lewis told Joshua. So they
never got married in the big house the way some
of the people on Live Oaks did. Instead they
waited until Neela could come over to Live Oaks
one night, and she and Joshua went to the
ground where Muhammad had been buried, and
where they named all the newborn children so
that the young could find direction from the elders; and there they stood and offered prayer
and confessed that they loved one another and
would from that day on. It had been a cold, rainy
night in April when they stood holding hands
and turning their faces toward the stars, but
a warm breeze came up and touched them. It
touched the broad shoulders of Joshua and dried
Neela's nervous tears, and Saran had said that

it was a blessing sent by Muhammad.

The ground seemed harder, seemed not to want to turn as they moved down the long rows. Suddenly the still of the warm air was broken by a single, plaintive note. It went higher, breaking into a different pitch, and then went even higher. Mister Joe Haynes jumped up and grabbed his rifle.

The note came down, picking up substance, broadening, stretching from person to person. A hoe hit the ground, and again, and then another hoe caught its rhythm.

"Sooner in the morning when I rise . . ." The song filled the field, calling to no one and everyone at the same time.

And there was an answer.

". . . The young lambs must find the way."
"With crosses and trials on every side . . ."
". . . The young lambs must find the way."

Across the field there were hoofbeats, and Lizzy looked up and saw Mister Joe Haynes riding across the edge of the field. She looked to see where he was going, and there, silhouetted against the sky, were some riders. There were four of them, and from where she stood Lizzy could see that they had somebody tied behind one of the horses. He was running along after them, falling down, being dragged for a while, and trying to get up the best he could. The dark figure, even a half a mile away, was too small to be Joshua. The song had been right. It was Lem.

Lem was Moses' boy. He was sixteen, three years older than Lizzy, and small, but tightly built. He had dark, quick eyes and a crooked smile that everybody liked, especially Lizzy.

She knew why Joshua had run away. He had gotten word that Mister Foster was going to have a sale of some of his people, and he figured that Neela would be sold. She didn't know why Lem had run away. Lem always did things that were different. His grandma, Dolly, said that he was like her grandfather. He was one of the first blacks that the Lewis family had bought. He had worked in the fields with the family and together they had built up the Lewis plantation.

"But every morning he would get up and say, 'I am a man!' " Grandma Dolly used to tell the children in the days before they were old enough to go into the fields. " 'I am a man!' "

When Mister Joe Haynes reached the figures in the field, he stopped his horse. He rode around Lem and leaned down and said something to him. Then he straightened up on his horse and pointed toward the big house.

When Mister Joe Haynes had finished with the riders, he came back and blew the horn for everybody to line up and start back to the quarters. It was already late in the day.

They walked briskly back, anxious to know what had happened. Moses started singing, and they all sang out with him.

"Sooner in the morning . . . when I rise . . ."

Mister Joe Haynes made a sign with his hand,

as if he wanted them to stop singing, but then he dropped it by his side.

The thing with Mister Joe Haynes was that he walked with a limp and couldn't go off to fight in the war. He told Old Master Lewis how bad he wanted to fight, how bad he wanted to kill Yankees. This was when Young Master Lewis was going off with a Georgia regiment. He looked fine in his uniform, but he wasn't going on about killing Yankees or nothing of the sort.

"Old Master Lewis said he just wanted to get it over with." Cuff worked in the big house and heard everything. "He said a lot of good boys was going to die in that war before it was over."

There were five cabins in the quarters. Two cabins stood on either side of a dirt road and a larger one was set off fifty feet down from the others at the end of the road. The larger cabin had been left over from the days when there were only five African men living at Live Oaks, and they all lived together. Now Moses lived in the larger cabin, and everyone used it as a praise house on the Sabbath and a gathering place in times of trouble. This was a time of trouble.

Lizzy found her cousin Annie, and they had some pan bread and cold greens left over from the night before. Annie went on about how she didn't understand why Joshua and Lem had run off.

"They're just gonna whip Lem something terrible!" Annie said.

"Hesh up, girl!" Lizzy gave her a cutting look.

"If you born with a taste for freedom in your mouth, you got to satisfy it," Grandma Dolly said. "And Lem and Joshua is both born with that taste. It runs in the family."

"I truly don't want to hear them old stories about no Hammad again," Annie said, sticking her lip out.

"Girl, have you lost your sense?" Grandma Dolly looked over from where she sat, braiding Cary's hair. "You been sitting in the sun so long you don't know how to talk to your elders?"

"I want to hear them," Lizzy said.

"Where's the boy?" Moses asked, speaking about his son.

"They still got him in the back." Bill was standing in the doorway, looking out toward the fields, away from the house.

"They know you looking over there," Ginny said.

"I knows that, too," Bill said, puffing on his pipe. "I knows that."

"You figure they gonna whip him?" Saran asked.

"Figure as much," Bill answered flatly. A curl of smoke went up from his pipe. "Hope that's the most of it."

"He ain't nothing but a boy." Saran was Lem's mother. The white folks all called her Sara, but her real name was Saran. "They got to take that into consideration."

Richard, Lem's brother, slid closer to his mother. Saran pulled him close, looking over at

Moses to see if he was going to say anything about her babying the boy.

"They don't got to take nothing into consideration," Moses said. "They the white folks and we's the black folks. That's all they got to take into consideration."

"Lord, Lord, Lord!" The words came from deep in Saran's bosom. There was a pot of turnip greens that had been simmering all morning, and there was a comfort to the odor that filled the small house, which took the chill off the waiting. In the soft glow of the fire Lizzy could see Saran's eyes, shining from the tears that brimmed them, wide with the strain of wondering what the white folks were going to do to Lem for running away.

"Wonder what Hammad would have done?" Lizzy asked, thinking of the African she had heard so much about.

"He would have done something," Grandma Dolly said. "He used to tell about the time he was on the other shore—

"It was a place called Bonce, or something like that," Grandma Dolly said. "It's hard to remember all what they told us. Anyhow, when he was a boy he got trapped by a Seen-Ba. That's a wild animal they don't have over here. He said he had to fight that animal with nothing but a short stick. The animal would not leave him alone and was surely trying to kill him. He said he fought that animal with all his heart and every bit of strength that was in him. When he finally killed it, he was laying down on the ground, about as close to it as I am to you. That's when the slave catchers came and got him."

"They had guns," Lizzy said, remembering what she had heard about the story.

"They moving the boy," Bill said, shifting his weight in the door. "They putting him on a horse."

"Oh, Lord, please don't let them kill him! Oh, Lord, please don't let them kill him!" Saran's voice rose and she lifted her arms to the heavens.

Moses got up and walked to the door.

"Don't do nothing foolish, Moses," Saran called out. "Maybe they just gonna whip him. Maybe that's all."

"Mister Joe Haynes!" Moses called out. "Where y'all going with my boy?"

"Don't question me, Moses," Mister Joe Haynes called back. "You should of kept your eye on him when you had the chance!"

"Don't do nothing until I talk to Old Master Lewis," Moses said. "I'll be right back."

"Haynes, you let a nigger talk to you like that?" One of the riders with the overseer half spoke, half whined the words. "That nigger needs whipping as bad as any I ever seen."

Moses started up the back path to the big house, and Mister Joe Haynes turned his horse around and galloped in front of him, brushing the big man back.

"Please, Mister Joe Haynes," Moses snatched his hat off. "Please don't hurt him bad."

"I ain't doing nothing Mister Lewis ain't told me to do," Mister Joe Haynes said. "And if you open your mouth I'll—You understand me?"

"I understands, suh," Moses said. He turned and walked back toward the cabin.

The men rode off with Mister Joe Haynes. Lem was tied to one of the horses.

"Oh, heavenly Father, look down on us to-night," Saran was praying, her thick voice even heavier than usual. "Look down on us and let us know You hear our prayers. O God, fill everybody's heart with mercy tonight—"

"Thank you, Jesus!" Grandma Dolly called out.

"Fill all our hearts with Your goodness and Your mercy and don't let sorrow touch us, sweet God."

"Amen!" Bill said softly.

"Touch them white folks, Lord!" Saran called out. "Touch 'em!"

Lizzy turned to see Saran standing in the middle of the floor, her lips bared back, fists clenched, legs apart.

"Touch 'em!"

The waiting was always the hardest. The waiting and the listening for some news, some sound of horses over the impatient chirping of the crickets, some answer to the hooting of the owls, some whispered echoes of their prayers on the spring breeze. The setting sun seemed to bring up the scent of fresh pine. The rim of the half moon was amber tinged, then silver white as the night drew on. The waiting was always the hardest. Bill stood at the door, tense, listening, every sense strained. Keeping so still, he had to remind himself to breathe.

"Here comes Miss Julia!" Bill moved away from the door, then opened it again as if it had been by chance.

"What you doing out so late, Miss Julia?" he said.

"Is Lizzy in there?" Miss Julia called to him.

"Yes, ma'am." Bill backed out of the door. "She want you, Lizzy."

Lizzy went to the door of the cabin and stood in it. Outside, Miss Julia stood fifteen feet away. She was wearing a dark shawl and carried a lamp in her hand, even though it wasn't nearly dark yet.

"Ma'am?" Lizzy tried to think if she had done anything wrong during the day.

"Lizzy, I want you to come up to the house and do some cleaning. Sara has left the kitchen in a mess, and I'm just tired of talking to her about how lazy she is!"

"Yes, ma'am," Lizzy said, knowing that Saran had never left the kitchen dirty.

"C'mon, now," Miss Julia said.

Lizzy looked at Saran and then followed Miss Julia toward the big house. She would probably have to sleep in the room with her tonight, she thought. That's what Miss Julia did, need somebody to talk to, and have her come up and do chores so she could have somebody to fuss at, and then make her sleep on the floor in her room.

The road to the back door of the big house was swept clear twice a day, and some of the men had been thinking about paving it, making it look as grand as the front pathway. All they had to do was to straighten it out so that it didn't go directly back to the quarters, and they could make a regular promenade out of it. But all that was before the war. Once the war started, all the white people talked about was how the South was winning and who they knew who had been killed.

All the white people were hoping that the South would win, and they told the blacks that they had better hope the same.

"A Yankee wouldn't a bit more mind killing you than he would a water bug," Miss Julia had told Lizzy once. "They even kill their own parents when they get old!"

Miss Julia was seventeen, four years older than Lizzy. She was pretty, and Lizzy liked to see her dressed up. Sometimes, on Sunday afternoons, they would both try on Miss Julia's clothes and promenade around the upper floor until Old Master Lewis would chase Lizzy back to the quarters. Old Master Lewis and Young Master Lewis had the same name, Manigault Lewis, except for the number on the end. When Young Master Lewis had gone off to war, Miss Julia had cornered Lizzy and made her pray to God that all Yankees dropped dead in their sleep. Lizzy had prayed it, like Miss Julia had told her, and had wondered if the Yankees felt anything that night. She knew it hadn't worked, though, because the next day news came about the Yankees still fighting in Tennessee.

"What they doing with Lem?" Lizzy asked.

"They should hang him from a fruit tree," Miss Julia said. "And they would have, too, if it hadn't been for me."

"What did you do?" Lizzy asked.

"I told them not to hang him because I knew you were sweet on him."

"Me?" Lizzy looked at Miss Julia. "I am not sweet on no boy."

"You want some tea?" Miss Julia asked.

"Okay with me," Lizzy answered.

Miss Julia dipped some water from a copper pot into a small kettle and put it on the stove. Lizzy looked around the kitchen and saw that it was spotless, as it usually was when Saran worked in it.

Miss Julia took the tin of English tea from under the cupboard and measured out two heaping teaspoons into the flowered teapot. "You like your tea with a lot of sugar in it?"

"Yes, ma'am."

"With all the troubles we've been having we sure don't need people running off like heathens!" Miss Julia said. "We just do not need people like that around."

Lizzy felt her stomach knot up. "Miss Julia, is Master Lewis going to sell Lem?" she asked.

"I don't know what they going to do with that wicked boy," Miss Julia said. "I don't think they really know, either. They are going to take him out to the woods and tie him up to a tree for

24

the night. Then in the morning, if he tells them
where Joshua—now, he's a grown man and has
got responsibility," Miss Julia interrupted herself. "What's he doing running off anyway?—If
he tells them where Joshua went off to all they
going to do is whip his hide good, which is a
lot better than he deserves."

"Suppose he don't say nothing?"

"Then I really don't know what they will do,"
Miss Julia said, checking the water. "Lizzy, what
the people down in the quarters talking about?"

"What they talking about?" Lizzy turned her
head sideways so she could see Miss Julia's face
from a different angle. "They talking about what
happened, the same as you and Master Lewis,
I guess."

"Daddy said that with all the talk about the
war and everything that y'all are getting rest-
less," Miss Julia said. The teakettle began to half
whistle and half hiss, and Miss Julia got two cups
and set them out. She poured the hot water into
the teapot and pushed one cup toward Lizzy.
"Over on the Foster place some of the people
got uppity and had to be put into the smokehouse with no water for a few days."

"Yes, ma'am."

"Lizzy, I've been good to you, haven't I?" Miss
Julia asked.

"Yes, ma'am."

"Well, if those people down in the quarters
get to talking about anything dangerous will you
let me know about it?"

"Yes, ma'am," Lizzy said.

"You know I've always thought you weren't just an ordinary hand." Miss Julia shook her head from side to side. "When this war thing gets over I'm going to buy you from Daddy, set you free, and you and me can go and live in Johnson City. Girl, you would just love Johnson City. You've been around here on Curry Island, but you haven't seen a thing until you see Johnson City. Women there get dresses down to the ground soon as they reach sixteen. It's nothing to see a Johnson City girl wearing genuine diamonds and being escorted around by two boys. And some of the Negro women are looking just as fine as the white women. Do you think we would make a fine pair walking through the streets of Johnson City with our parasols to keep the sun from our eyes?"

"If I had something good to wear I know I could look like a regular lady," Lizzy said. "Do the white ladies and the black ladies walk together in Johnson City?"

"No, but we could if we wanted to," Miss Julia said. "That's the way to live sensible. I just hope you don't get like Joshua and Lem. You think it's because they're boys that they run off like that?"

"Joshua is a grown man, Miss Julia," Lizzy said.

"It don't make a difference how old you are if you can't read," Miss Julia said. "Reading makes your mind mature. So if you don't read then your body gets stronger but your mind doesn't. Daddy says that's the biggest difference between a white person and a black person. A white person has a mature mind."

The tea was strong, stronger than Saran or anybody made it in the quarters. Lizzy liked it anyway. And she liked Miss Julia talking to her about going to Johnson City.

There was the sound of a door slamming on the second floor, followed by the sound of Master Lewis coming down the stairs. He leaned heavily on the banister, making small huffing sounds as he came down.

Miss Julia took the cup from Lizzy and put it down on the table. She giggled and put her fingers to her lips. "We're going to have to have us some tea tomorrow evening, too," she said.

"Joe Haynes is here," Master Lewis said. "Let him in and get that girl back to the quarters."

"Yes, Daddy" was all that Miss Julia said.

Mister Joe Haynes was already at the door when Lizzy opened it. "Come on in," Miss Julia said, all the time reaching around him to pat Lizzy's arm.

The door that led to the kitchen closed and Lizzy found herself in the back of the big house. The moon was bright enough to see the way, and even if it hadn't been she could have found her way in the darkness. The way between the big house and the quarters, and then from the quarters to the fields, was all she had traveled during her thirteen years.

"You find the other one?" she could hear Master Lewis's voice.

She didn't hear Mister Joe Haynes's answer but she heard Master Lewis curse.

"You got to teach them what they can do and what they can't do!" Master Lewis was saying. "Tomorrow, you take that boy and see if Foster or somebody wants him. Nobody want him, then you take him over to Oakes."

Lizzy glanced toward the kitchen door as Master Lewis's voice grew louder. Then she moved quickly down to the path toward the quarters.

When she got into the cabin, her breath was coming in fast gasps and there was a sharp pain in her side.

"Did they catch Joshua?" Saran asked.

"I don't think so," Lizzy said. "Master Lewis asked Mister Joe Haynes and I didn't hear the answer, but Master Lewis was cursing after that."

"Where's Lem?"

"He's tied to a tree out in the woods," Lizzy said. "They're going to leave him there tonight, and then Mister Joe Haynes is going to see if Foster wants him. If he don't want him, he's going to take him to Mister Oakes."

"Mister Oakes?"

When Moses pronounced the name of the slave trader, he turned and spat on the ground.

"Moses, what you going to do?" Saran asked.

Moses shook his head. "Joshua's gone, and

the boy's alive. I don't like it none, but at least he's alive."

"Oh, Moses!" Saran stood up and lifted her apron to her face. Dolly went over to her and put her arms around her.

Bill and old Cuff Green went over to Moses. Moses was a tall man, with a square black face and thick, flat lips that made his face look like somebody had carved it out of a banyan tree. Bill and Cuff weren't nearly as tall as Moses, so when Saran turned and looked him in the face she was looking right over their heads.

"Does that mean we're never going to see Lem again?" she asked. "Moses, we ain't *never* going to see Lem again?"

Moses set his face to say something, but it never came out.

Most of the talk was about Lem, but Lizzy knew they were all thinking about Joshua, too. She had heard about a man who had run off from a downriver plantation, and when they caught him, they had cut off the toes of one foot. The way the story went was that the man's foot healed up all right but that he just pined away. They sent for the doctor, thinking he had the wasting disease, but nothing helped. They had cut off his toes in the middle of summer, and he was dead before the next rainy season.

Lizzy sat next to Bill. "I think they both going to be all right," she said.

"What did Miss Julia want with you?"

"Just some foolishness," Lizzy said, knowing

that it was no time to talk about dressing up fine and walking down the streets of Johnson City.

"She looking to get on somebody's good side," Moses said. "What they can't get by whipping it out of you they gonna get by sweet-talking."

"She can't sweet-talk me!" Lizzy declared.

"What she promise you?" Moses asked.

"Nothing."

"Girl, Miss Julia didn't call you to no house just to let you know about Lem being tied to a tree," Grandma Dolly said. "And don't think you overheard nothing they don't want you to know. Anything you know is what they want you to know so they can use you. She can't stick her head in the door down here, so she turn your head around and stick it in here instead."

Lizzy didn't like Grandma Dolly talking like that to her. She thought of plenty of things to say but knew if she opened her mouth, she would get a backhand lick that would send her flying across the room. She didn't know what they would say that Miss Julia wanted to know about, anyway. All they were talking about was Lem and Joshua, and what was going to happen to them. Miss Julia didn't need to have her say it to figure that out. Only thing they could say was where Joshua was going.

"You know where Joshua is headed?" Lizzy asked.

"No," Saran answered. "No more than chasing his freedom dream north."

"His freedom dream?"

"Every black person who ain't dead sooner or later gets them a freedom dream," Saran said. "Sometimes it comes at night, and sometimes it just comes in the middle of the day. They out working a task and then they start dreaming of being free as one of them birds. Doing what they want to do, raising a family and working for themselves instead of some master. White folks know that, too."

"Moses, you think they tied the boy up in the woods 'cause they figure Joshua will come back for him?" Bill asked.

"The patrollers ain't found Joshua," Moses said. "They know Lem's his flesh and blood, so maybe they think he'll come back and try to free him. Joshua ain't no fool. If he's not long gone he's bound to know something is up if he sees Lem just out there tied to a tree like he's possum bait."

"He might not even see the tree Lem's tied to," Lizzy said.

"He'll see the tree, all right," Bill said. "If he's out there, and he's wondering what happened to Lem, he'll know what tree to look for."

"How's he going to know what tree?" Annie asked.

"Child, how come you still here? You better get on to your own place 'fore your mother think you done run off, too," Saran said.

"I'm fixing to go any minute," Annie answered.

" 'Bout six years ago," Moses said, "same year

that Lizzy's mama died and she come to live with us, two young men—field hands—got into a tussle with a white man. One of them cut the man on his arm with a hoe. Left a big gash in it, I heard tell. Anyway, they got all the hands, house and field, and brought them out to that meadow. They hung them two boys and made each and every one of us walk by the tree. They buried them right in that field.

"All those boys did was get tired of being beat down and tore down, and they gave up their lives for it. They didn't even let us mark their graves. Every time I go out in that field I want to do something for those boys, want to turn that field into something special."

"They ain't going to hurt Lem," Saran said. "Lizzy said so."

"I got to leave," Annie said. "Good night, everybody."

Everybody left and Lizzy went and lay down on Lem's bed.

"Get some sleep, girl," Moses said to Lizzy. "Come tomorrow we might need all the strength we got."

Moses turned out the lamp. Lizzy could hear his breathing as he went over to where his wife was stretched out in the darkness.

Lizzy lay in the darkness thinking about what Miss Julia had said. She thought of the two of them walking down the streets of Johnson City in fine dresses or maybe riding in a carriage. She tried to imagine what Johnson City looked like.

A long time ago she had met a man who lived in Savannah. He was a coachman for one of Master Lewis's friends. All the girls had gathered round the stable and looked at him. He was tall, with light skin and a face that was almost like a white man's face. He wore a red jacket with gold trim and white gloves. He looked about as elegant as Lizzy had ever seen a black man look. He went on about how good Savannah was and how the white folks treated black people different in Savannah.

"You can do just about anything you want to," he said. "Long as you gets your work done."

"Then how come you didn't get your work done and run off?" Moses asked.

"And be like them folks that call themselves free?" The man humphed and shook his head.

Moses asked him how the free black people were doing.

"They ain't doing no kind of good," the man said. "They were better off being slaves. Least they had something to eat and knew how to behave themselves."

When he said that, Moses spat on the ground and walked away. Afterwards he had called the coachman a poor excuse for a man.

"He might be a good coach driver, and I'm sure his white folks just love him to death because you can see he just love them to death, but he ain't no man," Moses said.

However which way she turned it in her mind,

Lizzy thought they would never see Lem again.

The thought of him being tied to the tree, remembering what had happened at that tree before, brought tears to her eyes. She tried to figure out why Lem had run away. She wondered if he had already had a freedom dream.

Lem had always been a little different. He always wanted to do something that nobody else did. Maybe he would try to lift something that none of the other boys could lift, or run faster. And it didn't make any difference if he couldn't do it; he would always try. Lizzy thought how she would feel tied to that tree, cold and scared, maybe hurting. She wondered what she would be thinking. She knew if it was her tied to the tree she would be afraid, afraid to death. Every noise would scare her, and the thought of what would happen in the morning would scare her, too.

The patrollers would be out, she knew, still looking for Joshua. The tree was on the edge of the plantation, though, and she knew where it was. Saran had told her not to go out at night, that the patrollers would see her as a young woman and might bother with her. But she wanted to say good-bye to Lem, wanted to say something good to him so he wouldn't feel so all alone.

Lizzy listened for the breathing, the way she always did at night. Usually, after a long day in the field, it was heavy and deep. Sometimes, in the winter, it would have a rattle to it if someone took down with sickness. She thought she remembered her mother's breathing, but she couldn't be sure. She remembered her mother, remembered when the small woman had curled up in her bed and died. Some said it was all the work she had done in the rice fields when she was young, before they had both been sold to Master Lewis. They said the dampness could get into your lungs and carry you off before you knew it. People on Live Oaks Plantation didn't die young. They worked dry, raising sweet potatoes, a little cotton for seed, and livestock. Old Muhammad, who had been so wild when he was young they had to drag him to Live Oaks in shackles, lived to almost a hundred and ten.

Lizzy thought she heard Saran's even breathing as she eased up. She slipped on her shift in the darkness and moved easily to the front of the cabin. She eased the door open and stepped out into the warm night.

The high-ceilinged cabin was cooler than the surrounding area. The sweet smell of the azaleas that were planted along the side of the big house came to her on gentle breezes, only to disappear as quickly as it came.

"Where you going?"

The flat, hard voice startled Lizzy. She hadn't expected anyone to be up and about, especially Grandma Dolly.

"Thought I would take a walk," Lizzy said. "Maybe go and see Lem in case I don't see him anymore."

"There were some riders here before," Grandma Dolly said. "Look like them Higgins brothers and some other trash. They got into it with Mister Joe Haynes, then rode off. Looked like they were juiced up."

"You think I should go and say good-bye to Lem?"

"You a woman, or almost a woman," Grandma Dolly said. "Might as well get used to the kind of troubles we face. It's always saying good-bye to somebody, or saying hello to somebody you know you might have to say good-bye to later on. You scared?"

"No, ma'am," Lizzy lied, holding her breath.

"Well, if you ain't scared, you're a fool," Grandma Dolly said. "You're dealing with folks who don't mind working you, don't mind whipping you, don't mind selling you, or anything else they get in their heads."

"Miss Julia said that after the war she's going to free me," Lizzy said.

"My father used to say—" Grandma Dolly had a pipe she was smoking. The fire had almost gone out, and she sucked on it until she got it going again. "He used to say they keep us in between the whip and the North Star. One hand holds out freedom and the other holds out a whip. Long as we sitting there turning our heads which way and that . . ."

She didn't finish what she was saying. That was the way Grandma Dolly was. Sometimes she would start saying something and just stop in the middle of it.

"I'm going to see him," Lizzy said. "Maybe bring him a cool drink of water."

"Just be strong, child," Grandma Dolly said. "If they can't turn your head, they can't turn you at all."

Lizzy found the clay jug and half filled it with water from the well. She drank some of it, letting the cold liquid spill onto her face and down the front of her dress. It felt good. Lem would like it.

The road down toward the tree skirted the fields that Master Lewis wasn't using. He was resting them, she heard Mister Joe Haynes say. They were marshy and cold. It wasn't mosquito time yet, but it had been warm and there were a few around.

Lizzy stopped. She should have brought Lem something more than the jug of water she had taken with her, something like a hoecake or a bowl of greens. No, she didn't want anyone stopping her and asking her what she was doing. Suppose he asked her to cut him loose? The thought stopped Lizzy again.

Lizzy had never been whipped by anyone except Miss Ruth, Master Lewis's mother, who used to whip her when she was small and just learning to help out in the kitchen. All the children helped out in the kitchen until they were old enough to work in the fields, and that old woman used to wear them all out with a birch rod she used to carry night and day.

Miss Julia used to slap her when they played together, but that wasn't much of nothing, either. She thought it was hard when she was hit, but the first time she saw a black person really being whipped, really being tied down and whipped by Mister Joe Haynes or another white man, she knew what it was.

She had seen Bill whipped once. He had just come in from the field on a cold day and was just about as tired as he could be and hungry, and Young Master Lewis had told him to bring some bolts of cloth from the back of a cart into the house. Bill had gotten mad and jerked the cloth off the back, and one had fallen into the mud.

Young Master Lewis had seen it and had asked him what he thought he was doing. Bill pretended not to hear him, picked up the fallen bolt, and took it on into the house. He put it on the kitchen table and went to leave when Young Master Lewis stood in his way.

"Bill, don't show your temper to me!" he said.

"I ain't showing my temper. I did what you told me to do!" Bill had said.

Young Master Lewis swung at Bill and Bill grabbed his hand and held it for a moment, and then let it go. "No use in you hitting me, Master Lewis," he said. "I done what you told me to."

By that time Old Master Lewis had come downstairs and seen the whole thing. It was he who ordered Mister Joe Haynes to whip Bill.

Two men took Bill to the barn and made him take his shirt off. Then they tied his hands together and hooked them over the harness rack.

Mister Joe Haynes laid it on Bill until the blood ran down his back. The sound of the whip cutting into Bill's flesh made Lizzy jump. She was crying and so were the other girls. Lem was crying, too. Ginny, Bill's woman, wouldn't even look at what was happening. She went around to the back of the house and cracked some rice with the other women.

Bill was told to say he was sorry to Young Master Lewis, and he did that. Then Master Lewis started telling him how to avoid getting whippings, and Bill stood there and listened to that for a long while. His hands were shaking and the blood was still running. Some of the women had prepared water and some salve to put on the places where the whip had cut him. They were standing on the side waiting for the beating to be through.

Lizzy didn't want to be whipped. There wasn't anything in the world she didn't want more than being whipped. But she had to say good-bye to Lem. And Lem was special to her. Maybe she was sweet on him, as Miss Julia had said, and maybe not. Only thing she knew was that she liked to look at him, liked to be around him. She had hoped to pick her own husband one day, instead of having Master Lewis pick one for her. Lizzy moved on, her legs growing suddenly heavier as she wondered what she was going to say when she saw Lem.

Some hounds were barking off in the distance. It sounded as if they were near the river. They were barking excitedly, so they hadn't found anything. They were just yelping, probably hungry if anything. She wished she had brought something for Lem to eat.

There was a small piece of the road that had a fence along it. Years ago a stream had cut across where the road was now. Lizzy remembered Moses talking about how he had helped the men move the stream.

An old man, a man who couldn't speak any English, who had just been bought by Old Master Lewis, was the one who knew how to move the stream, to divert its waters to the twisting path that it now took from the small inlet upland to the fields. The place where the stream covered the old road was so marshy, they built the fence alongside of it, to hold on to. The tree was only a little way from the fence.

Lizzy stopped at the fence and strained her eyes, looking through the darkness. She saw Lem all right, but she was scared to get closer. Suppose they had killed him, she thought.

"Lem?" she called to him.

"Huh!" came the reply.

"You okay?"

"Who that?" Lem's voice was hoarse.

"Lizzy." She moved forward toward the tree. As she neared she could recognize his form. She moved faster, even sorrier that she had only brought him the drink of cool water.

"How you doing, Lem?" she half whispered.

"Not good," Lem said. His voice was thick.

Lizzy saw that one side of his face was swollen, and there was blood on his cheek. She had seen the women tend the men who had been beaten by the overseer. She remembered how quickly they worked, how stern faced. She pulled up the bottom of the sackcloth dress she wore, found the hem and pulled it until it ripped. She tore a piece of it off, put it against the mouth of the jug of water, and wet it.

"It's going to hurt," she said.

She washed the blood from Lem's face and saw that there was still a trickle coming from the corner of his mouth. She looked down at his ropes. They were cutting into his arms.

"How they catch you?" she asked.

"I stopped to rest," Lem said. "Joshua told me to come on, to get across the creek, but I stopped. The dogs got me."

"Where did Joshua go?" Lizzy lifted the water to Lem's lips.

"I don't know—I don't know, he just kep' running." There was dried blood on the side of his chin.

She shifted the jug so that it was closer to his mouth. She didn't want to touch it, knowing that it must be really sore.

Lem sucked at the water, bringing it into his mouth in short, frantic gasps. She lowered the jug, let him take a few more breaths, and lifted it again before he could ask her the question she was afraid to hear.

She held the jug up, letting the water run across Lem's swollen lips and across her own arm. She glanced down at the rope. It was a strong one, and it was tied too tight for Lem to have even a chance to get free by himself.

CRRAACCKK!

The pain shot through her back as if somebody had stabbed her with a knife. Lizzy fell across Lem, and then went down to one knee.

CRRAACCKK!

The whip caught her across the ankle and knocked one leg across the other. She turned, lifting one hand. Mister Joe Haynes stood, his legs apart, playing the whip over the ground in front of him.

"You come to set him free?" Mister Joe Haynes asked.

"I just come to give him water, Mister Joe Haynes!" Lizzy said.

"You trying to set him free!" Mister Joe Haynes said. "You trying to make me look like a fool?"

"Please, Mister Joe Haynes." Lizzy pulled her legs under her and pushed her dress down. She could hardly see Mister Joe Haynes as clouds drifted across the moon, and the tears filled her eyes. "Let me go on back to the cabins, sir. Please."

"You know you got to get whipped," Mister Joe Haynes said. "You know that the same as me. Now you get right there next to that nigger."

"Please don't whip me, Mister Joe Haynes . . . please . . ." Lizzy pleaded.

CRRAACCKK!

The whip caught her across her hips, tearing the thin dress.

Lizzy looked up and saw Mister Joe Haynes put his rifle down by his side, the muzzle leaning across a bush, and roll his wrist back, making the long whip move almost as if it were alive, moving across the low, sweet grass.

"I thought it would be Joshua coming back for him," Mister Joe Haynes said.

"She weren't trying to free me, Mister Joe Haynes," Lem said. "No, she weren't doing nothing like that at all!"

Lizzy watched him as he took a step to one side.

CRRAACCKK!

The whip sent a shock through her, and she fell forward, reaching behind her as if she could take the pain away from her back.

"Whut the . . . !"

Mister Joe Haynes heard the sound the same time that Lizzy did. The grunting noise seemed to build for a brief instant and then rise as it neared them.

Joshua ran low and hard, a black fury in the darkness. Mister Joe Haynes lifted his whip halfway up, decided that it wasn't what he needed to stop the dark figure hurtling his way, and reached a moment too late for the rifle.

Joshua's body crashed into the thin overseer's bent frame and sent him backwards. The two men wrestled in the grass, with Mister Joe Haynes rolling on top of Joshua. He started pounding down on Joshua.

"Get the gun! Get the gun!" Lem said.

Lizzy looked to where the rifle still lay across the bush. She could see the glint of the moonlight on the barrel. She lifted herself to her knees, wincing as she moved her back.

The sounds of the scuffle behind her picked up as Lizzy moved the short distance to the rifle. She picked it up, stood, and turned toward where Joshua and Mister Joe Haynes moved in the darkness.

"Shoot him! Shoot him, Lizzy!"

Lizzy could hardly see the two figures, one white, one black, in the darkness. She had never touched a gun before—they didn't let blacks touch the guns—and she was trembling so that she could hardly hold the weapon in her hand, let alone aim it at anyone.

"Don't kill me, Joshua!" It was Mister Joe Haynes's voice. "Don't kill me!"

"You got a pistol in your pocket?" Joshua asked.

"I ain't . . . I ain't got nothing," Mister Joe Haynes said between gasps.

The moon came out from between the clouds and Lizzy saw that Joshua was kneeling near Mister Joe Haynes. He held one big hand on the white man's neck and went through his pockets with the other one. Then, satisfied that the white man didn't have another weapon, he stood up and came over to Lizzy and took the gun.

"What you going to do?" Lizzy asked.

"What I got to," Joshua said.

"Don't kill me," Mister Joe Haynes said. "Tie me up and get on away from here. But don't kill me. I got a wife and family."

"Please don't kill him," Lizzy said. Her back was still burning from the whip. "We can just tie him up, and then you can go."

"Then you best go, too," Joshua said. "If we don't kill him and he tell them that you helped us get away, your life won't be worth spit in the creek."

"I can't go . . ." Lizzy was shaking. "I can't go."

"Why?"

"She scared," Lem said. "Get me loose."

Joshua looked at Mister Joe Haynes. "Get the boy loose," he said. "If you try anything, I ain't got no choice but to kill you. Tell you the truth, I wouldn't mind it none, either."

Mister Joe Haynes stood up and went over to where Lem was tied to the tree. His hands trembled as he loosened the ropes.

"Joshua?" Lizzy's eyes were filled with tears. "I got to go?"

"Yeah, girl," Joshua said. "Ain't no matter what he say when we here. You stay here, they gonna beat you to death. You don't do nothing to a white man and get away with it. Don't matter if we kill him or not."

"I can't see Grandma Dolly and them no more?" Lizzy had begun to cry.

Joshua looked at Lizzy, then away for a moment. "I'll wait a bit for you to go say good-bye, Lizzy," he said. "Then we got to get going. I'm just about caught now, waiting around to get Lem out of here. Can't stand waiting no more."

"I'll go say good-bye," Lizzy said. "I'll be back."

"You just tell what happened," Joshua said. "So to ease their minds. And tell Moses I love him."

"You ain't going to kill Mister Joe Haynes, are you?" she asked.

"If you get back in a short while, I won't kill him," Joshua said. "If you don't, I'm going to have to break his neck. Stay away from the road. Now get on!"

Lizzy's bare feet splashed in puddles along the edge of the field. She stopped long enough to catch a breath and to fight back the tears that ran down her face. She was afraid. She stopped running when she reached the fence that separated the quarters from the first field and wiped off the tears.

She was afraid to go with Joshua and Lem, but she was scared to stay, too. She thought about the men who had been hanged and buried in the field. Moses had said he wanted to do something with that field one day, but the only thing that Lizzy could think about was her and Joshua and Lem being buried there with the others.

Lizzy was glad to see a dim line of light coming from where the door was hinged. Somebody was up. She went across the front and tapped gently on the door, the way she had been trained to when a light was on.

The light disappeared and the door opened.

Lizzy went in quickly and the door was closed behind her.

"I could see the light," she said softly.

"Bill, fix the blanket," somebody said.

There was a movement in the dark as Bill put the blanket over the door so the light wouldn't show through the cracks; then the oil lamp was relit.

"Miss Julia was over here—" Saran stopped abruptly. "What happened?"

"I went out to see Lem," Lizzy said. "Mister Joe Haynes was out there. He hit me with the whip and then Joshua come out from the bushes and knocked him down. There was a fight, and Joshua got the best of Mister Joe Haynes."

"Lord have mercy!"

"Joshua said that if they don't kill Mister Joe Haynes then I got to go with them." Lizzy looked into Saran's face, hoping that she would say something that would bring things back to where they were, that would make her knees stop trembling.

"Take that shift off!" Saran said. "Can't have nobody seeing it cut by the whip."

"Miss Saran—"

"Take it off!" Saran snapped. "That white girl already been around here looking for you. She see you got whipped, she know none of us did it."

Lizzy started taking off the thin dress. As she moved the pain in her back seemed to grow more intense.

"How Josh looking?" Bill asked.

"He looking okay," Lizzy said. Ginny had brought her another shift.

"It's still bleeding a little," Ginny said.

"Put some fennel leaves on it," Saran said.

The leaves, taken from a jar of water, felt cool on Lizzy's back.

"You got to let God be your guide, girl," Moses said. "Listen to Joshua. He know what he doing."

"He said to say he loved you," Lizzy said. "I think he's going to be all right."

"If he kill Mister Joe Haynes and they catch him and Lem, then it's going to be hard for all of us," Bill said.

"He said he wouldn't kill him," Lizzy said.

"If he don't kill him and Mister Joe Haynes come here and say what happened and they find you here what you think is going to happen?"

"I wish none of this didn't happen." Lizzy lifted her arms as Grandma Dolly put another shift on her. "We could all die."

"Girl." Saran took Lizzy's face into her hands. "When folks take your freedom, and the only way for you to get it is to risk dying for it, then dying comes when it wants to. You go on, you'll be all right. You young. You got plenty to live for. Just know who you dealing with, if they black in their hearts or if they white. Trust in God and what you feel."

"Somebody's coming!"

The light was quickly doused, and the door opened just enough to let Bill look out.

"It's Miss Julia!" he whispered.

"Girl, don't cry, and don't let her know you been hit with the whip!" Saran said.

In the darkness of the cabin, Lizzy could hear the others breathing. It was Moses who started praying.

"Show us Thy mercy, O Lord, and grant us Thy salvation. I will hear what God, the Lord, will speak. And so it will pass."

"Lizzy!" Miss Julia called from without.

"Hesh!" Saran whispered. "Let her call again. We told her you was sick and went out to the field."

"Lizzy!"

"Is you calling for Lizzy this time o' night, Miss Julia?" Saran called through the door.

"You heard me," Miss Julia said.

"Go on, child," Saran said. "Make like you sleepy."

Lizzy went to the cabin door, opened it, and stood in the doorway. She started to lift her arm up alongside the door, as she had so many times in the past, but the pain from where the whip had cut her made her pull it down again.

"Yes, ma'am?"

"Where were you before?" Miss Julia asked.

"I had to go into the field 'cause my stomach was growling," Lizzy said.

"I don't like you sneaking around at night," Miss Julia said. "Now you come on into the house with me."

"Miss Julia, I don't feel good," Lizzy said. "Mama Saran said I got the fever and it might turn into the heaves."

Miss Julia took a step toward Lizzy and held the lantern up. "Well, you do look a sight." Miss Julia twisted her hair in her hands.

"Can I come in the morning?" Lizzy asked.

"All right," Miss Julia said. "But I hope you come early before Mister Joe Haynes rings for the people to go to the fields. You don't look like you should be out in the fields tomorrow."

"No, ma'am."

"We women have to protect each other," Miss Julia said, a smile easing the hardness of her face. "Now you go on in and get some sleep."

As soon as Miss Julia turned and started back toward the big house, Lizzy stepped back into the cabin. She was trembling again, and when she found herself in Saran's arms, she began to cry.

"Talk to her, Moses," Saran whispered over Lizzy's head.

"You got to go on, now," Moses said. "Take our love with you. Take it to Joshua, and to my boy. You take it with you, too, 'cause we all love you. Now go on."

"If you get caught, act like you ain't right in the head," Saran said. "No matter what they do to you, or how bad you feel, or what you see. White folks ain't worried about simple Negroes. They just worry about Negroes that got sense."

"Go on, girl, before you break everybody's heart," a voice from the darkness said.

Lizzy felt somebody put something around her neck and knew it was a charm to keep off evil and sickness. In the darkness hands touched her, rough hands, some holding her arm, some patting her shoulders, some touching her hair. Lips touched her, kissed her. In the background it was Moses who was praying. It was Saran who turned Lizzy's shoulders toward the door.

"Don't turn back," she said.

The night was warmer. Darker. Lizzy wanted to turn back, to see the cabins, to see if Miss Julia's light was on, to see if anybody was standing in the quarters waving to her.

"Don't turn back."

Lizzy stopped, looked down, took a deep breath, and continued.

There was a noise. Lizzy leaned forward, and peered fearfully into the darkness.

"Joshua?"

"Over here." Joshua's voice was deep and calm. Lizzy turned and saw him coming toward her. Lem was behind him.

"Where's Mister Joe Haynes?" she asked.

"He's back there tied under that tree," Joshua said. "We'd best be getting on. It'll be light before long."

"Where we going?"

"Girl, I don't know where we going," Joshua said. "But I know we got to get away from here. They'll have the dogs out as soon as the sun rises."

"We going to get away, Lizzy," Lem said. He was limping slightly. "Don't you worry none about it."

"Where we going to get away to?" Lizzy asked, as the two men passed her. "You know where we going?"

"Just going," Joshua said. "Save your breath. Sound carry pretty good along here."

Lizzy knew Joshua was wrong. Sound didn't carry good over the fields, and it didn't carry good over the marshes, either. He just didn't want to talk, that was all.

She thought back on Mister Joe Haynes. Maybe Joshua and Lem had killed him. Maybe that's why they didn't talk much, because they had killed Mister Joe Haynes and knew they were headed straight for hell.

They walked as fast as they could. Sometimes Lizzy almost had to run to keep up with them. Lizzy knew if any white person saw them running across the fields they would be stopped. If they were stopped at Live Oaks all they would have to say is that they were one of Master Lewis's Negroes and nobody would bother them. But away from the plantation they weren't safe anywhere.

"Where we going?" Lizzy asked again, even though she had told herself that she wouldn't.

"I remember a place some miles from here," Joshua said. "There was a big house, and off from the big house there was a little brick house where they used to smoke hams before they built a new big house and a regular big smokehouse. If I can recollect where it was, maybe we can get in there until I see what's what."

"A smokehouse is gonna stink," Lizzy said.

"Dogs might not pick us up in there," Joshua said.

"We gonna be all right?"

"Keep quiet," Joshua answered.

They walked in silence, and Lizzy saw that Lem was having a harder time keeping up than she was. She saw that he was favoring his left leg, but he wasn't saying anything. Once he caught her looking at him and smiled through his still-swollen face.

When they finally stopped, it was on the edge of a field. The sun was just rimming the far edge of the field, and Lizzy saw a small band of Negroes walking, baskets under their arms, toward the fields.

"We can't make it to the smokehouse. They's a grove of trees over yonder," Joshua said, "we can stay there until night falls."

Lizzy was tired as they made their way to the trees, but it was a different kind of tired than from working the field. It was an excitement that she had never felt before. For the first time in her life, she didn't know what was going to happen next. There wasn't going to be a bell to

call her to the fields or the long rows to weed
and hoe. She was seeing more than the quarters
and the back of the big house at Live Oaks.

"I don't know if I can get up in a tree,"
Lem said.

"You can," Joshua said, simply. "You will."

Lem pulled himself up into a tree, using his
arms more than his legs. Lizzy climbed into the
branches of a twisted old tree that had partially
sunk under its own weight. The trunk of the tree
was covered with a soft moss that felt clammy
to her skin.

Joshua watched as Lem settled himself on a
branch. Then he said he was going to scout
around.

"If anything happen, don't give up," he said.
"Just keep going."

"You leaving?" Lizzy asked.

"Just looking around, trying to figure out
which way we got to go. Which way is the best
way north," Joshua said. He lifted a big hand
and, fingers curved, wiped the sweat from his
brow. "Just that we got to be ready for anything.
Being free is what we looking for. Everybody
got to look for his own freedom. Can't be no
children when we doing it, either. You understand that, Lem?"

"Yes, suh," Lem said.

Joshua shielded his eyes from the sun and
looked toward the heavens. Then he nodded and
started off.

"Lem, you scared?" Lizzy called out after Joshua was out of earshot.

"Naw," Lem called back. "We free, that's the onliest thing that matters to me. I'd rather die than go back to them fields again. How about you?"

"Don't know about dying," Lizzy said. "But I like running around out here. You think Joshua is going to look for Neela?"

"Don't know," Lem said. "Now hesh up. Here comes somebody."

Lizzy shut up and looked around. Across the field she saw two white men and two little children walking. She moved further along the branch.

She thought if they didn't see her they could surely hear her heart beating.

The two white men weren't hurrying, and they weren't headed straight for them. They were going directly toward a half-dried channel.

Lizzy knew she was about to cry again. She looked up to where the white men were looking at the channel. The two children were playing tag, running back and forth between trees and rocks.

That's what it means being free, she thought. Doing what you want. Using your time like you want to use it. She could imagine herself running with those kids. Of course, she wouldn't be playing a kid's game, but she could run with them. She could imagine herself in the field. Just walk-

ing along, maybe picking up some flowers for
her hair, or even to give to Lem. She closed her
eyes for a minute and pictured herself giving the
flowers to Lem and him looking stupid and act-
ing like he didn't know what to do with them.
It was just a dream of what she might do, but
it was a good dream. She took a deep breath
and opened her eyes.

The two white men had walked on, and the
children followed.

Lizzy wondered if Joshua had gone on without them. She thought that if he didn't get back
by dark she would tell Lem that the two of them
should go on.

The sun rose high in the sky, and Lizzy fell
asleep in fits and starts. She was hungry, and
already missing Saran and Grandma Dolly.

A few more white people went by, but none
closer to the tree than the channel. Once they
heard a dog in the background, but they never
saw him. All day they waited for Joshua to return, and he didn't.

Somewhere between the sun's being high and
it moving across the sky and losing its strength,
Lizzy decided that from that day, she was going
to be on her own. How could she go back? It
wasn't what had happened to Mister Joe
Haynes. Or what had happened to Lem. It was
what had happened to her. She was free. It was
a scary free, and it was a hungry free and a tired
free, but it was free.

Lizzy had fallen asleep and awoke with a start. For a moment she didn't remember where she was; then she did and felt her heart jump in fear. Across the open pasture a flight of dark birds swept upward, their black silhouettes graceful against the purple-and-gold-streaked sky.

Lizzy looked over toward where Lem had been, but she couldn't see him.

From the distance there was a booming noise, deep and ominous, that echoed from somewhere behind her. That was what must have made the birds take flight, Lizzy thought, and awakened her. Lizzy looked up but the sky was cloudless. She imagined that somewhere it was raining and that it was thunder she had heard.

She thought of staying in the tree, but couldn't bear the thought of being alone. She began to make her way down the branch, surprised at how low it was, and soon found herself on the ground. She was still hungry, still scared. She looked around and then went close to the tree to squat and release the water she had been holding.

She remembered which way Joshua had gone and started off in that direction.

"Lizzy!"

Lem's voice stopped her cold. She turned and saw him climbing down from another tree. Lizzy was glad to see him, glad to see his wide shoulders and the wide pants that Master Lewis had given out last Christmas.

"How you doing?" she asked.

"I'm doing okay," Lem said. "Josh ain't come back."

"We got to keep on moving," Lizzy said. "If they sent the dogs out they'll be coming this way soon."

"I don't think we gonna get away," Lem said. "I think that's why Joshua left. He come back to get me one time when Mister Joe Haynes caught me, but he ain't coming back again."

Lizzy looked at Lem, looked at him digging his foot into the ground, then looked toward where the birds had lifted into the air.

"You hear that noise?" Lizzy asked. "It sounded like thunder." She started walking slowly, hoping that Lem would start with her. He did.

"The sky's too clear for it to be thunder," Lem said. "I think that's where the fighting is."

They were walking alongside the channel, and Lizzy thought they were headed toward the river. It was getting dark fast, and they would have to find something to eat soon.

They walked for a long time, until the last light had faded from the sky and a cool breeze had lifted from the direction Lizzy thought the river lay in. Lizzy walked close behind Lem, neither of them speaking. As they passed a wild field they heard the sound of crickets close by. Lizzy knew that the wild field might have something to eat in it, maybe some yams, or sweet peppers. Lem didn't stop, and she didn't make the suggestion.

Lizzy thought about the song they had sung when the patrollers brought Lem in.

> *Oh, sooner in the morning when I rise,*
> *With crosses and trials on every side,*
> *The young lambs must find the way.*
> *The young lambs must find the way. . . .*

"Lem, you think being free means being all excited all the time?"

"You excited?" Lem asked. "Or you just scared?"

"Little of both, I think," Lizzy answered.

Lem reached out and took her hand. "You and me being scared together is all right," he said. "I can think of helping to get you some place safe, and that makes me feel good."

"Don't be thinking too hard on me, Lem." Lizzy swung the hand that Lem held. "You don't know what I'm going to be doing—"

They had heard it at the same time. The

hounds! Lizzy stood stock-still, holding her
breath. In the distance she could hear them.
Hounds barking in the night air, their yelps coming quickly as they moved along. Lizzy lifted the
bottom hem of her dress and started running
away from the sound.

Lem was running, too. He ran ahead of her
and she ran faster, trying to catch up with him.
She could feel her face contorting with the fear
of the moment, with the panic that she felt. Lem
was slowing down. Lizzy could hear him gasping for breath. She felt a sharp pain in her side,
but she didn't stop. She ran and ran until her
legs felt heavy and her thighs burned with the
effort. She stopped for a moment, leaning heavily against a tree and trying to stop the rushing
of her breath, the pounding of her temples, so
she could listen for the hounds.

She heard them. They sounded further away,
but she knew that if the dogs had their scent
they would pick it up again.

"We got to keep going!" Lem said. "We walk
for a while, then run for a while. But we got to
keep going!"

They pushed on, running for a while, walking
when they couldn't run, stopping as little as
possible. But each time they stopped, the dogs
seemed closer.

"There's some lights!" Lizzy looked ahead to
their left. She could see, in the brightening
moonlight, the tops of trees. In between the dark
shadows, the lights of fires flickered.

Lem moved next to her. She looked at his face. His eyes were wide and he held his shoulders high, trying to suck in enough breath to keep going.

"Those dogs sound like they're by the trees we were in," Lem said.

Lizzy turned around and looked in the direction from which they had come. She couldn't see anything. She looked back at Lem and saw him leaning over, his hands on his knees. She didn't know how much Mister Joe Haynes and the other men had hurt him, but she knew he couldn't run much further. Behind her the sounds of the dogs faded for a few seconds and then started up again.

"We got to head toward the lights," Lizzy said. "If there's any black people there, maybe we can hide with them."

Lem leaned toward the direction in which he wanted to go and started off again.

Lizzy didn't want to leave him. She wanted Lem to be all right, and she didn't want to be alone in the darkness. Even if they were caught, she wanted them to be caught together.

She thought about being whipped.

"I see the dogs!" Lem said.

Lizzy turned and looked, but she didn't see anything. She squinted and pushed her head forward. Then she saw them, four riders on dark horses, carrying torches, the dogs running ahead of them.

They weren't more than a few minutes away,

Lizzy thought. She turned and, grabbing Lem's arm, started off again.

They ran toward the lights, which soon were clearly campfires. They stopped. Soldiers weren't any better than the patrollers.

Lizzy turned and looked behind her. The riders had also stopped. "They pointing at us!" Lizzy said.

"No, I think they pointing at them fires," Lem said. He was down on one knee. Lizzy got down with him and looked at the riders behind them. They were still looking in their direction and pointing. But now Lizzy could see they were pointing at the fires.

One of them whistled and the dogs stopped in the field. They were whining and circling, eager to get on.

There were two more whistles, and the dogs circled one more time and headed back.

Lem and Lizzy stayed low as they moved toward the campfires. There were shadows among the fires, and once in a while they could make out a person. They couldn't see what they looked like.

"Hold it!"

Lizzy jumped and grabbed her arms. Lem started to run, and two men with rifles jumped in front of him. One swung his rifle, and Lizzy watched as Lem reeled backwards and fell heavily in the dark field.

"Contraband!" A voice near Lizzy spoke up.

Two other men went over and looked at Lem and then moved away.

"Get on into the camp if you want," the voice nearest Lizzy said.

Lizzy turned and saw the soldier. She couldn't believe her eyes. He was tall and broad-faced, and the rifle he carried looked almost taller than he was. But that wasn't what amazed Lizzy.

"You're black!" she said.

"Glad you noticed it," the soldier grinned. "I had just about forgot it."

Lizzy helped Lem up. Together they started toward the campfires.

"Are they Yankees?" Lem asked.

"I guess they are," Lizzy whispered. "They carrying guns, too!"

As they neared the fires they heard singing. It was black singing, all right, a low praise hymn being crooned sweet and strong in the night.

The Yankee camp was busy. The camp was filled with soldiers, half of them white, the others black.

Snatches of conversation drifted toward them. The voices weren't like the ones they had heard before, and Lizzy was having trouble understanding them. They seemed relaxed, busy with the work of soldiering. There were a lot of other blacks, too. Some of them were just sitting around; others were cleaning boots or saddles.

"You young folks looking for something to eat you can get it around by that wagon." An old man, his white beard contrasting sharply with his black skin, pointed toward a wagon.

"You got black soldiers here!" Lizzy said.

"There's four and forty thousand of them, seven hundred and threescore, all crying out to the Lord for strength," the old man said. "How can they fail?"

She went toward the wagon and around it.

A wide, heavyset woman wearing pants under her dress was serving food from a large kettle. She looked at Lizzy and Lem and reached for two tins.

"Where y'all from?" she asked.

Lizzy looked at Lem and put her head down. She didn't want to tell the woman she had run away.

"If y'all from around here they's some people down the way from around here, too," the woman said, putting some beans on the tins and passing one to Lizzy. "They's some bread in that basket. You know anything about cooking, honey?"

"Not too much," Lizzy said.

"They'll find you something to do," the woman said. "Don't worry none."

The beans were good and Lizzy ate them with her fingers, cleaning the tin with the bread and then licking her fingers clean.

"We're safe now," Lem said.

"Not if Mister Joe Haynes gets here," Lizzy said.

"The Yankees will shoot him," Lem said.

"Tree him like a possum and shoot him dead."

Lizzy listened to Lem talking, listened as his courage came back, as he relaxed. He had stretched out on his back as he talked. His words came slower and slower, and when she asked him if he was still hurting he didn't answer. Lizzy looked over at him and saw that he was asleep.

She had two dreams that night. One dream was about the hounds coming closer and closer, and everyone in the quarters standing around watching them bite her and not being able to do anything about it.

But it was the other dream that filled her, that moved her body in her sleep. It was a dream of being free, of walking across a wide meadow, not even following a road, just going any which way she wanted to go, not caring when she got there. She had the dream over and over again, each time wearing a different one of Miss Julia's dresses. It was a beautiful dream.

In the morning it was a black man who woke them up. He told them to get up and help get things ready for the white officers.

The cooks started making breakfast. Lizzy was given a pair of boots and told to get the mud off them.

"It's dry, child," a man said. "Just brush 'em off good."

The soldiers were awakened a little while later, and they took down their tents. They were ready to move out as soon as they finished eating. A soldier went among them and sorted them out.

Lizzy was put to work packing up some wagons. She didn't know much about what she was doing, just passing things when they came to her and watching them being loaded into the back of a ox-drawn wagon. Some of the black men were lined up, and Lem was told to stand with them. Lizzy heard the white soldier speak to them.

"They're starting a new colored regiment," he said. "If you're able-bodied, you can join it and help with the fighting. If you're not able-bodied, or if you don't have the stomach for fighting, you can drop out now."

Lizzy's eyes went straight to Lem. He was standing with the other men, as tall as he could.

"Okay, stand at ease while we get you some gear," the white soldier said.

After a while, some other men from the far side of camp came and joined the men already lined up. The white soldier came and gave some of them shovels and some of them rifles. One of the ones he handed a shovel to was Joshua!

Lizzy tried to catch her breath and caught the hiccoughs. It was Joshua, standing tall. When the white officer walked away, some of the black women ran over to the men. Lizzy went to Joshua and threw her arms around him.

"Joshua! Oh, Joshua!" Lizzy held him as tightly as she could.

"Heard a young girl and boy came in the camp last night," Joshua said. "Lord knows I was hoping it was you."

"Where did you go?"

"Looking for Neela," Joshua said. He looked away. "Couldn't get nowhere near her last night. But I still got my breath, and I still got my determination, and I'm going to find her again."

"I know you will, Joshua," Lizzy said. "I know you will!"

Lizzy found Lem and didn't know what to say to him. He had a shovel, too. She just put her fingers to his lips, and she thought he kissed them.

"Okay, okay! Let's go! Let's go! You women move back!" the white officer barked. Next to him a tall black soldier watched attentively. "Right face!"

The men turned right.

"Forward . . . march!"

They marched them off with neither Joshua nor Lem nor any of the other men looking back.

"What should I do?" Lizzy looked around as the soldiers and wagons started moving out. "What am I going to do?"

"Girl, you can go on with some folks who gonna try to make it North," a woman said. "Or you can stay with the soldiers and help them do what they want. They always need somebody to cook and mend."

Lizzy looked to where the black soldiers had gone down a road, seeing them turn and disappear around a bend. She couldn't see around the bend, or know what she was going to find when she got around it, but she knew she had to find out.

She ran as fast as she could, her feet slapping against the hard road. When she got around the bend, the men were still in sight, tall and proud. She followed them, never looking back.

APRIL 1900,
CURRY ISLAND,
SOUTH CAROLINA

THE LEWIS FAMILY, 1900

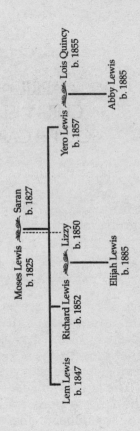

Moses Lewis ⚭ Saran
b. 1825   b. 1827

Lem Lewis   Richard Lewis ⚭ Lizzy   Yero Lewis ⚭ Lois Quincy
b. 1847   b. 1852   b. 1850   b. 1857   b. 1855

Elijah Lewis   Abby Lewis
b. 1885   b. 1885

"Sukey, if you think you fooling somebody by walking slow, I just want to tell you that you ain't!" Elijah Lewis called to the mule, knowing that he would be ignored. He stopped, pushed his hat back off his forehead, and wiped the sweat from his brow. He had been in the field all morning, and the rows seemed to get longer and the field wider. He looked over to the old field, knowing that he would see Grandma Saran's dark form somewhere in the square patch of rich earth.

When the War Between the States had ended and the Yankees had helped parcel out the land to blacks who wanted to stay and farm the only land that most of them knew, the Lewis family had been given the eight acres that bordered Live Oaks. The story went that Moses had led them into the field to pray, but that he was so filled with the joy of being able to look upon the people gathered around him, finally not having to share them with an overseer or a master, that he couldn't speak. After a long while, he lifted his face to the heavens and called out, "Glory!"

Afterwards, when they did pray together in the Glory Field, they pledged forever to sing and give praise to the Lord and to freedom.

Sukey had pulled the plow over and had stopped when she felt the lack of resistance. Elijah picked up the reins, angled the plow back into the dark earth, and clicked his tongue at the old mule. Sukey started again, turning over the new ground.

Life had been good, if strange, after the war. The white people around Curry had to learn that the blacks were free, and the blacks had to learn just what being free meant. To some it meant being hungry for the first time and trying to take care of themselves for the first time. To others it meant working the land as they always had, but working it for themselves.

Most of the people from Live Oaks had taken the name Lewis, so those who had been sold away could find them if they made their way back. Some had taken other names, wanting to establish their own families. There were Eppses, and Foxes, and even a few Oakeses. But the names weren't a problem. After the Yankee soldiers left, it was the whites who were trying to get things back to what they had been before the war. Blacks who had a little land were losing it to the banks and to taxes. And then there was the Klan. White men who rode at night, terrorizing blacks, pulling them out of their homes, and beating them for being disrespectful to a

white man or for not working hard enough in a
field they were sharecropping. That's why the
Lewis family worked so hard to hang on to the
land they owned. They didn't want to sharecrop.

"That's not just dirt out there," Grandma
Saran had said. "Somebody in our family been
working that land since we was first brought
over here. We've been up and down these fields
till we know them like we know our own hands.
Back in slavery times it was us who sweated over
those fields, bled over them, and Lord knows
cried over them."

It was good thinking, as far as Elijah could
tell. But on Curry good thinking didn't go too
far if you were black. Things were going hard
and they were back on their taxes. Grandpa
Moses Lewis and Saran had gone to the bank in
Johnson City to see if they could borrow the
money.

"This little pinch-face man said they didn't
lend no money to colored." Grandpa Moses
sucked on his pipe when they got back. "Said
the King Street Bank was for white folks."

It was something in the way the two old people had looked away from each other, not wanting to see the hurt they both shared, that sent
a chill through Elijah, a chill that turned to anger
when he thought about it.

"Sukey," Elijah called out. "What you think?
You think we ever going to keep this land?"

Sukey paced forward slowly, placing her front
feet carefully before her, jerking slightly with her

hips as she moved down the row.

"Sukey, you are the dumbest mule I've ever seen," Elijah called out. "I'm talking good sense to you about our future and you just ignoring me! You think you white or something?"

Sukey reached the end of the row and turned left to come up the next row.

"Least you could tell me what you think of Abby's idea of us being fishermen," Elijah said. "Beats sharecropping, I think. Don't know if it beats working in a pulp mill."

Elijah's father, Richard, had worked in two pulp mills in Georgia. The first had been near Savannah, and the other was in Valdosta. When he had come home this time, Elijah thought he looked different, older. There were small lines in his forehead and the front edges of his hair, over the ears, had grayed. He didn't talk much about his work, or about his and Lizzy's being away from the family, and Elijah didn't bring it up. He didn't bring up the boat, either.

It was Abby who had found the boat they had. Abby was fourteen, six months younger than Elijah, and a lot more carefree. Abby had seen the boat when he went searching for she-crabs down by the river. It didn't look like much, and the old man who owned it was glad to exchange two loads of firewood for it. They had loaded the boat up on a wagon and brought it home. Grandpa Moses worked on it with them, replacing some of the wood that had rotted away and pitching it with tar and crushed oyster shells until it was watertight. When it was ready, they went out in it as much as they could. Sometimes they went out in it on Sundays after church and, if Grandma Saran was off visiting her sister in Johnson City, even caught a few fish to sell before the old woman came home and found them working on the Sabbath.

Elijah looked up at the sky, shielding his eyes from the bright sun. There would be another two hours of daylight beating down on him, two more hours of trailing behind Sukey before he would call it a day. He remembered that it was Saturday and they would all have the next day off. They were going to bless the new cemetery in the back of the church after services and then have a picnic. Then he would have to sit with Abby and hear him talk about how they should give up farming and concentrate on fishing or maybe even go live in Johnson City and be "city folk." But Abby wouldn't say anything in front of the old folks, and he would do his share of plowing the same way all the others in the Lewis family did.

"Hey, Sukey!" Elijah called. "What you think about moving to Johnson City? You a city mule?"

Sukey stopped at the end of the row and turned left.

"Lord, bless this precious earth." Moses Lewis stood at the head of the oldest grave in what had been the African burying ground on the Live Oaks Plantation.

Elijah watched as the old man, his wide black hands like tree limbs gripping his felt hat, swayed gently. The grave was covered with shells and outlined with small pieces of colored glass.

"Bless this ground, and keep it holy in Your sight," Grandpa Moses went on. "Keep it holy in Your sight as it is precious in ours."

"Amen!" came from the back of the small gathering of people.

"Lord, we have raised up from this ground and have lain down in it for nearly one hundred and fifty years," Grandpa Moses went on. "And we know we might not be able to hang on to it. But Lord, everybody we ever loved is buried here. From the time . . . from long before the war, we was burying our people right in this ground. We got their places marked. Some was born here and some crossed the water, but they resting together."

"Walk together, children!" Loote Epps had lost a leg to sugar, but he was out behind the church the family had built along with the others who had come to consecrate the burying ground.

"Lord, look down on us and help us to walk in Thy holy way. Amen."

Grandpa Moses nodded, pleased with what he had said, and then reached down and took little Mary's hand and walked away. Grandma Saran stood for a long moment looking down at the graves before turning away herself and starting toward the table they had set up for the picnic.

"What your mama make for the picnic?" Elijah grabbed Goldie's basket and started carrying it toward where the table was already filling up with food.

"What difference it make?" Goldie said, stepping in front of Elijah so he'd have to stop short. "You'd eat it if it was streak-a-lean pudding."

"I might," Elijah said, "if I thought you made it."

"If that's suppose to turn my head, you got another *think* coming, Elijah Lewis!" Goldie's smile lit up her dark eyes.

Elijah put down Goldie's basket and sat on the table's edge for a moment, then jumped up when he saw Grandma Saran giving him a look. Goldie took the tablecloth off the sweet grass basket and looked down approvingly at the dish holding her mother's rhubarb pie.

"I might have to marry you quicker than I planned," Elijah said.

"Marry *who*?" Goldie put her head down and rolled her eyes up toward Elijah. "Just because you a Lewis and think you good-looking don't mean you got a right to cast your eyes on me! How old are you anyway? Twelve? Maybe eleven?"

"Girl, you know I'm nearly sixteen and ready!"

Goldie put her lips close to Elijah's ear. "Then you better get *un*ready, Mr. Elijah Lewis."

Goldie pulled her skirts up in front of her, gave Elijah a look over her shoulder, and sashayed away.

Elijah wasn't sure he wanted to marry Goldie. His father, Richard, had always said that marriage was a serious thing. And one thing that Elijah wasn't sure about with Goldie was how to be serious. Every time he came around her he just started feeling happy inside, and for the life of him he couldn't stop the silly grin that would come over his face.

"Boy, are you possessed by something?"

"Ma'am?" Elijah turned and saw Grandma Saran standing behind him. "Possessed? No, ma'am."

"Don't tell me you're in love," Grandma Saran said. When she smiled, the corners of her eyes wrinkled.

"I could be in something," Elijah said.

"Well, I want you to come down here once a

week and help keep the burying ground nice,"
Grandma Saran said, turning toward the small
square of land.

"Grandma Saran," Elijah said, "how come the
white people ain't got nothing on their graves
but a stone? And our graves got shells and all
kinds of decorations on them?"

"Child, how do I know what's wrong with
white people?" Grandma Saran asked.

"And how come we keep a grave up for Uncle
Lem when he's not even buried in there?"

"Don't mean nothing that his body ain't in
there," Grandma Saran said. She walked to the
edge of the burying ground and pushed some
stones with the toe of her shoe. "Lem went away
from here and fought in the war. They brought
his body back. Brought my son home past the
oak trees, the same way they brought back Old
Master Lewis's boy. Master Lewis wouldn't let
Lem be buried here. Told us to take him down
to the river and put his body in that cold water.
We went down to the water, but we didn't put
Lem in it. We buried him in the Glory Field. We
didn't mark it lest Master Lewis find the grave."

Grandma Saran shivered slightly. She looked
up at the sky. Elijah looked up, too. In the distance there was a mass of dark clouds. The wind
was picking up, too.

"Looks like that storm they were talking about
is coming," Grandma Saran said. She knelt and
started pulling some weeds out of the ground.
"I remember back in '90 we had a storm that

messed up just about everything you can think of. It was bad around here, but it was a real mess in Johnson City. Real mess."

"You saw it?" Elijah asked.

"Saw the mess afterwards," Grandma Saran said.

"Here comes Sister Clinton." Elijah saw the heavy, light-skinned woman coming down the path from the church.

"I think the Lord put that Clinton woman here just to test my faith," Grandma Saran said under her breath.

"Sister Lewis, is that you?" Sister Clinton stopped and leaned back, as if she were having trouble recognizing Grandma Saran. "Ain't you got a job taking care of that little blind white boy?"

"Thought I needed a day off, Sister Clinton." Grandma Saran put her hand in Elijah's and pulled herself up. "And this burying ground needed some praying over. You sure are looking well. I saw your granddaughter at the praise services this morning. Child sings like an angel."

"She sure is something," Sister Clinton said. "But, you know, I saw that little white boy this morning when I was taking some ironing into town. He was with that man who runs the telegraph office. You know who I'm talking about, always wearing them dirty suspenders and talking loud!"

"Well, he can be with whoever his daddy want

him to be with," Grandma Saran said.

"Is that man sickly?" Sister Clinton leaned a little closer. "Because I could swear he seems like he don't walk too steady to me."

"I haven't seen him lately," Grandma Saran said. "You know this is spring planting and weeding time."

"Tell me about it!" Sister Clinton said. "Did I tell you how much I like that dress? Well, I just love it to pieces!"

"That's nice," Grandma Saran said.

"Nice seeing you again, Elijah." Sister Clinton smiled, adjusted her hat, and started back toward the church.

"She so glad to do washing and ironing for the white folks she don't know what to do with herself," Grandma Saran said.

"How come you're not watching that Turner boy? What's his name? David?" Elijah put a pebble on the back of his hand and balanced it out in front of his chest.

"He's staying the weekend with that trashy Foster. I know who Sister Clinton was talking about. And she know he was probably half juiced up. He's always half juiced up. I don't know why Mr. Turner let him take that boy out. They were supposed to go fishing in Foster's boat," Grandma Saran said. "Why you got that rock on the back of your hand?"

"Showing how steady I am," Elijah said. "Uncle Joshua said that when he was in the army they had to stand next to somebody shooting a gun and hold a pebble just like this to show they weren't afraid of the shooting."

"What's that up in that tree, boy?" Grandma Saran shielded her eyes from the sun.

"Where?" Elijah looked up.

Whack!

Grandma Saran knocked her grandson's hand into the air and watched the rock sail across the low azalea bush and onto a shell-covered grave. "Guess you're not as steady as you thought you were," she said, laughing.

"Grandma, you're just sneaky!"

"I thought you were just so steady!"

"I didn't even know Foster had a boat," Elijah said. "He must got a rowboat, because me and Abby are out on the river all the time and we don't see him."

"I don't know what Foster's got." Grandma Saran turned and started toward the picnic tables. "But I do know Mr. Turner don't need to have his child out with that old Foster. Foster just trying to soup up to him so he can borrow some drink money once in a while."

"Old man Turner got a lot of money?"

"More than most people around here," Grandma Saran said. "His daddy didn't have no whole lot of debts before the war. They owned a little hotel in Wraggstown."

"He had black people?"

"About six or so," Grandma Saran said. "They

worked in his hotel. Thought they was better than everybody else. You know them Smiths over in Pine Grove?"

"Them red-headed Smiths?"

"Yep. They used to belong to Turner. When the war was over, he fired all of them and hired some new people."

"And that boy was born blind?"

"David? They say he could see when he was first born," Grandma Saran said. "But when he got about two they saw he was walking into things. . . ."

Grandma Saran's voice trailed off, the way it often did when she was thinking hard.

Elijah wondered if she was thinking about little David or the taxes.

"My daddy tell you he's thinking about going North to look for work?" Elijah asked.

"Yes, he said it," Grandma Saran said. "He wants to help get the money but I hate to see the family so far apart. You know, it just puts me in mind of slavery times when they would sell people away. We didn't have nobody from our family sold away but I seen it in other families. It's a hurting thing, Elijah, a hurting thing."

Elijah wanted to talk to his father more, to say something to him that would make him happy, that would make him look not so tired. Once in a while he would look over at him and see him looking back, and they would both smile. Maybe, Elijah thought, that was the way it was with black men. The weight of it all just held you down so that you didn't do a whole lot of smiling.

The praise sermon had been spirited that morning. The church itself had been built from the boards of the cabins the older people in the community had lived in during the long period of their enslavement. They said they wanted to keep it as a reminder of what God had freed them from.

Grandma Saran went to help Sister Aiken with the small kids, and Elijah moved down the table and sat an arm's length away from Goldie.

"Somebody say grace so we can sit down and eat," said a tall woman with shiny black skin and teeth as white as the bleached cotton dress she wore.

"Stick your eyes back in your head, Elijah Lewis!" Goldie Paige hissed at Elijah.

"I got to look—" Elijah started.

"Go on, Elijah," Grandma Saran interrupted her favorite grandson. "Let's hear you bless this food this fine Sunday afternoon."

"Oh, Lord . . ." Elijah looked down as Goldie giggled. "We are truly thankful for the food we are now about to receive. . . . And, uh, we're glad . . . that You are glad that we are getting it. Amen."

"Amen!" said Richard. Lizzy was sitting at the far end of the first table and she nodded approvingly at her son.

"Elijah, how you know the Lord is glad we're getting this food?" Elder Dexter asked, settling on the bench behind the hot rolls. "How you know that?"

"The Lord loveth a cheerful giver," Elijah said quickly. "And all this food was given by . . . us."

"And I do hope He love a cheerful eater." Uncle Yero was a little touched in the head and crippled in his left leg, but he was always fun.

The table was filled with food. There were collard greens seasoned with ham hocks, mustards, sweet potatoes, rice, fried chicken, bacon, hot bread, and several pies. Elijah picked out his food with his eyes as he waited for the elders to fill their plates.

"Grandma Saran." Mary Hardin, Abby's girlfriend, gestured with a napkin. "Do you think it would be right for the boys to race on a Sabbath? The only reason I ask is that Henry said he could beat all the Lewis boys one by one or all together if they wanted to run like that."

"He ought to be able to run," Abby said. "When them white boys chased him from Mr. Parson's store, I thought he was going to leave his shadow behind he was moving so fast. All you could see—"

"They was seven of them wh-white b-b-boys!" Henry protested. "Whut you want me to do?"

"Better leave them white boys alone!" Richard

Lewis said. "You bother with them white boys and first thing you know there's going to be trouble. Things get out of hand quick with the Klan running around."

"I heard they ride around in sheets and say they dead people!" Henry went on.

"When I was young," Moses Lewis started, "I was about the fastest thing in these parts. Wasn't I, Saran?"

" 'Cepting for that boy over on the next plantation with that long head," Grandma Saran said. "Whatever happened to that boy?"

"Married a high yellow girl and took her up North," Grandpa Moses said. "She's faster than he is, if you know what I mean."

"Some of them high yellow gals think they's white," Henry added. "D-d-don't they, Goldie?"

"You better watch your mouth!" Goldie's mouth tightened as she spoke, knowing that Henry was referring to her light skin.

"All y'all hesh up," Lizzy spoke in a harsh whisper. "Here come old man Turner!"

Grandma Saran took the tea towel off the hot rolls, broke one off, and pulled it carefully apart. The steam from the roll drifted up, and Grandma Saran watched it intently as Mr. Turner crossed the ground between the road and the shady spot under the oaks where the tables sat.

"Afternoon, Mr. Turner," Lizzy said. "I guess you smelled those greens clear over to town."

"They sure smell good." Hamlin Turner took his hat off and wiped a band of sweat from his forehead. "I see your azaleas are up early. Probably from all the rain."

"Probably that and it hasn't been cold this winter," Grandma Saran said.

"You could take them into Johnson City and do real well with them," Mr. Turner said. "I saw a woman selling some from a cart down there on King Street. She was selling little bouquets."

"You want me to fix you a plate, Mr. Turner?" Goldie asked.

"No, I was just passing and thought I'd drop by and say hello," Mr. Turner said. "Y'all go on with your picnic. Have a nice time and all."

"Well, thank you," Lizzy answered.

"You haven't seen Foster, have you?" Mr. Turner leaned the top of his body backwards as he spoke.

"He ain't been around here," Elijah said.

"I didn't think so," Mr. Turner said, glancing at Grandma Saran. "Well, I guess I'll be getting along."

Grandma Saran let Hamlin Turner walk nearly out of earshot before she couldn't stand it any longer and called out to him.

"Mr. Hamlin!" she called, half standing at the long table. "Where's David?"

The balding white man turned slowly, lifted his hands upward, and exhaled deeply.

"Aunt Saran, I don't know where they are."

Elijah watched as Hamlin Turner shook his head, wiped at his neck with a dirty handkerchief, and started back toward his rig. Mr. Turner's rig wasn't fancy, but it was well made. He raised one foot to the small step on the side of the covered surrey and then pulled himself up to the seat with his arms. When he turned back toward the picnic, he looked directly at Grandma Saran, nodded, and shifted the reins over the broad back of the dappled mare in front of him.

"Serve him right," Grandpa Moses said.

"Hesh!" Grandma Saran looked down at the table and shifted two biscuits so they were arranged neatly on either side of a chicken thigh. "He may deserve it but little David don't!"

"Nothin' we can do," Lizzy said. "White people don't like colored in their business."

"Lizzy, ever since you were up North, you've been talking trash about white folks." Richard Lewis looked over at his wife. "Must be something in the water up there."

"I heard those northerners are just as swell as they want to be." Sister Lois rocked back and forth as she sewed.

"Most of them were really nice," Lizzy said. " 'Cause some of them didn't like colored people at all. I heard a grocer man say that he had never even seen a Negro before he came south and that he was scared of us when he first saw us. Then he didn't like us."

"Why didn't he like us?" Goldie asked.

"He said he didn't have no particular reason," Lizzy answered. "He said he just didn't."

"That's the way some folks are," Grandpa Moses said. "They can't like you just 'cause you're a human being. What they got to do is find some reason for liking you. And that reason is mostly that you doing something for them, or maybe—"

"Or if you sharecrop for them," Sister Lois interrupted. "Work their lands for next to nothing."

"Woman, are your lips so loose you can't keep your words in until I finish what I got to say?" Grandpa Moses asked.

"Moses Lewis, you say that little bit you got to say so slow it's going to be next Sunday before we get to hear it," Sister Lois said.

A fly flew over the food, and Grandpa Moses swiped at it with his hand. "Girl, I got more to say right now than you gonna have the rest of your natural life," he said.

"I didn't say you didn't have something to

say," Sister Lois went on. "I just said you sure take your own sweet time in getting it past your lower lip."

"What are we going to do about little David?" Grandma Saran asked.

Elijah knew that little David was on Grandma Saran's mind. Shortly after David was born, she had been called over to the Turner place. Mrs. Turner had become ill, and Hamlin Turner had turned to the woman who had been his nanny as a child. She had practically lived at the Turner place during the young bride's illness, and she stayed with the husband after the woman had passed away. Mr. Turner had never remarried. When little David became blind, he hired an Irish nurse to take care of him.

"I didn't even know Mr. Foster liked fishing," Elijah said.

"He don't like fishing," Grandpa Moses said. "You can bet anywhere he went he got his jug with him. I saw him once on that little island near Key. He was having a picnic lunch with that cousin of his, you know, the one with the store."

"Why would he go all the way over there?"

" 'Cause he can follow the tide out," Grandpa Moses said. "A lazy man always follows the tide. Then he can follow it right back in if he wasn't too juiced up to get the boat going."

"You want me and Abby to go and see if they need a hand looking for them?" Elijah asked.

"She didn't say nothing about me going," Abby protested.

"It would be nice," Grandma Saran said. "It don't hurt to make believe you were awake when you went to church this morning."

"I was awake," Abby said.

"I think he was dozing off when Reverend Dexter passed the plate," Goldie said.

"Y'all going on to town you better get going before it gets too late," Grandpa Moses said. "This looks like what the old folks used to call *yende* weather. Looks like it's turning real ugly."

As if in response, the wind picked up, lifting a corner of the tablecloth and whipping it against Sister Lois.

"Better put a jacket on, too." Elder Dexter nodded, as if he were agreeing with his own advice.

"Too bad Goldie can't go," Abby said, standing. "But she got to keep an eye on Henry. She told me she thought Henry was looking better every day."

"Abby, why don't you shut up your mouth!" Goldie answered, throwing a biscuit toward him.

"Don't be throwing no blessed food around!" Grandpa Moses said. "What's wrong with you children?"

"Daddy?" Elijah tried to think of something to say before he left. He knew his parents had to start back to Savannah and would be gone when he returned.

Richard pulled his son close and whispered in his ear. "You a Lewis, boy. Don't forget that."

"I won't, Daddy."

Richard Lewis turned and went back to the

table and sat next to Grandma Saran.

Lizzy lifted her son's chin up and looked at him. "When the crops are all in and the Glory Field is turned and ready for next year, I expect to see you coming over to Savannah to spend some time with us. I know I ain't going to be disappointed, right?"

"No, Mama, you know me better than that."

"Boy, look how your eyes are tearing up." Lizzy wiped at her son's eyes with a tea towel. "You're just a mush melon like your daddy. How can men as strong as you men are be so tender inside? You gonna answer that question, or you gonna kiss me and go on before I make a blubbering fool of myself?"

Elijah kissed his mother and turned away.

Elijah and Abby hitched up the dray that the church's part-time sexton used to haul wood. Abby ran his mouth on the way into town but Elijah didn't have much to say. Abby asked his cousin if he knew what time it was, and Elijah just grunted and shrugged.

It took nearly an hour to travel into town when the roads were dry, longer when they weren't. The sun had been high all day and the ground was firm, but not hard. Elijah looked at the sky. It was looking bad. The wind was picking up more, and there were brief smatterings of rain. In the distance the low boom of thunder rolled along the horizon.

"It's raining over the water," Abby pointed off to their right. Elijah pulled the top of his shirt together and wished he had worn a jacket. "We've had the boat out in the rain before. Plenty of times."

"It's getting cold," he said.

"I can't see how Grandma Saran can like white folks the way she do," Abby said. "She was born a slave and stayed a slave most of her life."

"She can like who she wants to like," Elijah said.

"I didn't say she couldn't," Abby said.

"And she don't have to like white folks to like little David, or even Mr. Turner," Elijah said.

"I heard she asked him for the money for the taxes," Abby said. "And he said he couldn't give it to her because the white folks around town wouldn't like it."

"Who told you that?"

"Sister Clinton," Abby said. "I know she like to run her mouth, but that's what she said."

A spray of rain and dust hit Elijah's face, and he turned away from the road. He took his bandanna from his pocket and wiped the dirt from his face.

"Abby, if I got an idea you gonna go along with it?"

"Yeah," Abby said. "You got one?"

"Maybe," Elijah answered. "Give me a minute to think it through."

"I got an idea, too." Abby took a pebble from the back of the cart and threw it toward the high grass on the side of the road. "I'm thinking about buying a guitar."

"If you thinking about playing that fast music you better find some other place to play it than around the house," Elijah said. "You know Grandma Saran said that ain't nothing but the devil's music."

"Ragtime ain't the devil's music. The devil ain't got no music. You think they got music down in hell?"

"If they do you sure gonna find out," Elijah said. "You start playing that music around the old folks, you're going to be in some big trouble. What you want to play it for anyway?"

"Something different," Abby said. "We ain't like Grandpa Moses and Grandma Saran. You, me, and Goldie are a different kind of black folks. We what you call the new breed and we got to make new moves and new music."

"That's what my idea is about, making a move," Elijah said. "I'm thinking to tell Mr. Turner I'll find little David if he lends Grandma the money to pay the taxes. He don't lend her the money, then I won't go out looking for his boy."

"You know where he is?" Abby asked, surprised.

"No, but you and me got as good a chance of finding him as anybody else," Elijah said.

"Man, you too hot-blooded. You say something like that to Mr. Turner and he's liable to get mad and start some trouble."

"I thought you and me and Goldie was the new breed. You mean all the new breed does is play fast music?" Elijah asked.

"You know the Kluxers shot a man over in York about a week ago?" Abby asked. "And all he did was to tell a white man he wasn't moving off the sidewalk when the white man told him to move."

"He dead?"

"No, but he shot!"

"He may be shot," Elijah said, "but at least he's a man."

"What you doing this for?" Abby asked.

"Something I saw in Grandma Saran's eyes," Elijah said. "She was talking about how the bank wouldn't lend them the money to pay the taxes, and her eyes looked empty. I never seen a person's eyes look like that before. You could look at her eyes, the way she put her head down, and you could almost feel how much she hurt. Then I looked at Grandpa Moses. . . ."

The mule shied away from a flurry of leaves that danced along the side of the road and then lifted into the air like some kind of leafy animal. Elijah steadied the reins and shifted his seat on the buckboard.

"So what did Grandpa Moses say?" Abby asked.

"He didn't say anything," Elijah said. "What's he going to say? He can't stand up to the bank."

"Yeah, what makes you think you going to stand up to Mr. Turner?" Abby asked.

"I don't know if I can." Elijah was grinning. "Just know I'm going to try."

"What you grinning about? You gone simple or something?"

"Could be," Elijah said. "That's from hanging out with you so much."

"Love is making you simple," Abby said, leaning back. "Goldie must got you good."

"I'm sweet on that girl," Elijah said. "So you can just keep your mouth off of her."

"You crazy, cousin," Abby said. "I ain't getting married until I'm forty, maybe even fifty."

"You ain't getting married till you find a one-legged blind woman," Elijah said. " 'Cause she won't see how ugly you are, and even if she hear about it she won't be fast enough to get away."

"Get on with yourself, man."

They passed a field of long-grain rice, and Elijah saw it swaying in the wind. The tall stalks looked almost like waves as they bowed before the wind. Elijah remembered stories that Grandma Saran used to tell him when he was young about how some people could call the wind to them.

As they neared the beach, they saw a bolt of lightning zig and crackle its way across the sky. A horse pulling a light rig danced sideways as it passed them and then broke into a gallop as the thunder boomed around them.

There was a knot of men down by the riverside, gathered around a fire built in an iron drum. Elijah stopped a distance down from them. He tied the reins to the seat and hopped down. Abby crossed over and came down beside him.

Sheriff Glover was talking with his back to them as they approached. The sheriff was thin and didn't have any backside at all. Mr. Turner saw Elijah and Abby first and signaled them to come over even though they were headed directly toward him.

"Glad you came," Hamlin Turner spoke through his teeth. "We still don't have any word."

"What you going to do?" Abby asked.

"You boys got to stand on top of me?" The sheriff turned and looked at Abby.

Abby looked away and took a step backwards.

"Mr. Turner is offering a twenty-five-dollar reward," one of the other white men in the small group said. "For anybody who finds the boy. We looked about where we thought they would be but nobody saw them. It's got to be a danger to go out too far."

"Dangerous to stay out there, too," Mr. Turner said. "I think they're on one of those islands waiting for the storm to blow over. The weather's bad but it's not impossible."

"Close to it, Mr. Turner." Wood Wilson, an old-timer, looked out at the sea and shook his head. "It's going to be a big one before it gets settled. And they could be back and safe already."

" 'Could be' ain't 'sure'!" Mr. Turner said. "You know I'm looking for 'sure,' Wood. Now you know you haven't seen Foster in any place where you'd expect him to be, have you?"

"You're right there," Wood said.

The men who were gathered were the ones who had boats. Some of them were just boaters, and some of them were fishermen. Elijah saw two of them turn and walk away from the beach.

"Only place to look is to go past Jeems Bank, which is too dangerous to go in dis wedder, Cap'n." Macon Smith was one of the few black fishermen in the area, and he knew the waters well.

"Macon, Elijah, I'll give you ten dollars if you find the boy. Macon?" Mr. Turner said.

Two more men started off, away from the beach. Mr. Turner kept his eyes dead on Macon Smith, not wanting to let on that the others had given up on finding his son.

Macon shrugged and put his head down.

Elijah looked out at the water. The whitecaps near the shore were already fifteen to twenty feet wide and the waves in the distance were cresting into longer and longer lines. Out at James's Bank, which Macon Smith had called "Jeems" the way the old folks did, the water looked about as rough as Elijah had ever seen it. The waves would be two to three feet high over the submerged bank. The rain hitting the side of the drum came in short sporadic bursts as the gusting, spiraling wind drove it now toward the shore and now out to sea. The storm was already too strong for them to take a boat out safely, and Mr. Turner knew it. Macon Smith nodded, smiled awkwardly, and walked away. There was only Sheriff Glover and two other white men left facing Hamlin Turner. Elijah looked at Abby, took a deep breath, and turned to Mr. Turner.

"My grandma needs the money to pay her taxes," Elijah said, looking down at the ground.

"What you mean, Elijah?" Mr. Turner's voice was flat as he turned.

Elijah lifted his head and looked at Hamlin Turner. "She needs the money to pay her taxes," he said. "She don't need no ten dollars."

"That's what I'm offering if you find my boy."

"You were offering twenty-five dollars to the others," Elijah said, his head down.

"You don't have a boat as good as theirs," Mr. Turner said.

"No way their piece of boat could get past James's Bank." Frank Petty had hired them once to row his boat on a fishing trip.

"It'll go," Abby said. "Me and 'Lijah is the best sailors out here."

"You think you worth twenty-five dollars?" Mr. Turner asked.

"We ain't going unless we get thirty-five dollars," Elijah said. "Cash money."

Sheriff Glover unsnapped the black leather holster and put his hand on the butt of his gun. "You know why young niggers like you don't get to be old niggers?" he asked.

There was thunder in the distance. The sound

of the surf whispered behind them. Elijah avoided Sheriff Glover's stare.

"You think you know where he might be?" Mr. Turner's words were slow, even.

"Naw." Elijah glanced at Mr. Turner and quickly away. "But we can look. We've been to near about every little island around here. If he's out there, we can find him."

"Anybody else want to go out looking?" Hamlin Turner asked the other men.

"Can't go out now," a short, heavyset man with gray eyes said. "Liable to break your boat up before you got it out into the channel. Wouldn't do nobody no good."

Mr. Turner looked at Elijah. "I've done your family a lot of favors," he said. "This is no way to treat me."

Elijah turned and started walking away.

"Nigger!" Frank Petty's voice whined through the growing cold. "Don't you be walking away from no white man when he talking proper to you!"

Elijah turned and looked at Frank Petty, then faced Hamlin Turner. He saw first the anger and then the concern in the white man's eyes. Sheriff Glover shifted his eyes from Elijah to Abby and back again. For a long moment the small knot of men stood silently, only Frank Petty's collar flapping in the wind. It came to Elijah at that moment, that very moment, that he was an absolute man for the first time in his life.

"You take twenty dollars?" Turner asked.

Elijah looked down without offering any answer.

"Ten dollars is more cash money than this nigger ever seen in his life," Frank Petty said. He shifted his feet in the sand.

"You taking out that fishing boat you got?" Sheriff Glover turned his head and seemed to look toward Abby's feet as he spoke.

"Only one we got," Abby said.

"It's strong," Elijah said.

"Get it down to the old pier," the sheriff said. "I'll go with you."

Elijah looked up at Hamlin Turner.

"I don't like your attitude, boy," Mr. Turner said. "And I know your people don't know what you're doing. But if you go out and find my boy, I'll give you the thirty-five dollars."

"Sheriff, you got a idea where they are?" Frank Petty asked nervously.

"I told you before I didn't have no idea," Sheriff Glover said. He hunched his shoulders forward against the cold. "I spoke to Foster before he took his boat out, but he didn't say nothing about where they were going."

"Then how come you going out with the niggers?" Petty asked, taking a small step sideways.

" 'Cause they ain't likely to get me kilt," the sheriff said, "and that's the only thing I'm worried about."

Elijah walked ahead of Abby as he went down the beach toward where the Negro fishermen had their boats. Just the week before he had told

Goldie and Mary Hardin that he was going to hit the next white man that called him a nigger even if it meant that he had to go to jail. But he knew you didn't raise your hand against a white man in Montgomery County. Not if you wanted to live to talk about it.

"Hey, 'Lijah." Abby caught up with his cousin. "Why you think the sheriff going out with us?"

"It's Elijah," Elijah said. "It's not 'Lijah!"

"You sure hate to be called a nigger, don't you?" Abby said. "You should have been born white."

"Uncle Lem fought and died to be free," Elijah said. "Uncle Joshua fought and got wounded to be free. They didn't fight to be called no niggers."

"Did I say they did?" Abby answered, hurt. "I still wonder why the sheriff is going out with us."

"He wants a piece of the money," Elijah said, swallowing hard. "I ain't giving it to him, though."

Abby didn't answer or ask Elijah how he was going to stop Sheriff Glover from just taking the money.

They called the boat the *Pele Queen*. Elijah had told Goldie that when he married her he was going to call her his Second Queen. The seventeen-foot boat had been designed as a plantation pleasure and sporting boat, with a small sail and room for three sets of oars. Sometimes the cousins just took the boat out for fun, but mostly it was for fishing. What they usually caught were mullets, yellowfin, and, if they were lucky, some bonitos. Mullets didn't bring much of a price, but when they went out and caught bonitos or salmon trout they could sell them in Johnson City. And if they could get someone else to go with them to catch and crate the crabs that clung to the sides of the net, they could sell them as well. At the very least they could scare up a dinner of plate crabs or mullet-gut stew nearly any time they wanted it.

"I bet Sheriff Glover knows we're the best sailors out here," Abby said.

"He's thinking something," Elijah said as he looked on the ground between where the boat was beached and the water. He didn't want to drag the boat over rocks or other sharp objects. "I know he didn't like what I was talking to Mr. Turner."

" 'Lijah, you was talking some big talk," Abby said softly.

"You scared?"

"Some."

"I got to be who I got to be," Elijah said. "I can't fit into a place just 'cause somebody say that's what I got to do."

"I didn't say you did," Abby said. "I just said you were talking big, and you know white folks don't like that."

"It'll blow over if we find David," Elijah said.

"We going to go look for him out on Key, where Grandpa Moses said?"

"Yeah, I guess so," Elijah answered. "Just hope he's okay if we find him."

"You think we going to make it out there and back?"

"I don't know about you," Elijah said, "but me and the *Pele Queen* are going to make it."

The *Pele Queen* was nearly flat-bottomed. It had a rounded prow that rose in a shallow arc from the water and rounded sides that took in too much water when it had a heavy load in high seas. But it never tipped, and that was what was important.

The rigging on the *Pele Queen* was cumbersome, but it was tight. Abby pulled the boat into the water until he was knee-deep and then jumped up on the boat. Elijah pushed, wading into the water until he felt the sudden incline of the ground beneath his feet, and pulled himself into the boat.

"How far you think they went?" Abby called down to him.

"Had to be far," Elijah said. "Or the others would have found them."

The spray of water in his face was colder than he thought it would be, but its salty taste made him feel good. Overhead brown-winged plovers flew in tight, noiseless circles.

"You think the sheriff is going to try anything funny?" Abby asked.

"Naw," Elijah said. He looked to where Mr. Turner was standing with the sheriff. "Look under the seat and see if that gutting knife is there."

Abby stopped rowing, felt under the old train seat they had found and were using as a boat seat, and nodded.

In the distance, the clouds were darker than Elijah had ever seen them before. If he had just been out fishing, he would have turned the boat for shore. The gulls, even the ones that weren't foraging for food, were flying low.

We're the best sailors out here, Abby had said. Elijah recalled the words, reassuring himself. As Elijah watched the whitecaps rise and change angles as they headed away from shore, he knew they had better be the best.

Sheriff Glover met the boat just opposite the cannons. He was carrying a bundle, which he threw into the *Pele Queen*, and then, without saying a word, he started pushing her nose toward the open sea.

Once the boat was turned, Sheriff Glover lifted himself easily over the side. Elijah watched as he opened the bundle he had thrown aboard and took his gun from it. He put the gun in his holster and then took the seat behind Abby and held the rudder.

The short sail was useless in the squalling wind, and Abby had tied it firmly to the mast. The boat was turned straight out toward James's Bank, and Elijah spread his legs and braced himself between the oarlocks. He held the oars forward as he watched Abby's smooth rhythm and then fell in with him. The pull of the oars felt good in his arms and shoulders. He knew it would take a few strokes to get loose, maybe even more than that, but the roll of the boat was good, even joyful. The rounded oar handles, worn smooth by years of pulling through the lowland waters, warmed in his strong hands. Over Abby's shoulder Sheriff Glover hunched over the tiller, his face dark as he worked out whatever thoughts he needed to be working out.

The water just beyond the first bank was rough with the breaker line running at a sharp angle to the shore. Elijah knew that the tide was coming in and it was just the wind that was forcing the waves sideways.

Beneath the roiling waters lay the sinister and

treacherous sand banks. The water near the banks often changed direction abruptly, or produced a foam that suggested the danger that lay below. The distance between the first sand bank and the larger James's Bank was usually fourteen minutes of strong rowing on a good day. It was going to take them longer today, Elijah knew.

But it was what lay beyond the bank that worried Elijah. If there was a strong undercurrent, they would be in it once they went past the sand bank.

Elijah and Abby pulled together, struggling with the breakers dispersing over the bank. As they got nearer and nearer, the rowing got harder. The muscles in Elijah's shoulders started burning, and he was breathing harder. They were drifting left, just as he thought they would, and he eased up on his right oar to turn the boat slightly.

"Sheriff, we need to go into the current!" Elijah called out. "Toward Gray Rock!"

Sheriff Glover brought his forearm alongside the tiller and pulled it toward him. The breakers were coming over the bow when the boat dipped forward and smacking against it when it was on the lift.

"Pull, Abby! Pull!"

Abby put his back into the rowing, and they pulled quickly past the breaker line over the first bank.

"Hold . . ."

Elijah started to yell to Sheriff Glover to take

a hard hold onto the tiller when the boat began
to spin again, first one way and then the other.
Elijah looked back and saw Sheriff Glover holding on to the sides of the boat. Abby had seen
it, too. He pulled his oars into the boat and held
onto the sides.

"We're going too fast!" Abby called out.

Elijah knew what Abby meant. They were ap-
proaching Gray Rock, a small island, less than
two acres in area and approachable only from
the side that faced Johnson City. The other side
was little more than a rocky projection that invited small boats to their demise. There was a
submerged marsh area some hundred feet in
front of it. On the far side of the narrow island
was a channel through which the ocean seemed
to get faster, threatening to carry a vessel out to
the cold, inhospitable sea. It was no place to be
during a storm. Beyond Gray Rock lay Key Island, which Grandpa Moses had seen Foster on
before. But they needed to go to the right of
Gray Rock if they were going to have a chance
to reach Key Island.

Sheriff Glover put his hands to his brow,
trying to shield his eyes from the spray that was
picking up. It had begun to rain harder.

"There's no way we can get out there!" he
called. "We'd better start back!"

"No!" Elijah called out to Abby. "Keep going!"

Sheriff Glover unsnapped the leather flap on
his holster, pulled the long-barrel revolver from

its nesting place, and pointed it at Abby. "I said turn back, boy!"

Abby looked at Elijah.

Elijah pulled the oar handles into his lap, lifting the blades from the water, letting the boat pick up speed and roll with the sea. Sheriff Glover whirled, pointed the gun at him and extended his arm.

Elijah took a deep breath and held it. He looked over the gun barrel into the sheriff's frightened face. For a long moment the two of them, Elijah and Sheriff Glover, stared at each other as the boat bobbed and turned in the water.

The officer first put the gun down by his side and then lifted it and replaced it in its holster. He turned away from Elijah's glance.

The rowing had been hard, but now it was harder, as both boys pulled with all their strength to get past Gray Rock and on to Key. Every muscle in Elijah's back began to ache as he pulled them away from Gray Rock and closer and closer to Key Island. He imagined Abby's face, knowing that his cousin would be in as much agony as he was, but wouldn't be showing it.

There was a line of whitecaps between them and Key Island, but also a lot of white and green foam near the island. Abby stopped rowing and pointed. Elijah nodded and stopped rowing, too.

"What's the matter?" Sheriff Glover called out.

"Could be rocks!" Elijah called back. He peered into the water but it was moving too much to be sure of anything. A lot of the islands were in shallow water and had submerged rocks around them. They rowed the boat a little closer, saw what looked like a sand bank under the breakers, and stopped again. They were less than twenty-five yards offshore.

Elijah let himself down over the side of the boat and held on until his feet touched solid ground. He walked toward the shore and felt the jagged rocks beneath his feet. He pointed down at them with his thumb. If Foster and little David had allowed their boat to get too close to the island, it could have been damaged.

Sheriff Glover saw what was going on and took out his revolver and wrapped it in the same cloth he had used to bring it to the boat.

"Stay with the boat!" Elijah called to Abby.

Abby dropped anchor as Sheriff Glover went over the side of the boat. Elijah led the way on the short walk. He was breathing heavily by the time he passed a large turtle that had disappeared under its shell. Sheriff Glover was right behind him, and alone, out in the water on the bobbing boat, was Abby.

"You start looking one way, and I'll start looking the other," Sheriff Glover said. "We can't stay out here too long."

"Sheriff, why did you come out here with us?" Elijah asked.

"Your grandma might needs the money, boy." Sheriff Glover wiped his nose with the back of his hand. "But round here, poor ain't just for niggers. Now let's get on with this."

Key Island was no more than an eighth of a mile across at its widest part. What could be seen of it was shaped like the large keys that opened parlor doors, but surrounding it and just below the water's surface was a rocky shelf that extended irregularly along the leeward side and with some regularity along the side of the island that faced the open sea. Growing throughout the island were wild grasses, weeds, and cane plants, and what looked to Elijah to be an untamed bush somewhat like palmetto, but with small, purplish flowers growing out of the very tips of the leaves.

"David!"

Elijah heard Sheriff Glover call the boy's name, pronouncing the "a" as if it were an "i," the way some white people did. He knew the sheriff was scared. He was scared, too.

It was growing dark quickly, and the warm rain, which had been coming down steadily since they had started out, was now falling much harder. Elijah's clothes were soaked, and the rain, washing the sweat from his brow into his eyes, blinded him. He pulled his already wet shirttail from his pants and tried to wipe the water and perspiration from his eyes.

"Da-a-vid!" he called out.

It wouldn't have made any sense for them to go to the other side of the small island, he thought. The weather would have been worse there, and they would have a better chance of being seen on this side. Elijah looked back to where the boat was bobbing in the water, tossing and turning, straining against the small anchor that he and Abby had bought on King Street back in Johnson City. For a moment he let his mind wander back to Johnson City, and then he quickly forced himself back to the little island.

"Da-a-vid!"

He moved toward the center of the island, walking gingerly over the marshy footing. A sudden flash of lightning stopped him in his tracks, and the boom of the thunder, too close to the flash for him to brace himself, seemed to rise up from the island itself.

"Da—" He started to call out again, realized he had his eyes closed, and forced himself to open them. The wind howled and pushed at him, and the trees at the crest of the island looked like shadows dancing wildly against the distant sky.

Elijah looked around and saw nothing. He was sure that they weren't on Key Island. He wished he hadn't made Abby come out with him. He stumbled, catching himself with his hands, feeling them sink into the soft earth as he scrambled to his feet.

As he neared the crest of the island and turned back he couldn't see the boat. He looked again, not sure if he was looking in the right direction or if the boat had gone under! He pulled his shirt up, shielding his face from the wind and the driving rain, but he still couldn't see the boat.

Everything in him wanted to run back to the shore, to scream out Abby's name, to jump into the water and search for the boat. The footing on the island was heavy and the bottoms of his pants were soaked as he headed toward the crest of the island. He clenched his jaw and ran the last few yards sideways. He got to the top and looked over.

"Da-a-vid!"

The wind roared and whipped his wet pants around his legs. His shirt stood almost straight back from his body as he leaned into the wind.

"Da-a-vid!"

He thought he heard something. It could have been the cry of a trapped gull, or the wind whistling through the tall grasses, but it was something.

"Da-a-vid!" he called again.

"Help!"

The cry was weak, but it was clear. Elijah looked to his left and saw the boy's thin arm swinging over his head.

"Sheriff! Sheriff!" Elijah called to the darkness behind him. "He's over here!"

Elijah didn't know if Sheriff Glover was near or if he could hear him. He started down the slope toward where he had seen David, slipping as he did, trying to catch hold of tree limbs, trying to keep his eyes open. He didn't want to lose the boy now.

He wiped his eyes again as he reached David Turner. The boy was trembling with the cold and sickly looking. At his feet, half covered with wet grass, was Foster.

"He's hurt!" David said.

Elijah looked at Foster. His eyes were open and his teeth were gritted. Then Elijah saw why they were on this side of the island. Foster had both arms around David's leg in a death grip. He had been hurt on this side of the island and he wasn't going to let the boy leave him.

"Let me get David to the boat and . . ."

Foster was already shaking his head and working to get a tighter grip on the boy's frail, white leg.

"Where you hurt?" Elijah asked David.

"I ain't hurt," David answered. "Mr. Foster's leg is hurt. Is my daddy here?"

"No," Elijah said. "He sent us."

"Who are you?" David lifted a tentative hand.

"Elijah," Elijah answered. "Elijah Lewis."

David reached up and touched Elijah's face and then his hair.

"Elijah!" A voice came from the storm. It was the sheriff calling.

"Here!" Elijah answered. "We're over here!"

Elijah first heard and then saw the sheriff coming down the slope toward them. He heard him curse once as he fell.

"Foster has a hurt leg and he's scared to let go of David," Elijah said.

As Elijah explained the situation, the sheriff cleared the branches from around Foster. The round-faced man stared at the sheriff.

"It's broken," the sheriff said. "I'll set it best I can. You get the boy out to the boat."

"Take me with you!" Foster held on tighter, and David winced from the pain.

The sheriff slowly, deliberately, withdrew the pistol from its protective wrapping. Without a word he put the muzzle against Foster's forehead and cocked the weapon. Foster let go of David's leg. His mouth opened and he began to whimper.

Elijah lifted David into his arms and felt the boy's arms go around his neck.

"Elijah!" Sheriff Glover was putting the gun back into his holster.

Elijah looked over his shoulder.

"If you don't come back I'll find you and kill you," he said. "You hear that?"

Elijah looked at the two men—the sheriff with his forced sneer, Foster still whimpering—and turned away.

The wind picked up sand and bits of twigs

and sent them flying into Elijah's face. David clung to him desperately as he picked his way over the crest and down the other side toward the spot where he hoped to find Abby and the boat.

The water had risen, and Elijah had to stop a distance from where he had first come ashore. At the water's edge, he stooped to put David down and saw the boy tremble. The child was shaking from cold and fear, but there were no tears coming from the blind eyes. He just put his arms around his knees and waited.

Elijah searched for the boat, trying to focus on shadows in the dark waters. The crackle and hiss of lightning overhead startled him, making him recoil as it arced across the open sky. It was by the last light from this lightning that he saw the boat.

"There it is!" he called to David. "I see the boat!"

He took David's hand and pulled the boy to his feet. He began walking and David, holding Elijah's hand with both of his own, followed him into the water.

The boy could swim, so he wasn't afraid of the water. Still Elijah held onto his shirt as tightly as he could. When they got to the boat, he could see that Abby was having a hard time keeping it moored.

Maybe because he was tired, or maybe because of the weight of the boy in his waterlogged clothes, but it was all that Elijah could do to push

David over the side and into the boat.

"I'm going back for Foster!" Elijah called.

"You want me to go?" Abby asked.

"No, I'll go," Elijah said.

The sheriff had Foster on the beach by the time Elijah got back. He had tied Foster's leg to a fairly straight branch and had dragged him down to the shoreline.

Sheriff Glover didn't say anything when he saw Elijah. His face was flushed with the effort he had made to get Foster to the beach. Together they grabbed the still-whimpering man and started for the boat.

Foster screamed and called on God to help him as the sheriff and Elijah dumped him into the boat. Abby helped the sheriff into the boat and then pulled in Elijah.

It was several more minutes before they could get the anchor up. Abby had taken off his shirt and wrapped it around David, but the boy still shook almost as badly as he had before. On the floor of the boat, Foster seemed to be going into and out of consciousness.

Even with the wind pushing them toward shore, the rowing past Gray Rock and then in toward James's Bank was all pain. They had to prevent the boat from drifting into a line with the bay where an undercurrent could push them back out or carry them down below the pier area. The wind was gusting harder than Elijah had ever seen or felt it, and he wasn't sure if they were going to make it.

There were strong eddies just in front of James's Bank and Elijah thought the tide was going to start out. The *Pele Queen* rolled hard and its stern came completely out of the water. The line snapping against the spar sounded like gunshots in the darkness. Abby dropped an oar, and they watched it move along a wave, fly into the air, and clatter loudly against the side of the boat. When it fell into the water they only had three oars left.

Once they were past James's Bank, the rowing was just as hard but they weren't afraid of being swept out to sea. Elijah thought that the worst that would happen would be that the boat capsized and they all had to swim for it or that they would drift upland.

"Fires!" Abby's voice was strained, just loud enough to be heard over the sound of the sea. Elijah looked and saw the fires ashore, like orange stars in the darkness. He and Abby took turns rowing the boat the rest of the way.

Two men, one of them Macon Smith, came out to throw ropes on the boat to steady it while they got David and Foster out. Abby got out and helped the men pull the boat toward shore.

"Elijah, I'm letting you have half the rescue money," Sheriff Glover said as he slid over the side of the boat. "Don't say nothing about it. Just be glad you getting what you getting."

"Sheriff"—Elijah's face was inches from the sheriff's—"my grandma needs that money. All of it."

"Yeah, I guess she does if you say so," Sheriff Glover said. "I don't know anybody around these parts that don't need cash money. I told you I'm letting you have half of it, so there ain't no need to go talking about it."

Sheriff Glover pulled his wet shirt away from his skin and turned away.

Elijah closed his eyes and tried to think of something else to say to the figure that moved away from him. He thought there must be something to say, some idea, some word that would make things right. He heard voices behind him, familiar voices, and, wearily, turned toward them.

Grandpa Moses, Grandma Saran, and Goldie were waiting for them along with Mr. Turner and the others. Elijah saw that the storm had torn down some of the trees along the waterfront green and had blown over a buckboard. Mr. Turner had some men right the buckboard and put Foster on it. They had to walk beside the mules to lead them as they went to find a doctor.

Elijah and Abby were shaking hands all around, and Macon Smith was saying that he would see to it that the *Pele Queen* was secured. Grandma Saran was crying as she hugged Elijah, telling him that she knew God would take care of him and Abby. As she talked with her head against his chest, Elijah saw Sheriff Glover walking with Hamlin Turner. He was carrying David.

The *Gazette* carried the story of the storm the next day, saying how much it had cost everybody and how much damage had been done. Four people had been killed, and two were still missing. On the bottom of the first page was a story of how Sheriff Virgil Glover had rescued David Turner and James Foster from Key Island, but that during the night Mr. Foster had died from an apparent heart attack.

"We don't never get no credit." Grandpa Moses was carving on a piece of driftwood. "It don't make no difference, though. When the Lord does the tallying up, then *everybody* is going to be in for a big surprise!"

Elijah looked over to where Abby was sitting in his long johns, cradling a cup of sassafras tea. Elijah could smell the sassafras from across the room and realized that as soon as Grandma Saran knew he was awake, he would be getting his. He had felt her come in to him in the middle of the night, had felt the mutton tallow on his chest, and had fallen asleep with her rubbing in the remedy against colds and consumption.

Later that morning Elijah faced Abby over a breakfast of fried hominy and bacon. "Don't say nothing to Grandma Saran," he said. "No use in worrying her over it."

"You think we going to get any of the money?" Abby asked.

"How Mr. Turner going to fix his mouth to say we didn't do nothing?" Elijah asked.

"They're white folks," Abby said. "Maybe their mouths just come fixed wrong."

Elijah told himself four times that he wasn't

going to run in and ask Mr. Turner for the
money. Right was right, he told himself over
and over again. But he was wondering, too. He
knew that Sheriff Glover had talked with him,
and he remembered seeing the sheriff carry
David as he walked alongside his father. But
David knew who had found him, knew who had
carried him to the boat. And there wasn't any
reason for the boy to lie. No, none at all.

It was two days before Elijah Lewis got back
into town. He had to pick up some washing from
the white folks for some of the women who did
it for twenty cents a load, and he needed to take
in some baskets to the market. He did that and
then he went down to check on the *Pele Queen.*
Abby had checked on it once and said it was all
right except for the oar they had lost, but Elijah
wanted to check it again.

Elijah saw that the oarlock had pulled out and
fallen inside the boat. That was why Abby had
lost the oar.

"Why don't you lend me your boat over the
weekend." The voice came from behind him.
"Give you half of what I catch."

Elijah turned and saw Frank Petty and his
uncle, J. D. Petty, standing with some crab baskets. "I don't lend my boat," Elijah said.

"How come you such a uppity boy?" Frank
Petty spat a stream of tobacco juice on the
ground.

"I don't want any trouble from you, Mr.
Petty," Elijah said, looking away.

"You still didn't answer his question, boy."
J. D. Petty had a reputation for not liking black
people.

Elijah looked again at his boat and then started
to walk away. Frank Petty stepped in front of
him and pushed him back against the boat.

Elijah reached into the boat, grabbed an oar,
and whirled around to face Frank. "Come on!"
he said, holding the oar with one hand and beck-
oning with the other.

A few men from down the beach came to see
what the commotion was all about. Half of them
were black.

"What's the matter, Frank?" an old white man
asked.

"Boy here can't take no joshing, that's all,"
Frank Petty said, picking up his crab basket. "He
needs to relax a little."

Elijah watched as the Pettys walked down the
beach. The other men watched them, no one
speaking. The blacks drifted off first, and the
whites returned to their business. Elijah had a
feeling that he might have to fight Frank Petty
some time before this whole thing was over.

"So he just reached over and give you the money!" Grandpa Moses' voice lifted with disbelief as he looked from Elijah to the money the boy had put on the table in front of him and Grandma Saran.

"No, he didn't say anything when we got back the other night," Elijah said.

"He was just taking care of little David," Abby said. He and Grandpa Moses were laying out oak strips they had cut during the winter for baskets.

"So when I went to town this morning, I went around to his back door. I was halfway afraid to knock."

"I can't imagine being afraid of Hamlin Turner." Grandma Saran still had the ends of the snap beans in her lap.

"So he sits me down and asks me if I wanted a cool glass of lemonade," Elijah said. "And I said yes because I didn't want to look like I didn't have no manners or something."

"That's right," Grandpa Moses added. "You got to have manners."

"I was ready to remind him of what me and Abby had done," Elijah went on, "when he goes into the other room and comes back and starts counting out the money. Thirty-five dollars!"

"Just counted it out?" Grandma Saran looked at the money again.

"He said that all the money in the world wasn't as precious to him as his boy," Elijah said. "He looked real touched. Then he told me how Sheriff Glover talked to him about the money, too."

"He wanted a piece of it, too?" Grandpa Moses looked up from the strips.

"He wanted half of it," Elijah said. "But Mr. Turner told me not to worry on it. He said he took care of the sheriff."

"Oh, my goodness!" Grandma Saran shook her head. "You boys are something!"

"Mostly it's Elijah." Abby straddled a chair he had turned backwards. "I said, 'Look at old 'Lijah talking to them white folks like he a regular businessman!' "

"We can't take all this money," Grandma Saran said. "You got to buy yourself something nice with a part of it. Then we can take the rest what's left over and pay the taxes."

"I ain't seen thirty-five dollars stuck money since Skippy was a pup!"

"What's stuck money?" Abby asked.

"Stuck money is money what comes in your hand and sticks there for more than two minutes," Grandpa Moses said. "A black man don't see no stuck money. What we see is scratch money. The white man give you money in one hand, and then he scratch on his paper to see what you owe him, and then that money go right back to him."

"What you boys—what you young men— want for supper tonight?" Grandma Saran asked.

"What you gonna have?"

"I was just thinking on having some fried chicken, collard greens, and some candied yams. But now it looks like I'm going to have to add a rhubarb and store cheese pie to it."

"Sounds good to me," Elijah said. "It sounds real good to me."

Elijah worked the sunny side of the Glory Field, and Grandpa Moses and Abby worked the shady side. He felt good, better than he ever remembered feeling. This was what it felt like, being a man, he thought. Working out in the fields with your family and knowing your taxes were paid and having somebody like Grandma Saran fixing your supper. It was as if he was stronger than he had ever been—and taller.

Elijah couldn't be still. He couldn't sit still and he couldn't stand still, either. Not with the way Grandpa Moses and Grandma Saran had looked when he gave them the money. That was the way it was supposed to be, everybody excited and thinking about what they were going to be doing. He reached down and picked up a handful of dirt, saw the way it looked in the light part of his palm, and squeezed it as tightly as he could. It was Lewis land, and it would be Lewis land.

He remembered Henry's mother saying how she knew when the colored boys went off to fight in the war that they were going to win it for the Union. They had gone out scared, she had said, and had come back strutting so tall and proud it had brought tears to her eyes. Some of the men who had fought with the Union got a hard time from the old Confederate soldiers when they came back and had to leave Curry. Uncle Joshua had had to leave, but he left standing like a man.

Then Elijah let his mind wander. He imagined a rich white man coming all the way down from Philadelphia and going out sailing with his family. Then there would be another storm and he would lose his little boy just like Mr. Turner had lost David. Then Elijah changed his dream so that the man from Philadelphia would lose a little girl, just to make it different. Then he thought about it some more and thought he'd better make it a little boy.

In his dream it was twice as hard as it was with little David. He had him and Abby hanging on to the side of the boat, and maybe Sheriff Glover would jump off and swim back to shore shouting something about how nobody could save the child 'cause the storm was too bad.

But he and Abby would save the child, and the man from Philadelphia would give them one hundred dollars cash money. How did Grandpa Moses call it? Stuck money! Yes, that would be it. Stuck money.

The storm had given the ground a good soaking, which meant they would have to weed again before the week was out. Weeding was backbreaking work, but it had to be done. Elijah thought that if he and Abby could earn some money with the boat, maybe they could get their own field. It would be part of the Lewis family land, but they would buy it on their own. Then he smiled at the thought of him being a landowner.

Off in the distance he saw a lone rider on a big, black horse. He watched as the horse stopped at Linda Road, then shifted direction toward the Lewis house. He could tell it was Sheriff Glover and turned back to his weeding. He pushed the hoe under a small patch of weeds and rocked it gently until they came up. He looked to see if he had gotten the roots, saw that he had, and then chopped through it. Out of the corner of his eye he could see Glover coming, in no big rush, his hat pulled down over his eyes.

If he thought he was going to get any more of the money, Elijah thought, he was dead wrong. They hadn't needed him out there in the first place. All he had done was to tie up Foster's leg to a branch and drag him down to the shore. Foster had died anyway.

The next weed he didn't lift. He just chopped it through, jabbing the hoe deep into the ground even when he didn't see the weed anymore.

Sheriff Glover stopped at the edge of the field, then went past him to the house.

Elijah kept chopping the hoe into the ground, walking the row slowly, as Grandpa Moses had taught him to do. He saw Sheriff Glover talk to Grandma Saran from the back of his horse, then wheel the animal around, and start back down the road, as casually as he had come.

From the distance Elijah saw Grandma Saran gather her skirt in her hands and go quickly into the house. He turned and looked at Sheriff Glover as he rode slowly past, not looking at Elijah or even apparently mindful of his presence. Soon Goldie appeared at the front door and came tearing across the field, her skirts flying behind her. Elijah rested his hand on the hoe and waited. He turned his head slightly and saw that Sheriff Glover had already crossed Linda Road.

"Elijah, we got trouble!" Goldie's face was already streaked with tears.

"What's the matter?" Elijah turned again and saw Sheriff Glover almost out of sight.

"Sheriff Glover came and told Grandma Saran that some men are going to come tonight to give you a whipping!"

"Ain't nobody . . ." Elijah felt the anger well

up in him. He looked away from Goldie, across the neatly kept fields, and then back into her tear-stained face. "Ain't nobody giving me no whipping. He better bring about ten guns if he's gonna whip me!"

"Grandma Saran said to come into the house." Goldie was pulling at Elijah's arm. "Come on!"

Elijah wouldn't run. He walked slowly across the field, ignoring Goldie's pleas for him to hurry. He thought about Sheriff Glover, and wondered if he could take him. He could, he thought, if the sheriff didn't have the big pistol on his belt.

"Goldie tell you what he said?" Grandpa Moses met Elijah in the yard.

"He ain't whipping me!" Elijah said. "I ain't letting him whip me! He didn't try it just now with just me and him in the field and he ain't whipping me later."

"It ain't him," Grandpa Moses said. "It's Frank Petty." Behind him Grandma Saran came out of the house. She was dressed to go to town.

"Goldie, you go get Abby, and Henry, and everybody else you can see," Grandpa Moses said. "Tell them to get over here right away. We got trouble."

"Grandma, I didn't do nothing," Elijah started to explain to his grandmother. "I was in town and he . . ."

Grandma Saran threw her arms around her grandson and held him tight.

"But he ain't whipping me, Grandma," Elijah

went on. "He ain't whipping me."

"That's why you got to go!" The old woman was crying. "I knew you weren't going to let him whip you. That's why you got to go!"

"Grandpa Moses . . ."

"Sheriff Glover said that Petty got a bunch of men in town and they getting all liquored up," Grandpa Moses said. "He told them he wasn't going to stand for no killing, and they said they were just going to whup you. But you can't trust them when they sober, so how you going to trust them when they liquored up?"

"Can't we stop them?" Goldie asked.

"Best we can do is to get all the men folks we can who got guns and just sit here and wait for them to come," Grandpa Moses said. "Then we can tell them that you gone and hope that they're satisfied with that. If they ain't, then we'll just have to hope there's no killing."

"Sheriff Glover said I should go?"

"No, he just come out to warn us to expect trouble. He said you got to do what you got to do." Grandma Saran's body was heaving up with her grief, and the tears ran freely down her face. "Why can't they leave our men alone!"

"That's the way things are," Grandpa Moses said. "The only way some people can see their own manhood is by pushing somebody else down. If you want us to fight them, we'll get the guns. Ain't no Lewis scared. If that's what you want us to do. If you want to go, you can head up to Chicago way like Joshua and Neela.

Joshua is getting old now, but he can get you a place to stay if that's what you want to do."

"Grandma Saran." Elijah's eyes filled with tears. "You know I can't stand for no man to whip me. I'm as much man as anybody alive."

"I know, Elijah," Grandma Saran said. "I know."

"You fix me something to eat on the way?"

Grandma Saran nodded and turned away.

Elijah put his good pants and two clean shirts in a sack with his good shoes and a fresh-pressed collar. Abby couldn't talk. He just sat in a corner and stared at his hands until it was time to hitch up the team.

It was Grandpa Moses who brought out the shackles. He brought them out and stood in front of Elijah.

"The first black man that we can remember in our family come here wearing these," he said. "This is where we come from, and what we overcome. It's up to you where you go from here. You hear that?"

"I hear that," Elijah said. "I hear it."

The waiting room at Elksdale had been closed since the war. The windows were boarded, and debris was piled against the side wall. Cary Epps had driven them to the small water stop six miles from town. Cary sat on the wagon, a shotgun across his lap, alone in his thoughts. Goldie stood next to Elijah beside the wagon, both of her arms around him, her head against his shoulder. The first train out was headed north, toward Canada. Elijah would have liked to have caught a train toward Savannah where his parents were, but one wouldn't be along until the next evening. It wasn't right, he thought, to have to go where the first train took you, to have to follow the tracks instead of what was in your heart.

"You remember when you was little I used to rock you and tell you how me and you was going to ride in a fancy rig down King Street?" Grandma Saran looked up at the tall, black man before her.

"I should be back there with the men," Elijah said. "I can handle a gun same as any of them."

"Elijah . . . Elijah . . ." Grandma Saran rubbed the back of his hand. "It ain't about handling a gun. It's about going on. And looking for a better day. And that's what you got to do. You a Lewis. And you got something in you what's been passed down from generation to generation, from man to man. We come a long way, from them shackles to now, but we still got so long to go."

"Everything was so good this morning—"

"It's still good, Elijah," Grandma Saran said. "It's still good. As long as God is still ruling heaven, it's still good. Just don't forget you're a Lewis, and we're family. I know you going to make that mean something. You write us and we can figure out what's what down here and let you know. . . ."

Grandma Saran was crying again.

What made him feel worse than anything was the seventeen dollars he had in his pocket. She had made him take it to have something to live on until he found some work.

An old white man in overalls and a straw hat pulled a buckboard up next to the closed station. He saw Grandma Saran, Goldie, and Elijah and nodded. Grandma Saran nodded back.

The whistle of the train seemed to come from a thousand miles away.

Goldie had helped make the basket of food he was taking. She handed it to him and whispered in his ear that she loved him.

Elijah kissed Grandma Saran, who turned quickly away and went to the wagon.

"You ain't going to marry nobody till . . ."

"I ain't going to marry nobody till you get back, Elijah," Goldie finished the sentence for him. "I won't even think of nobody or nothing until you get back."

Elijah took her shoulders in his hands and pulled her to him. Her face, as they kissed, was wet with tears and puffy from crying. The kiss itself was quick and salty from the tears. It was the first time that they had kissed like this, like a man and a woman, and both of them knew that it might be the last. He moved away from her and saw her eyes searching his face, looking for some sign that things would be all right.

"I know I'll be back," Elijah said, softly. "Don't you worry on it."

There wasn't a colored car so he had to sit on

a crate in one of the boxcars. The conductor said that when they got to Illinois he could ride where he wanted.

The train rocked through the darkness, through the night. Elijah Lewis closed his eyes and felt the weariness in his bones come down on him. He closed his eyes and waited for sleep, wondering if he would ever wake to a better day.

MAY 1930,
CHICAGO, ILLINOIS

THE LEWIS FAMILY, 1930

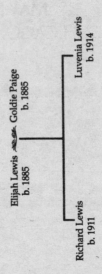

Elijah Lewis   Goldie Paige
b. 1885   b. 1885

Richard Lewis
b. 1911

Luvenia Lewis
b. 1914

"I'm just not going and that's it!" Luvenia Lewis put the curling iron back on the stove with a bang and then adjusted it so that the curler was not directly in the fire.

"You ain't going to do *what*?" Etta Pinckney adjusted the sheet that Luvenia had put around her shoulders. "I guess you didn't read what that letter said!"

"Miss Etta, I know what the letter said." The tall, dark-skinned sixteen-year-old was combing pomade through her godmother's hair. "But just because Daddy's going to send me the money to go down to Curry doesn't mean I have to go."

"You looking out for gray hairs, girl?" Miss Etta was in her mid-fifties.

"You're okay on top," Luvenia said, "but I'm going to have to put some henna near your temples."

"I don't want no red hair," Miss Etta complained. "How much gray I got?"

"Not much. And I'll match you up," Luvenia

said, carefully avoiding a small mole on the back of Miss Etta's neck.

"Well, I don't know what you're going to do if your daddy says he wants you down there. You know Elijah's always had his heart just set on going back home. He talks more about that Glory Field you people got down there than he do about his apartment."

"Mama says he just uses it as an excuse not to buy new furniture," Luvenia said. "Anyway, Miss Etta, I'm a city girl! Let him take Richard on down there with him. I don't want to live on nobody's farm."

"Well, call me when you're fixing to tell him so I can buy a front-row seat." The kitchen chair groaned as Miss Etta shifted her weight. Mr. Harrison, her boyfriend, had repaired the chairs twice, but the joints still creaked.

"He wasn't talking about it that much before he went down for Grandpa Moses' funeral," Luvenia said, picking up the curling iron again. "What I think happened was he went down there, got to thinking about the good times he had when he was young, and then started talking about staying down there. What does he know about farming? He's been up here since he was my age."

"I hear what you saying, Luvenia, but I don't see how you can just up and—*ow*, girl! You got to burn my neck? *I* ain't sending you down South!"

"I'm sorry, Miss Etta, but I'm really upset."

"Yeah, well be upset on your own neck!"

"Daddy's got to realize that there are city folk and then there's country folk. I was raised in Chicago and I'm a Chicago girl. You have to explain that to him in your letter."

"*What* letter?"

Luvenia lay the curling iron down and put her arms around Miss Etta's neck. "You have to help me out," she said. "You understand Daddy and you can be convincing when you want to be. I saw that letter you wrote to your cousin in Detroit."

"Writing a letter asking my cousin to send me a quilt because I get cold in the wintertime ain't no big thing," Miss Etta said. She held the mirror up and looked at the job that Luvenia was doing on her hair. "But Elijah is a strong-minded man and you know it. I sure don't hear you talking about sending a letter to Goldie."

"You know Mama is going to do just what Daddy says," Luvenia said. "Lean forward so I can finish your neck."

"You going to finish my neck or the hair on my neck?" Miss Etta asked, smiling.

"Anyway, I've got plans for being here in Chicago," Luvenia said. She pushed Miss Etta's head gently forward and started curling the short hair on her neck. "I'm going to college."

"Yeah, you talked about that before, but Elijah didn't say he was going to send you, did he?"

"I can raise some money doing hair," Luvenia said. "You know I can do some hair, right?"

"Yeah, you can do hair."

"I went down to the bank this morning and asked them to lend me the money to go to the university."

"You thinking about going to the University of Chicago?"

"Yep."

"Girl, you got some nerve on you," Miss Etta said. "You think I should get a hair piece?"

"If you get one, get it from Mr. Johnson over near Wabash," Luvenia said. "You know him?"

"No, but if he gets his hair from dead people, I don't want it, because I don't want to be wearing nothing dead on me."

"I don't know where he gets his hair, but a lot of people sell hair. I know some white ladies that sell hair."

"What did the bank say?" Miss Etta got up and took down a box of saltines from the cupboard.

"They said I had to have a guaranteed income," Luvenia said. She held the mirror in front of Miss Etta. "Somebody who will sign a paper that says that they'll keep me working until I get the money paid back. I have to make at least eleven dollars a week, too."

"If you making eleven dollars a week you don't need to borrow no money!" Miss Etta said.

"Anyway, I'm going to ask the man I work for if he'll sign a paper saying he'll guarantee me a job," Luvenia said.

"You going to ask him first or you going to tell your daddy first?"

"You can put it in your letter." Luvenia moved the curling iron away from the flame.

"I don't know how you can stand no live-in work, anyhow," Miss Etta said. "Looks to me like a girl as young as you are would want to be around some place where she could find some entertainment in the evenings."

"They're not bad to work for," Luvenia said. "I stay there five days a week—six days when Mr. Deets is out of town, which isn't that often—and then I can come home."

"Your folks ain't home, so you got to live in that empty apartment by yourself. Child, a place that don't have family in it ain't h-o-m-e. You hear what I'm saying?"

"Miss Etta, it's not that bad," Luvenia said. "The Deetses don't have any young children or anything, and Mrs. Deets said that if I ever needed anything she'd help me out."

"She needs to help herself out," Miss Etta said. "I saw Mr. Deets's picture in the paper. Man's so old he's starting to rot around the edges."

"Miss Etta, will you be serious! You have to listen to this stuff so you can put it in the letter to Daddy."

"And the University of Chicago is going to let you just waltz on in the door?"

"I finished high school!" Luvenia protested.

"Least I got enough credits to get my diploma, and there's no use of me going on to another year at that school if I can start in at the college."

"You finished the *colored* school and you are smart, but they don't let that many *colored* people in their college. They don't want us over there, and I'm telling you what God loves and that's the pure D truth!"

"If Mrs. Deets gives me a—what's that noise?"

There was a clatter that seemed to come from behind the wall, followed by a bang.

"It ain't nothing but that stupid high yeller girl on the fifth floor throwing her garbage in the dumbwaiter without putting it in a bag!"

Miss Etta braced a large dark hand on the sink, pulled herself out of the chair, and went to the dumbwaiter and opened the door just in time to see the dumbwaiter with the loose garbage passing. She waited while the small chamber for garbage went down on the chain and pulley system that took it to the basement where Mr. Harrison would put it in cans and out on the sidewalk in the mornings for the trash collector.

"If there's anything I can't *stand*," Miss Etta called up the dumbwaiter shaft, "it's a stupid, skinny, and dirty heifer!"

Miss Etta slammed the door shut and went back and sat heavily in the chair.

"Why does she do that?"

"Because she thinks she's Miss *It* and what she really is rhymes with what she thinks she is! You know she tried to talk to Mr. Harrison!"

"Get out of here!"

"She was out all night one time and come home all liquored up, and he was putting out the garbage." Miss Etta was rocking. "She come grinning at Harrison like a Chessie cat what just hit the number."

"She has her hair done at that parlor near the park and then goes around telling people it's just naturally straight."

"So you think Mr. Deets is going to guarantee you the job?" Miss Etta asked. "You know college is a long haul. You got to go four years."

Luvenia curled the hair over Miss Etta's ear tightly, held it for a long moment, and then loosened it gradually until it fell just right. "Sometimes, before I get up in the morning, I lie in bed and think about going to college, hurrying in with my books and pens. Then one day, when I'm finished, I think I might teach school. Maybe high school or even college."

"You got you some big dreams, girl."

"Miss Etta, I know I can do it." Luvenia straightened up and clasped her hands. "I think it's what God wants me to do. That's got to be why I think about it all the time. I can see myself at the same school as Florenz."

"Who?"

"Florenz Deets, their daughter. When I clean her room I look at her books. They're not that hard. Once I read a chapter in her history book and at the end there were these questions and I answered every one of them."

"Just by reading that book once?"

"I can be just like Florenz," Luvenia said. "It'll be hard, but I know I can do it!"

"Well, you ain't got to convince me, you got to convince your daddy to let you stay in Chicago on your own." Miss Etta lifted the strap to her slip and scratched under it. "You know, Chicago is a fast city—especially for a young girl. I don't think your daddy is going to go for it."

"He will if we work on him," Luvenia said. "You want me to do these dishes?"

"No, I'll do them—well, go on if you don't mind," Miss Etta said. "A friend of Harrison opened a fish place over near Boyd Street. That's where we're going tonight. You know that man had the nerve to tell me he like to spend money on me?"

"And never takes you any place!"

"Ain't that the truth!" Miss Etta said. "If he kept his gas the way he keep his money, he'd be one of those dirigibles!"

"Miss Etta, why you talk about that man like that?"

"I talk about him but I love him," Miss Etta said. "And if I ever see that little skinny heifer upstairs talking to him again, I'm going to grab her by her skinny ankles, you know the way you do the wishbone in a chicken?"

"Uh-huh."

"Then I'm gonna snap her butt in two pieces and wish she don't never get herself together again."

Luvenia laughed as she started putting away her hair comb and curling iron. She watched Miss Etta survey herself in a hand mirror.

"How you like it?"

"You do know how to do you some hair," Miss Etta said.

Luvenia started doing the dishes, and Miss Etta went into the bedroom to get dressed. Miss Etta had one heavy skillet that she used to cook everything in and a porcelain pot that was cracked on one side, creating a shape that looked, to Luvenia, like a frog. The older woman knew she was washing the dishes to get her to write the letter, and Luvenia knew that her friend would probably write it, too.

Miss Etta, in addition to being her godmother, was Luvenia's best friend. Before Luvenia was born, she had been her mother's best friend. When Elijah left home, Goldie had stayed behind on Curry until she felt she was woman enough to be with him. After he got a job in a meat-packing firm, she had come up to Chicago, they married, and she had found a job cleaning offices for a trucking company. Richard was the first child, looking more like Goldie than his father, and then Luvenia had come.

Her mother, Luvenia knew, had always done the right thing. The right thing was to work hard, hand in hand with her husband, to save and to send money down to Curry to keep the Lewis land up. The babies were the right thing, too, and so, finally, was the return to Curry with the man she loved. Elijah was so looking forward to "getting back home," and his wife was going to be at his side. Luvenia was keeping the apartment until her parents were sure they wouldn't have to return.

Goldie had sent her a postcard from nearby Johnson City, the kind with a picture of the waterfront and some colored men sitting on crates. She said that Johnson City had changed so much she didn't remember much about it and that the actual docks looked just like they did in the picture. She wrote that Richard, Luvenia's brother, loved Curry Island. She also sent her love. Elijah had signed the card, too, but Luvenia knew that her mother had probably made him do it.

Not that Elijah was an unfeeling man. He was as kind and as gentle a man as Luvenia had ever met. He was what Miss Etta called a "choice" catch.

"You can find them with decent jobs, and you can find them built up good and good-looking, and once in a while you can find them sweet. Your daddy is all of that and then some more."

But Elijah Lewis was also possessed. What he wanted was to own all the land that the Lewis family had been working for years and on which, before the Civil War, they had worked as slaves. Every spare dollar went to Curry, holding the Lewis family together even when white families in the area failed. Elijah was their bank, their holder of burial insurance, their emergency fund.

Richard Lewis was three years older than

Luvenia, and when the family had talked about going down to Curry, he just went along with it.

"Is that really what you want to do?" Luvenia had asked him once.

He had answered yes, that of course it was what he wanted to do, and she hadn't asked him again.

Luvenia was proud of her daddy, but she didn't want to be like him.

"Luvenia, you want to go out with me and Mr. Harrison tonight?" Miss Etta came in wearing a green, short-sleeved dress and her good brown shoes. As usual she hadn't rubbed the deodorant in well, and there was the telltale sign of white under her brown arms.

"No, I think I'll stay home and take a long bath tonight," Luvenia said. "You going any place after dinner?"

"Going to try to get that cheap man of mine to take me over to the Metropolitan," Miss Etta said, lifting her dress and pulling down what needed to be pulled down and twisting around what needed to be twisted around. "Phil Terry and the Nightingales are going to be over there. I could just eat that bass player of theirs up."

"Bunny Fields?"

"I didn't know you knew nothing about the Nightingales." Miss Etta cocked her head to one side.

"They were putting up posters on the street," Luvenia said. "I think they're all cute."

"Well, he sure is," Miss Etta said. "I was saying my prayers the other day and put in a direct request to the Lord that if I didn't get into heaven when I die just send me to wherever Bunny is."

"Miss Etta, you are a mess," Luvenia said.

"You come on by tomorrow, and we'll sit down and see if we can't scare up a letter for your father," Miss Etta said over her shoulder as she went into her bedroom. "Though as far as I know, there's going to have to be a strong wind to change that man's mind."

It had been on Palm Sunday, on a trolley car headed toward Wabash, that Luvenia Lewis had first put words to what she had felt for a long time, that there were two distinct kinds of colored people in Chicago. Most of the blacks in the crowded city were country-type people, with sleeves that always ended up several inches too short and shoes that were scuffed and worn down at the heels. And they always seemed to be carrying something.

When the trolley passed the railroad station, two black families got on. They were clearly country folk. One of the men, tall and thin and holding an envelope in his incredibly long fingers, asked the white trolley driver directions to a certain address. Behind him, settling onto the trolley's wooden benches, were two women, a girl about Luvenia's age, and two small boys. Luvenia imagined them being from some place called Waycross, or Gee's Bend, or even Curry

Island. The women's dresses were too long; the men's sleeves were too short, as usual. They carried two baskets, one filled with clothes and the other with plates. One of the boys carried a dark-colored wooden trunk around which a rope was tied. The girl looked at Luvenia and a slight smile flickered across the dark face from beneath the perfectly round straw hat. The girl was pretty. Luvenia had smiled and nodded back and then turned her head to look out of the window.

On the street two well-dressed colored men were talking on the corner. They were the other kind of colored people, the kind that usually referred to themselves as "Negroes" and spoke as proper as white people, and sometimes even more proper. Both of the men wore three-quarter-length coats, and one had on a bowler. Luvenia turned and saw that the young girl on the trolley had seen the men, too. Her eyes widened with wonder at such elegance.

There was something about the way that colored people went back and forth to their jobs, the hardness of it and the grimness of it, that bothered Luvenia. Her father said that it was because they didn't own what they worked for, but she wasn't sure. It seemed to Luvenia that among the poor people, the ones who had jobs were trapped by the little pocket of hope the jobs offered. And the ones who didn't have jobs were trapped by the hopelessness of it all.

You need land, her father had said. *That way you're working for yourself. You get up in the morning and you're getting up for you, and when you go home at night and lay yourself down, you're tired from working for yourself. That's worth the working!*

She knew what he meant, but the year they had gone down to Curry for a visit and she had seen the people walking the rows on the Lewis land, the hoes probing the ground before them, she felt as if the land owned them as much as they owned the land. She didn't want to be owned by a job, or by the land, or by anything else for that matter.

"You want to wear one of my hats?" Miss Etta asked. She slipped a wide rubber band over the top of her stocking, rolled the top of it down slightly and smoothed it out over her thigh.

"You going to let me wear the blue one?" Luvenia asked. She put a dusting of powder on her nose and spread it with a sponge as they got ready for church.

"Sure. It's on the top shelf of the hall closet. I'm going to try to get Mr. Harrison to come with us."

"He's not coming," Luvenia said.

"We'll see," Miss Etta said.

Luvenia followed Miss Etta out of the bedroom into the dining room where Mr. Harrison sat in his undershirt at the table with the Sunday paper.

"You ain't ready yet?" Miss Etta's voice registered mild surprise.

"Ready for what?" Mr. Harrison asked.

"Church!"

"My back hurts." He put a hand on the small of his back and rubbed it.

"Well, come on to church and we can pray for your back to get better," Miss Etta said, nudging Luvenia.

"Reverend Bradley always says a prayer for the poor in body," Luvenia added.

"Y'all go on ahead," Mr. Harrison said, standing. "I got some things I got to check on in the basement and then maybe I'll see you at the service."

"I'll be sitting up front, Honeybunch," Miss Etta said as he headed for the door.

As far as Luvenia knew, Mitchell Harrison had never seen the inside of a church unless the doors were open when he passed one on his way to the hardware store. He was a good man, though. He just wasn't a church man.

Bethel Tabernacle was twelve years old. Its members had been originally part of Pilgrim Baptist, but had broken off when Reverend C. J. Jones passed away and the congregation had bypassed Reverend Bradley in favor of hiring a new minister from Tennessee. The rumor was that Mother Jones, the late reverend's wife, was the one who didn't like Reverend Bradley.

The original Pilgrim congregation was in a storefront off Wabash. When the supporters of Reverend Bradley had broken away and bought their own storefront, it was with the idea that they would be the first to build their own regular church or to buy an existing one. But it was the original congregation that had been the first to buy a building. They bought the Jewish synagogue on Indiana Avenue and invited the breakaways to the dedication. No one from Reverend Bradley's church went back to Pilgrim, and all of them decided that the new Pilgrim building was as ugly a building as anyone could have found.

The choir put on their robes in the basement, the girls in the small office and the boys in the gym. The boys just put their robes over their clothes, while many of the girls, especially in the summer, took off their dresses. Luvenia decided to take off the sky-blue dress she had worn.

"We starting late," Johnnie Mae Stokes announced. She was a big girl with a sweet voice that could effortlessly leap octaves.

"Why?"

"Reverend Bradley had to go to the hospital to see Mr. Graham," Johnnie Mae said.

"He's about gone," Laurel, a Chicago-born girl with freckles around her nose, said.

"I just hope we don't start too late," Luvenia said.

She glanced at the clock on the wall. It was nearly twelve-thirty already. If they got started exactly at twelve-thirty they would be just about finished with Sunday services by two. Reverend Bradley never skimped on services or cut them short because somebody was in a hurry, and he didn't like the choir members leaving before services were done.

"Anybody got a safety pin?" Johnnie Mae asked. "This bra strap broke again."

"You ain't got nothing to hold up so what you need it for?" A voice from the back of the room spoke up.

"They might not be much, but I don't want them going catty-cornered," Johnnie Mae said.

"I'm not going to even get dressed until Reverend Bradley shows up," Mary Turner said.

"You just want everybody to see you in your slip," Laurel said.

"She wants Billy Haskell to see her in her slip," Johnnie Mae said.

"Watch your conversations in the House of the Lord." Sister Maslan was, at fifty-seven, the oldest singer in the choir.

"I'm not steadying about no Billy Haskell or any other boy," Mary said. "It is hot down here and it's going to be hot upstairs and I am trying to stay cool."

"Anybody know what we singing first today?"

" 'Standing in the Need of Prayer,' " Laurel said.

There was a knock on the door, and a youngish male voice announced that they were starting in three minutes.

The swishing of material as the robes went carefully over freshly straightened hair and bodies that ranged from light tan to deep black was joined by the muted humming of "Over My Head," the song that the choir was known for throughout the South Side gospel circuit.

Luvenia saw Johnnie Mae rocking to the beat of the song she was humming and joined her.

This is how the choir entered, as they always did. They came in from the back of the church, walking slowly down the center aisle, clapping the beat, rocking with the rhythm, and humming "Over My Head."

When they were seated, Sister Maslan came over to Luvenia.

"Sister Graham wants you to sing 'Never Grow Old' for Elder Graham," she whispered.

"Did he die?" Luvenia asked.

"No. She just wants you to sing it, that's all," Sister Maslan said. "You know that's his favorite song, and he loves the way you sing it."

"Yes, ma'am."

They sang what Luvenia thought was a lifeless version of "Standing in the Need of Prayer," and then Mother Bradley greeted everyone and made the announcements, including the fact that Elder Graham had taken a turn for the worse overnight and that they were going to have a special prayer session for him that evening and everyone was welcome. Reverend Bradley announced that they were going to take their text from Luke.

He went on about how God searched for the lost soul and how the angels rejoiced more over the recovery of one sinner than they did for all the righteous people.

"For a sinner who's come back into the arms of Jesus is a sinner who has slapped the face of the devil!"

"Amen!"

"A sinner who has turned away from evil and from wrongdoing is showing that there is a God in heaven and that He rules!"

"Amen!"

"What am I talking about? I'm talking about the lost sheep of this world! The sheep way over yonder in that part of the pasture where evil dwells and Satan delights! God reaches out to that lost sheep! He stretches out His forgiveness and a hand full of love and says 'Come unto Me and rest!' "

"Amen!"

"He said, 'Lay down, thou weary one, thy head upon My breast!' "

Luvenia glanced at the clock at the back of the church. The time was edging on to one-thirty, and Reverend Bradley was still going strong. In the second row, Miss Etta was caught up in the sermon.

"In ancient times . . . huh! . . . in ancient times," Reverend Bradley went on, "a wealthy man had two sons. And the younger son came to the man one day and said to him, 'Father, give me the portion of goods that falleth to me. . . .' "

The tale of the prodigal son was played out slowly, but Luvenia was glad to hear it. It sounded like the kind of story that Reverend Bradley would use to end his sermon. But right in the middle of it, Sister Graham stood up, waved her handkerchief over her head, and passed out.

The choir sang "Steal Away" while the attendant nurse and two older sisters got Sister Graham on a bench and rubbed her neck with cold water until the woman had revived. They offered to take her to the office, but she insisted she wanted to stay and hear Luvenia sing "Never Grow Old."

"If she passes out again when I sing, I'm going to throw some cold water on her myself," Luvenia said to Mary Turner.

". . . When the boy came back home he admitted to his father that he had sinned against heaven . . . against heaven and before thee . . . and I am not worthy to be called your son any longer . . ."

In the back of the church, Luvenia saw a heavyset man wearing a white suit with a yellow checked vest. He was Norman Chesterfield. She had only seen him once in a while when he came around to the neighborhood collecting numbers. In the neighborhood, he did not look like a disreputable character. But in the back of Bethel, he looked like one of the gangsters they had in *Ten Nights in a Barroom*, a film she had seen in the Regent Theater.

A few other people in the congregation had seen him, too, including a few of the men who played their numbers with him and who sunk down in their seats.

By the time Reverend Bradley finished his tale of the prodigal son and a collection had been taken, it was twenty-five to three. Guy Loving, the organist, was obviously ready to leave and started the introduction to "Never Grow Old."

Luvenia stood and started to sing.

"Go on, girl!" Miss Etta called to her.

When she was in trouble, she could sing. It was as simple as that. All the emotion within her seemed to rise from a place deep in her soul and pour from her throat. She sang, her feet apart, her face to the tinned ceiling. She sang the song with all her heart while Sister Graham screeched through the whole number.

The song finally ended after a woman called for a second chorus, and, after one last collection for the Building Fund, the services ended.

"If Sister Graham passed out again, I was just going to get up and leave!" Johnnie Mae said.

"No, you weren't," Mary Turner said. "You were going to sit right there and sweat down the front of your dress just like the rest of us!"

"I'm going to join the Lyceum church," Laurel said. "At least they got some fans that work."

"That's not a church," Luvenia answered. "That's a movie house!"

"We can start our own church in there," Laurel said. "We can call it the House of Bojangles or something like that."

"Have you forgotten that you are in the House of the Lord!" Sister Maslan was bone thin but wore a corset nevertheless.

"No, Sister Maslan."

"I do believe you have," Sister Maslan said.

"Did anybody see that man in that white suit in the back of the church?" Mary asked, trying to switch the subject to something neutral.

"All are welcome in the House of the Lord," Sister Maslan said. "Didn't you hear today's sermon? That might have just been the lone sheep that the Lord will delight in saving today!"

"Amen!" Johnnie Mae turned her back quickly and suppressed a smile.

In the church basement, Miss Etta was waiting. Several other people, including Sister Graham, stopped Luvenia and told her how beautifully she had sung.

"As hot as you people looked up there, it was a wonder you all didn't pass out," Miss Etta said. "What they need is to get you some summer robes instead of those year-round things you all wear."

"We're lucky to have them," Luvenia said, remembering that they had only gotten those robes a year before. "I sure hated to go to other churches to sing wearing those white-blouse-and-black-skirt outfits."

"Especially since none of you could agree on what kind of blouses you wanted to wear," Miss Etta said. "We can go on by my house and start on that letter."

"I think I'm going to go home and rest a while," Luvenia said. "Why don't you go on home, and I'll be there a little later."

"Come on and lay down at the house," Miss Etta said. "Ain't nobody going to be there except me. We can listen to *Bibleway* on the radio."

"Miss Etta." Luvenia took a deep breath. "I'm going to clean up the Deetses' place tonight. I'm going to clean it real good and then talk to her about what the bank said."

"Well, I hope she's listening to what you got to say," Miss Etta said. "I hope she's listening."

Luvenia's room in the Deetses' house was on the third floor. She arose at five-thirty each morning except for Thursdays and Sundays, her days off. Her first task was to put on water for Mr. Deets's tea, and to bring in the paper from where the delivery boy had tossed it on the porch. Mr. Deets would be the first in the white family to rise, and he would clump noisily to the breakfast table where he would find his paper and tea waiting. He never spoke to Luvenia, and never looked directly into her eyes.

When Luvenia arrived Sunday evening, Mrs. Deets was listening to the Victrola. The sound of Mrs. Deets's Victrola was deeper than a lot of ones that Luvenia had heard, and she loved it.

"I like some opera," Luvenia said.

"You don't know enough about opera to say that you like some of it," Mrs. Deets retorted.

Luvenia adjusted a crocheted armrest cover. "Do you think," she asked, "that Mr. Deets likes me?"

"He, of course, likes you, or you wouldn't be

here," Mrs. Deets said, peering over her rimless glasses. Precious, the brown-and-white Pekingese that slept at her feet in her bedroom, settled deeper into the cushion next to his mistress.

"Then do you think that he would guarantee me a job?" Luvenia put down the damp rag she was using to wipe the dust from the crevices of the mahogany breakfront.

"Mr. Deets does not like to deal with the hired help," Mrs. Deets said. "He feels quite strongly that he should not have to consider those he hires beyond paying them on time and seeing to it that they are honest."

"I'm honest," Luvenia said.

"And why ever would you be interested in college?" Mrs. Deets asked, already holding her hand up, palm out, the way she did when she didn't want an answer to her question.

"Yes, ma'am." Luvenia felt the tears stinging her eyes as she watched the thin woman turn the switch on the lamp that sat on the end table near her chair. She turned it once and then again.

"It doesn't work." Mrs. Deets looked at Luvenia. "If you can't keep a simple lamp operating, why do you think you can be successful in college? Well, can you tell me?"

"I think I could learn a trade. . . ."

"You have a trade," Mrs. Deets said. "You are a maid. Reaching beyond yourself will just be a disappointment. I'm sure you don't understand that now, and maybe you never will. But I know about such things. I never went to college. Instead I looked for and found my place in life, and, as you see, here I am."

"I see, ma'am."

"Well, so much for that!" Mrs. Deets stood, shaking her head slowly from side to side as if Luvenia's stupidity was just too much for her to bear. She crossed the room, Precious prancing at her heels, and Luvenia held her breath as she heard her going upstairs to the bedroom next to that of Mr. Deets.

Well, then it will have to be Florenz, Luvenia thought. She turned the lightbulb, found that it was loose, tightened it, and tried the switch. It came on, and she turned it off again. Florenz would have to guarantee her the job. Perhaps that would even be better. Florenz was not much older than she was and always had her way.

And she had asked Mrs. Deets all wrong. She had stammered her way through it, intimidated by the older woman. She would practice how she would speak to Florenz. If she wanted to go to the University of Chicago, she should surely be able to explain to Florenz why she wanted to go.

Sleep came in small snatches, the mind drifting into the nothingness of her darkened room. Luvenia tried to think of what she would say the next day to Florenz, but all that came to mind was the dry, almost brittle voice of Mrs. Deets.

And why ever would you be interested in college?
she had asked.

The words came at Luvenia from different angles. They were words she had heard in the
Deetses' parlor and words she had seen in the
eyes of the man at the bank. *And why ever would
you be interested in college?*

Her dreams were tortures. The first one she
had two times, one after the other. It took place
downtown, just off State Street. Someone, Mrs.
Deets perhaps, but clearly someone who could
say such a thing, told her to take Precious home
and to be very careful with him. She had lifted
the small dog into her arms and started across
the street. How she stumbled at the curb wasn't
clear or how the dog seemed to fly from her
arms into the street in front of the trolley.

She had the same dream again. This time it
was Mr. Deets who was telling her to take
Precious home. In the dream, she knew, without
it ever being said, that if she got the dog home
safely, then she would have the guarantee of a
job that would get her the loan and would get
her into college.

When she approached the curb, she held the
dog tightly against her bosom. She placed her
feet carefully onto the street. Then, suddenly,
she felt herself falling. It was as if the street had
given way beneath her weight. There was nothing to stop her, and she clutched the dog tighter
and tighter, searching, even as she hurtled

through space, for the other side of the street. Finally she stopped falling and was on the other side of the street. She looked down at Precious, and he, too, was safe. She put him down carefully but missed his leash. As he ran past her back into the street she knew what would happen. She turned quickly as the small dog disappeared beneath the trolley.

She woke. Turning on the bedside lamp, she looked at the clock. Two-thirty in the morning. Her throat was dry and she took a sip of water from the half-filled glass on the nightstand. She looked at the lamp. The soft light coming through the colored glass globe pleased her. She would have liked to have left the light on for the rest of the night. It was not that she was afraid of the dark but that the light was so pleasing.

She knew that Mr. Deets often got up in the middle of the night and went about the house turning off lights and checking the doors. Luvenia turned the lamp off and pulled the pillow next to her and put her arms around it for comfort.

In her next dream, she was at a rent party at Miss Etta's apartment. The Victrola was turned up as loud as they could get it, and a "Fats" Waller record was playing. The front door was open and so were the windows, in the hope that somehow a stray breeze would make the July heat more tolerable.

Mr. Harrison was selling drinks for ten cents

a glass, and a high yellow girl was complaining that the homemade liquor was going down rough.

In the dream, as she had done when she first went to a rent party at Miss Etta's house, Luvenia watched the women dancing, moving hips that had worked all week long in factories and legs that had knelt scrubbing the floors of rich whites.

"Rent parties are good for people," Miss Etta had said. "They get a chance to let go, and that gets them loose for the next week."

There had been more men at Miss Etta's party than there had been women, and there were more men in Luvenia's dream. But it was the women she watched. In the dream she saw the women growing somehow larger, more big-boned. She saw their hips widen and their bosoms swell. This was what black women could do. They could dance and sing and snap their fingers and show off hips and bosoms that made promises to men who could spend the dime for a drink and maybe a dollar or so to help buy a layaway coat for the coming winter or to catch up on burial insurance payments down at the Mutual Insurance Company.

"Get into it, girl," Miss Etta had said to her. "You old enough to shake that thing!"

In Miss Etta's apartment, she had smiled shyly and sipped the soft drink Mr. Harrison had given her. But in her dream, she found herself in the middle of the dancers, trying to keep up with the rhythm, growing large with the other women until they almost reached the ceiling, dresses pulled up to their knees, some in heels and some in saddle shoes, "shaking that thing." In the dance she was trying to get off the dance floor, trying to get away from the music, from the jelly glasses of cheap whiskey and out of the cold-water tenement. But try as she could, she couldn't leave. No matter what wall she found, it didn't have a door; even the fire escape window was closed to her. There were men there, all explaining how fine she looked, all holding dimes to buy drinks, all patting their feet in perfect rhythm, all friendly, all smiling, all holding their hands out to her.

This time when she woke, she sat up and, taking the Bible Mrs. Deets had left in her room, read from Leviticus until it was time to make breakfast.

Luvenia knew that, except on Wednesdays when Florenz Deets's first class at the University of Chicago was at nine-thirty, the seventeen-year-old girl's day never began before ten. She would get up some time between ten and eleven-thirty and have Luvenia fix her a small lunch, which, if her parents were not home, she would have with a cigarette. Katie Hornung, as fair-haired as Florenz was dark, would often come over in the mornings, filling the Deetses' parlor with high-pitched conversation about how the world was coming to rack and ruin as she consumed endless cups of black coffee.

This Monday morning, Luvenia made breakfast for Mr. Deets, two poached eggs with a small square of butter on one slice of slightly browned toast. Then she went upstairs to make her bed. When she came back downstairs, Mr. Deets had left, as always, and she removed his dishes from the mahogany table.

Luvenia had chores to do—Mrs. Deets always left a list of them—and she hurried through them as quickly as she could. It had been several days since Florenz had asked if she would join them for tea on this Monday, and Luvenia wanted to be finished with her work as early as she could. Katie was already over, and the two girls had spent most of the morning on the sun porch playing cards and whispering between themselves. Katie had said hello to Luvenia earlier but hadn't mentioned the tea. By one o'clock Luvenia thought the girls had forgotten the invitation.

"Lulu, whatever are you doing?" Florenz came in at one-thirty, calling Luvenia by the name she had invented for her.

"Making sure the books are dusted," Luvenia answered, smiling. "Mr. Deets must have a thousand of them in here."

"He hasn't read half of them," Florenz said, leaning against the heavy oaken doors that led to the library. She was wearing a dark skirt, a white cotton blouse that Luvenia had ironed the day before, and an ivory-colored cashmere sweater that went to mid-thigh.

"I think it's good just to have books around so you can read them if you want to," Luvenia said.

"Why don't you come to tea with us and tell us what you read," Florenz said. "You haven't forgotten that I asked you, did you?"

"No, ma'am." Luvenia returned Florenz's smile.

"Do you drink tea at home?"

"Yes. Do you want me to make some?" Luvenia asked quickly, putting down the dust mop she had been holding.

"No, the tea is already made," Florenz answered. "Katie has done the honors. All that we have to do is to sip it like the ladies we are. Come along, now."

Luvenia honestly liked Florenz despite the older girl's annoying explanations of why "the coloreds," as she put it, were inferior to whites. At first Luvenia had thought she was just silly, but there was a real vitality to her, a kind of bubbly air that Luvenia had always liked.

"Miss Deets, that is a fine sweater you're wearing," Luvenia said. "And you *do* know how to wear it."

"Chicago has fine clothes," Florenz said. "Anything you can buy in New York City you can buy in Chicago. It just costs more in Chicago."

Florenz led Luvenia into the parlor and gestured toward the seat across from where Katie, slightly round-shouldered in her suit jacket, pushed the wire-frame glasses up on her nose.

"Good afternoon, Miss Luvenia," Katie lowered her voice and spoke in an accent that could have been intended as British. "Welcome to the Deets mansion. Will the Earl Grey tea be to your liking?"

"Yes, Miss Katie," Luvenia said. "It would be, indeed."

The Deets family empire consisted of delicatessens in Chicago, Cicero, and Oak Park, as well as hams and cheeses imported from Italy and the Netherlands, which they sold throughout the nation. Mrs. Deets was active in the arts and local charities and enjoyed the sports of tennis and croquet.

"Now, you were telling me about the books you read," Florenz said.

"A teacher from my old high school gave me a book by Dr. Du Bois, and I've been reading articles by Mr. Locke on the New Negro," Luvenia said, conscious that she was rushing the words out.

"And whatever is the 'New Negro'?" Florenz asked.

"A Negro who can do anything that he wants to do," Luvenia said. "If he wants to write poems, or play an instrument, or be a scientist, or go to college, then he can. He doesn't have to be a laborer, or a messenger, or a maid."

"Does all this mean that you're unhappy being a maid?" Katie asked. "Because if it does, I don't blame you one little bit. I couldn't see myself as a maid."

"That's because she thinks she's going to be trapped into something because she's a woman," Florenz said. "I don't think a woman has to be trapped in anything. Especially if she's as pretty and as smart as you are, Katie."

"That's being trapped in something," Luvenia said. "Having to be smart and pretty."

"You'd rather be dumb and ugly?" Florenz

asked, annoyed. "Is that part of being the 'New Negro'?"

"No, ma'am."

"What she means, Florenz—"

"I *know* what she means," Florenz interrupted. "We study the Negro at the university. She's been listening to a lot of radicals who want to force the Negro on people. I think those Negroes who are deserving will do very well for themselves, and those who aren't, will not. You cannot make people socially and politically equal by noisy rallies or those radical labor unions."

"I don't think she meant all that, Florenz," Katie said, pouring the tea. "And if she did, she might just be right."

"I thought," Florenz said, looking directly at Katie, "that we were having tea and being ladies, not radicals!"

"Of course," Katie answered. "What else?"

"And how are you getting along these days?" Florenz asked, her voice mellowing and the sudden anger that had flushed her face clearly subsiding.

"Oh, fine," Luvenia said. She looked down at the table before her. "But I'll do even better if you could do me a favor."

"Oh?" Florenz shifted position and pushed the sleeves of her sweater up almost to her elbows.

"I went to the bank—no, first I went to the University of Chicago and asked about how to apply and how much it would cost and everything," Luvenia said, glancing quickly up at Florenz. "They told me how much it would cost and I went to the bank and asked if they would lend me the money. I didn't think they wanted to lend it to me. But they said they would if I had a guaranteed job, if Mr. Deets would say that he would keep me working here for four years until I graduated."

"So what do you want me to do?" Florenz asked.

"I asked your mother if she would ask Mr. Deets to give me a letter to the bank. . . ."

"And naturally she said no," Florenz answered. "She doesn't believe in education. Don't you use sugar in your tea?"

"Sugar? Oh, yes." Luvenia took the tiny teaspoon and carefully put two scoops of sugar into her tea.

"There must be nine or ten Negroes in the law school alone," Katie said.

"Well, we can't guarantee that Daddy will write a letter for you," Florenz said. "Daddy does whatever Daddy chooses to do. Some people are like that. They simply have the determination to do just anything. I think if we were living in the olden days he would have discovered America instead of Columbus. Then it would be called Deetsania or something like that."

"Deetsania?" Katie winced. "That's awful! I wouldn't live here if it was called Deetsania!"

"That doesn't solve Luvenia's problem," Florenz said. "I'll speak to Daddy. He'll do what he wants but he does listen to me more than most people."

"I'm sure he'll do it if you say so, Miss Florenz."

"And do you think you can go to college on what my father pays you?"

"I can do hair on my days off," Luvenia said. "I can do white hair and black hair. I'm really good."

"I'll ask him, but that doesn't solve my problem," Florenz said.

"She thinks we have a crisis," Katie said.

"Of course, we have a crisis," Florenz said. "And we need the help of every woman in the house, including yours, to resolve the crisis."

"Yes, ma'am." Luvenia felt herself smiling as Katie poured her another cup of tea. Already she was picturing herself gathering her books before making a rush to classes at the university as she had so often seen Florenz do.

"The problem, again, is her silly father," Katie announced.

"Daddy has his new car, which he drives to work every day, and the old one, which just sits in the garage gathering dust."

"Yes, ma'am."

Precious came into the room, and Florenz, who hated the small brown-and-white fluff of a dog, quickly slipped off a shoe and tossed it at him. The dog scampered quickly away, turned at the doorway, and gave a staccato scolding to his tormentor.

"Lulu, get my shoe and kill that dog!"

"Yes, ma'am." Luvenia retrieved the shoe and shook it at Precious before returning to the table.

"I once made the mistake of asking Daddy if I could drive the Ford, and he just about laughed in my face," Florenz continued. "He said that I didn't know a thing about driving. This is not true, of course, because I've driven plenty of times in cars owned by some of the boys at school. Of course, I can't tell Daddy that, and he wouldn't count it anyway."

"He should trust you," Luvenia said.

"Of course, he should," Florenz said. "But, as we were saying before, Daddy doesn't always do what he's supposed to do. So we have hatched a small plot."

"And you are part of it!" Katie leaned forward.

"Am I going to get into trouble?" Luvenia asked.

"Of course not," Florenz said. "We've got this whole thing worked out. Daddy takes this new car—"

"The Oldsmobile—" Katie added.

"The Oldsmobile," Florenz went on, "to work almost every day. I think he wants to hire a chauffeur, and I don't see why he doesn't, but he hasn't so far—"

"The guilt of the nouveau riche," Katie chimed in. "How many sugars, Lulu?"

"Two, please," Luvenia added in the same tone as the two white girls.

"*Anyway*," Florenz clucked at Katie for interrupting, "so what we want to do is to call him and tell him that we have to take you to the hospital."

"Me?"

"Right. You're perfect," Katie said. "This part is my idea."

"What we're going to tell him is that you have these terrible cramps and that we have to take you all the way across town to a colored doctor," Florenz said.

"We're going to tell him that we made a dreadful mistake," Katie added. "We tried to get a car service to take you, but when they realized that you were colored and that you had 'female trouble,' they refused."

"I don't have female trouble," Luvenia said.

"Of course not," Florenz said. "But Daddy's too old-fashioned to ask me questions about it. And there's five dollars in it for you if we pull it off."

"He won't be mad at me, will he?"

"How can he be mad at your being sick?" Florenz asked. She was already picking up the telephone. "Now, the only possible hitch is if he asks to speak to you. You must just tell him that you feel terrible."

"Then moan a little and give the phone back to Florenz," Katie said. "Then we'll all hop into the car, take a spin around the park, and come back!"

"And I will have established my driving!" Florenz said.

Luvenia wasn't at all sure about the adventure, but the idea of it was exciting. She put her hands under the table and clasped them tightly. She was hoping for all the world that Mr. Deets would not ask to speak to her.

As Florenz dialed and waited for someone to answer the telephone, Katie held her stomach and pretended to be in great distress, which almost made Luvenia laugh aloud.

"Hello? Country Star Products?" Florenz exhaled heavily as she got into her part. "Yes, this is Florenz Deets. May I speak to my father? And please hurry. It's an emergency!"

The girl rolled her eyes up as she listened to the secretary on the other end of the telephone. She signaled silence from her co-conspirators with a finger on her lips.

"No, I have to speak to my father," she said in a response to some question from the other end of the telephone, adding just the right touch of authority.

She waited again, and then her eyes widened as she got back into her role. "Daddy, I just made the biggest mistake. Lulu's here and she's sick. *Female* trouble. I think she might even be in the family way."

Luvenia swallowed hard. She wasn't "in the family way" and didn't want anyone to think she was.

"I called a car service, but none of them will take her to a colored doctor, and I just have to drive her over there before she . . . before something drastic happens! . . . No, if you don't let me take her there, I'll have to just put her out. Mother will have a fit even to think of any Negro babies dropping out here in the parlor. Daddy, I know what I'm talking about. Yes, I'm sure I can handle the car. I'll drive slowly. I'll just take her there, let her out, and come right back. Yes. Yes. Of course, I wouldn't stay over there! Yes. Yes. Yes, all right, I'll be leaving right away! Yes, of course."

Triumphantly she hung up the telephone.

"And?" Katie leaned forward.

"Ladies, shall we go?"

The very pit of Luvenia's stomach seemed suddenly absent, and her breathing became shallow as she walked behind Florenz and Katie toward the driveway. Florenz slid in behind the wheel, and Katie slid in beside her, leaving the rear of the big car for Luvenia. She hadn't liked it a bit when Florenz told her father that she was in "the family way." The white girl meant it only as a trick on her father to get the use of the car, but to Luvenia it was what so many whites expected of Negroes: that one day they would show up and announce that they were pregnant or call to say they had been arrested. That was what Luvenia had wanted to get away from, those vicious things that grew like vapors in the minds of people distant from her community, from Miss Etta, from the sisters at the church. They would grow like vapors, but word of them would be passed from mouth to ear, from mouth to ear, sometimes with a laugh and other times with a sneer, until they were no longer the vapors of rumor and myth, but the edges of a hard reality into which it was so easy to stumble, pitfalls for which one searched in the darkness.

It was why Luvenia wanted to go to college, to be a teacher, or perhaps even a lawyer, anything but someone else's expectations of her.

The drive started out with a bit of excitement as Florenz put the big car in reverse, and pushed too hard on the accelerator, sending Katie into the dashboard and Luvenia, sitting in the back, nearly over the front seat. The gravel kicked up as Florenz first slowed down and then sped up again.

"So far, so good," she said as the car reached the street.

The drive was more pleasant than Luvenia had expected. When they stopped at street corners, people would stare at them, and two men with straw hats asked Florenz if the car belonged to her.

"Of course," she announced, proudly.

There were a few near misses and curses sent in their direction, curses that Florenz answered with a wide smile as she cruised toward the park.

"How long do you think we have before your daddy is on his way home?" Katie asked.

"As long as we want," Florenz said. "I'll just tell him that after we took Lulu to the doctor, we were so upset we went for a relaxing ride in the park."

"You do think of everything, dahling," Katie said, affecting a southern accent.

On Katie's signal, Florenz also assumed what she imagined to be a southern accent, and the two girls pretended to be driving around their plantations. Katie commented on how well the crops were doing and how pleasant things were now that the "silly old Civil War" had ended.

Luvenia wanted to join the conversation, to be silly with the white girls, but the words never seemed to come. She liked, no, she *adored* Florenz's light manner, the way that she considered only those things serious that made the first page of the morning paper. She adored the girl's lightness, but somehow could never even imitate it. What Florenz was, the way she acted, was somewhere between imagination and humor, between the cloud and the rainbow, bubbling and airy, so far from reality. It was appealing on Florenz and sometimes on Katie, although Katie was always more serious. But Luvenia sensed that her life was, and always would be, that of a bird always aware of just where the ground was and more comfortable on her feet than in flight.

"What I hope," Florenz was saying, "is that Daddy just gives me this car. I mean, if something's not being used and I have a use for it, then I should have it."

"And you will, too," Katie reassured her.

"Unless, of course, he wants to buy me a brand-new Jordan. Now there is a fine car. Maybe a tan one to match my new coat."

"My father says he doesn't believe in cars," Katie said. "He talks about cars as if he's talking about some ancient religion."

"Isn't that Tom Pawley over there?" Florenz's voice rose in pitch.

"Where?" Katie was looking through the park. "Yes! Yes! And he's with that biology major from Kentucky."

"He's not that much—" Florenz was leaning on the horn. "There, they see us!"

Florenz pulled the car to the side of the road, putting the wheels up on the sidewalk.

"Hi there, Florenz, Katie. Where are you girls going?" Tom put a foot on the running board.

"For a spin. Want to come along?"

"Sure. Who's your friend in the back?"

"Oh, that's Lulu. She helped us with the scheme to get the car today." Florenz opened her pocketbook and took out some bills. "Lulu, I'll let you out here. Don't say a word until we get our stories straight. Don't go back to our house. Go right home and don't call in. We'll tell my parents something about your being ill and how we took you to the doctor. You can just come in tomorrow. When you do come in, stay out of Daddy's sight. Okay?"

"Yes, ma'am."

Lulu took the offered bills, got out of the car, and stood smiling as Tom and the other boy got into the backseat.

"Lulu, are you going to be all right?" Katie asked. "Should we drop you someplace?"

"No. I'm all right," Luvenia said.

"You sure?" Katie asked. Tom smiled at her as he loosened his tie.

"Sure."

Luvenia walked the entire way home. She was angry, not with Florenz or Katie, but with herself. Florenz and Katie had done what they always did. They had fun the way they knew how and with the people they admired. There was certainly nothing wrong with that, she thought. The only thing that was wrong was her part in it. It wasn't that Florenz and Katie and the two boys were mean, or even unkind; they just weren't *her* friends, and they didn't know about her life or about the life of any Negro. They didn't know how she felt being so close to the girls in age, so close in so many ways, and yet so distant. They were college people and they were rich. They were white, too. And Luvenia, never having been white, wasn't sure how much that mattered, although she felt it must have mattered some.

There were moments, as when she began to tire while crossing Wabash, that she was almost on the verge of tears. In her mind, she was telling the story to Miss Etta, each time with a different emphasis.

Eventually the thought came to her that Florenz wasn't that good a driver. The thought amused Luvenia more and more as she thought about it. The girl was smart, rich, and pretty. Her family had two cars, and she went to college.

And the worst thing that Luvenia could think about her was that she couldn't drive very well.

When she arrived home, she went right to her room. She knew she was going to cry. She just didn't know when.

There was a knock on her door, and she opened it to Mr. Parrish. He was known to be at home all day every day and was the unofficial message center for her building.

"There's a telegram for you," he said, looking properly worried. "I told the boy that he should take it over to that place you work, but he wouldn't."

"Did you give the boy a tip?" Luvenia asked, her eyes already misting.

"Just a dime," Mr. Parrish said. "You need anything, you just give me a call. You hear?"

"I will," Luvenia said.

When he had gone, Luvenia took the telegram, opened it quickly, and read the brown type.

> YOUR SERVICES WILL NO
> LONGER BE REQUIRED
> —JOHN DEETS

The crushing feeling seemed to rise from her knees, careen through her trembling body, and settle heavily in Luvenia's chest. When the tears came, they came as they never had before, rushing to her eyes and pouring down her cheeks even as she tried to muffle them by pulling the pillow tightly into her face. She cried, her body twisting with the misery that filled every conscious part of her.

What surprised her, lying in the darkness, was that she couldn't think. There was a sense of panic, and the memory of sitting behind Florenz and Katie in the back of the car, trying not to think of what Mr. Deets would think of her. She closed her eyes tightly, trying to bring on the relief of sleep, trying to move away from the pain that was now as real as any she had ever known before. But sleep would not come or even one clear thought that did not renew the well of tears or the quilt-muffled sobs. It was when her arms began to jerk, when her hands, still clutching the telegram, seemed to move on their own, that she knew she had to get out of the house, to see some person, some thing that would bring sanity back to her.

Luvenia more ran than walked to Miss Etta's house, her eyes swollen, her vision blurred. Fragments of thoughts tumbled through her mind in a mad rush that seemed to mirror the crowded Chicago streets. She imagined herself taking the bus to the Deetses' home, finding Mr. Deets, and begging him to take her back.

Through the crystal prism of her tears, she ran hard into a tall black man. He was thin, the stench of old sweat mingled with new announcing his presence as much as the gold tooth in the front of his mouth.

"I'm sorry," she mumbled as much to herself as to the man.

"Hey, baby, I got some good news for you," the man said. "Whoever done hurt you, he ain't worf it!"

Whoever done hurt you, the man had said. What had hurt her, what she knew would hurt her as soon as she heard it coming from Florenz's mouth, was that Mr. Deets would think of her as just another colored girl with 'female trouble,' and had fired her for that very reason.

Miss Etta's door was partially opened, and Luvenia pushed in and saw the woman sitting at the table in her slip, sewing a dress where it had split under the arm.

"What happened?" Miss Etta's voice was flat

and hard as she looked up from the dark blue dress before her.

"I got fired from my job." Luvenia sat down heavily. She felt her face contort into a mask of sorrow, felt the bosom fill, and heard the sobs coming even before they reached her throat. "I'm just going to Curry. I just . . ."

"Girl, we got problems here." Miss Etta examined her work on the outside of the dress. "You know Sister Stovall died. Well, they got her laid out all proper, but the casket done broke open."

"Miss Etta, I lost my job!"

"Girl, a black woman losing a job ain't no big thing!" Miss Etta paused as she broke the thread with her teeth. "It ain't the last job you going to lose. Mr. Harrison's mother was over at the sitting today, and she said the casket broke open at the corner. The funeral's tonight."

"Can't they . . . can't they just nail it up or something?" Luvenia asked.

"Uh-unh. It's one of them cheap caskets and the wood warped. They tried to nail up one side, and the other side started splitting."

"That's . . ."

"I know what it is." Miss Etta stood and slipped the dress over her head. "It's a shame but that undertaker—that walleyed fool that used to live in the colored 'Y' and whoever heard of an undertaker who lives in the YMCA?— won't be back until tonight when they have the funeral."

"I thought you didn't like Sister Stovall?"

"That's right. I couldn't stand the two-faced heifer," Miss Etta said, straightening out her dress, "but she's gone now, and everybody got a right to a decent burial. I'm going over there to see what I can do. You coming with me?"

Luvenia spoke, didn't hear the words coming out, and nodded that yes, she would go.

"I thought you would so why don't you go on in the bathroom and wash your face and take yourself a good pee," Miss Etta said. "That sometimes helps you to get yourself together."

"I . . . lost . . . my . . . job." Luvenia said the words slowly, letting them sink in to Miss Etta.

"Honey, I hear what you're saying." Miss Etta put a big hand over Luvenia's. "But you will either go hungry or get you another job, and I don't think you gonna go hungry. That poor woman ain't gonna have her but one funeral, and everybody deserves a decent funeral. Can I count on you, baby?"

"Yes."

Luvenia went into the bathroom and looked at herself in the cracked mirror of the medicine cabinet. She looked bad and she didn't care. She sat on the toilet, felt another shiver of desperation, and somehow stopped the urge to scream.

Sister Stovall's body was laid out in the Dudley Free Will Baptist Church. Dudley was the oldest, and largest, storefront church on the South Side. Inside the church itself, it didn't look like a storefront institution. The second floor had been taken out and a two-row balcony had been installed in the back. A picture of a stained-glass window had been painted behind the stands where the choir stood.

"I didn't know she went to Dudley," Luvenia whispered as she looked at the small casket on the front of the stage. It was illuminated by two floor lamps on either side. There were pictures of a white, blue-eyed Jesus on the shades of the lamps.

"She didn't go to no church except on Christmas and Easter," Miss Etta said. "She's lucky to find a place that would bury her. And she didn't have a penny when she died."

"She didn't?" Luvenia thought of the fox stole Sister Stovall wore around the neighborhood.

"Everybody thought she had money," Miss Etta said. "But her Unity Insurance wasn't even paid up."

Miss Etta pointed toward the corner of the coffin as a dark man shuffled from an office behind the pulpit.

"Y'all relatives?" the nearly toothless man asked.

"Friends," Miss Etta said.

"I'm Deacon Brown. I just come to see what's what. Can't do nothing with that coffin." The deacon bent over from the waist and ran his fingers along the edge of the mahogany-colored wood.

The wood had come apart at the corner, the division flaring out at the top of the coffin, revealing the satin lining and part of the stiff batting beneath it. Sister Stovall's heel, in a taupe-colored cotton stocking, was just visible.

Miss Etta put one of her large arms on either side of the corner and pushed with all of her strength. The wood creaked and a piece of the top slat chipped off.

"What is this stuff made of?" Miss Etta asked.

"This is like one of them one-day boxes they used to use down around Berea, in Kentucky," Deacon Brown said. "They used to bury people within twenty-four hours of them dying because they didn't have no way of preserving the bodies and people didn't have money for no fancy coffins."

"You tried nailing it?" Miss Etta asked.

"If you nail the top slats, then the bottom starts splitting. Like when you was trying," Deacon Brown said. "You got you a good grip there."

"We can put a cover on it," Luvenia said. "Put a sheet around it first, and then put something over that."

"I got that black lace shawl Mr. Harrison bought me from a Coast Guard fellow," Miss Etta said. "It's all the way from Spain."

"We got a sheet in the back we can donate," Deacon Brown said. "That might be a good idea."

Luvenia looked at the foot, then at the closed coffin. She took a deep breath.

"I'll go on home and get the shawl," Miss Etta said. "Why don't you see what kind of sheet they got here?"

Miss Etta started down the aisle of the small church and Deacon Brown went for the sheet, leaving Luvenia alone with the coffin. She leaned on it, her thoughts instantly back to the telegram that Mr. Deets had sent her.

A part of Luvenia Lewis said that she should go back to the Deetses' house and ask to see her employer and that he would understand how much she needed the job. She would say that Florenz had only been pulling a trick on him and that she would explain.

Then she thought that she wouldn't have to go back at all, that Florenz would tell her father what had happened and he would send another telegram. There was nothing to worry about. There was nothing at all, she told herself, to worry about.

"She a close friend of yours?"

Deacon Brown's voice startled Luvenia.

"Not really, but everyone deserves a decent funeral," she answered.

"You're a decent young person," Deacon Brown said. "That's a rare thing these days. Young people don't have respect like they used to in the old days."

Luvenia took the sheet and first wrapped and then unwrapped the end of the coffin. Then she took it again and folded it carefully so that it laid over only the foot of the coffin, barely covering the corner.

"Can we tack it on like this?" Luvenia asked.

"Yeah, I guess so." Deacon Brown went back to the office to find a hammer.

Luvenia thought of the Deetses' home. In the evening, only Mr. Deets answered the phone.

Miss Etta returned with the shawl and, after Deacon Brown had tacked the sheet to the end of the coffin, laid it carefully over it.

"It don't look too bad," Miss Etta said.

"Looks a lot better than her foot sticking out," Deacon Brown chuckled and then caught himself.

Luvenia pulled gently at the sheet, saw that it was not going to come off, and turned toward Miss Etta. "It'll last if they don't tug at it too hard," she said.

The wind had picked up, sending cold gusts that whipped the ends of Luvenia's dress. Miss Etta took her hand as they walked briskly down the nearly deserted streets, both women leaning into the wind. A clock in the window of a furniture store read nearly eleven o'clock. A street lamp flickered above them when they reached Miss Etta's block.

"How you feeling, girl?"

"Okay, I guess," Luvenia said. "I think I might get my job back. All that has to happen is that Florenz tells Mr. Deets what she did. Then I'm sure that . . ."

"Oh, baby." Miss Etta turned away. The half-moon was barely visible as it drifted over the tenement roofs. From the distant darkness came the easy rhythm of a horse's hooves on cobblestone.

"You don't think I should call Mr. Deets?"

"Sure. Call him from the basement," Miss Etta said. "Mr. Harrison's got a telephone down there."

"He does?"

"Yeah, some people say that he takes numbers sometimes and calls them in from down there. I don't believe that. Do you?"

"I guess not," Luvenia said. "But what do you think? Do you think he'll give me the job back?"

"I think you should ask for it back if that's what you want to do," Miss Etta said. "But I think you can be just as hurt getting it back as not getting it."

Miss Etta took Luvenia's arm as they walked the rest of the way to the tenement the older woman had lived in most of her life. They went down the tin-covered stairs to the basement apartment that came with Mr. Harrison's job as building superintendent. They found him working on the plumbing, and Miss Etta told him that Luvenia had to make a private telephone call. He gave Luvenia a look and asked if she had finally caught her a beau.

"No, and mind your business!" Miss Etta said.

The telephone at the Deetses' home rang five times, and Luvenia was ready to hang up when she heard the heavy voice announce that she had reached the Deets residence.

"This is Luvenia," she said. "I wonder if Florenz told you what happened today?"

"That you were part of a lie?" was the quick answer.

Luvenia hesitated, searching for a response. "I wondered if it would be all right . . . if I came in to work tomorrow?"

"I'm sorry, but I don't think so," Mr. Deets answered. "I can't compromise on the standards I have for my domestic help. However, because I basically think you are a decent person, I will give you good references. In the future I hope you will maintain your personal honesty under all circumstances. Good night."

When Luvenia came out of Mr. Harrison's apartment Miss Etta didn't have to ask her what had happened. She took the young girl in her arms.

"You can stay with me for a while," Miss Etta said.

"Miss Etta." Luvenia took a deep breath. "Is there any place around here where I could do hair and people could . . . you know, come to, and I could charge them?"

"You mean you going to try to make it on your own?" Miss Etta asked. "Child, I know you can do some hair and stuff, but . . ."

"I think I can do it, Miss Etta. I know I can!"

"You really hate Curry that much?"

"No, I don't." Luvenia wiped the tears away with her fingertips. "It's just that Curry isn't my dream, it's my daddy's. You know I really love that place."

"You do?" Miss Etta's hands went to her hips. "Since when?"

"Since the first time I saw how my daddy loved it," Luvenia said. "I love it and I want to save it and be as proud of it as he is, but I don't want to live it. Does that make any sense?"

"You know, you are deep for a skinny girl," Miss Etta said. "Skinny girls usually ain't deep but you are deep!"

"I want to be part of what Negroes are doing today. I want to be . . . building something, making something, I don't know. I feel like I could even discover something. That's what the New Negro is doing."

"What we Old Negroes supposed to be doing?"

"You're supposed to be doing anything you *want* to do, anything you have the *mind* to do," Luvenia answered.

"Girl, just look at your face! You look like you're fixing to fight or something!"

"I'm sorry, Miss Etta."

"Don't be sorry. As determined as you look, I'm just glad I'm on your side. Mr. Harrison can help you find a place. It won't be much, probably, but it'll be something for you to get started. And I can get up a rent party for you."

"I don't think I need a rent party," Luvenia said.

"What do I care if you think you need one or don't think you need one," Miss Etta said. "I throw rent parties because I like to have parties. If they pay somebody's rent, that's okay, too. And since it's for my only godchild, this is going to be a get-down, swinging, New Negro rent party. How about that?"

"Sounds good to me."

"Sure it do. Now why don't you come on upstairs and tell me how you going to do my hair and make me beautiful so Mr. Harrison will get down on his knees and beg me to marry him."

"On his knees?"

"On his knees!"

> *Dear Daddy and Mama,*
>
> *It was so good to get your postcard. Thank you for sending your blessing and your love. You know how much I need them. I know I will miss you but I will visit Curry as much as I can. You can feel sure that I will stay close to Miss Etta, and that I will attend church every Sunday, and stay in the choir.*
>
> *In your letter you say I should never forget that I am a Lewis, and come from a proud tradition of good and God-fearing people. I promise you that I will never, never do anything that will make you ashamed of me. I love you and Richard and I will always keep that love as the most precious thing in my life.*
>
> *Your daughter,*
>
> *Luvenia*

The hardest part of the week was writing the letter to her parents. The next hardest part was not having a job to go to every day. She did some baby-sitting and worked for two days in a glove factory, but she couldn't keep up with the other girls on the sewing machines. It made the visit of Miss Katie, Florenz Deets's friend, all the harder and the position she talked about all the more difficult to turn down.

"It's in Oak Park," Katie had said, referring to the small, white community just outside of Chicago. "And I know the family."

Katie had felt bad about Luvenia's being fired by Mr. Deets and wanted to help. But what Luvenia needed was a way to make the decision to strike out on her own. She would miss her parents and even her brother Richard. And she had seen so many young women struggle from week to week, finally ending up getting married to any man who had a steady job.

"Miss Katie, I think I want to start my own

business," Luvenia had said. "Just to see how it'll work out."

"It's hard enough for a woman to get a job in Chicago," Katie said. "I can't even imagine starting my own business."

Luvenia had forced a smile and had responded to Katie's embrace. If they had been men and had shook hands instead of embraced, Katie would have felt the sweat in Luvenia's palm and would have known how terrified she felt inside.

On the day of the rent party, Luvenia saw a sign about the party in the barbershop window, and on the way to Miss Etta's, she saw one in the window of Mobley's Grocery and Fine Meats Store. When she reached Miss Etta's, the door was open, as usual, and she went in and saw that Mr. Harrison was standing at the end of the table. Miss Etta was telling him what to do, who had made the potato salad, and who was going to bring the collard greens.

"You think you want some hopping John?" she asked, knowing that black-eyed peas were his favorite.

"Yeah, I guess so," Mr. Harrison said. " 'Course I'm going to have to dance a little harder to work 'em off."

"Just don't be ducking no place I can't see you," Miss Etta said. "Now go on and get the stuff so I can see if everybody doing what they said they would."

When Mr. Harrison had left, Miss Etta told Luvenia to put some vinegar in the ribs on the stove and to make sure that the fire was low. "And cut up some of them peppers on top of the icebox," she added.

Miss Etta, for some reason, always used white vinegar instead of cider vinegar, and Luvenia poured it liberally over the simmering ribs.

She started cutting the hot peppers into small pieces and adding them to the bowl of chopped okra and onions that Miss Etta had already prepared.

"I got a letter from Daddy," Luvenia said.

"And he told you to get your butt down to Curry, right?" Miss Etta held a girdle in her hands and was pulling it in different directions.

"No. He did say he was disappointed, though. But things aren't going so well down there, either. He thinks he might have to come back to Chicago from time to time and work to send money down there."

"Lots of folks do that," Miss Etta said, still pulling on the girdle. "I guess half the people in Chicago sending money down South."

"Miss Etta, what are you doing with that girdle?"

"These cheap girdles get shrunk when you wash them," Miss Etta said. "And sometime they don't get shrunk evenly so you got to make sure you stretch them a little bit here and there before you try to get into them. That ain't something you're ever going to have to worry about."

"I think he thought things were going to be a lot better down on Curry."

"Did you tell him about losing your job?"

"Nope!" Luvenia shook her head. "I think I can do something to help out so it won't be bad. As long as he understands."

"Your mama have anything to say?"

"Said she loves me," Luvenia said, smiling.

She did think she knew how her father felt. He had dreamt about returning to Curry and a life he had just remembered as a boy. But it was a way of moving on for him, a way of reaching within himself and becoming . . . for a moment she searched for words and meaning . . . what would her father become? And then it came to her that what he would become, what his dream was all about, was becoming part of a tradition. And for Elijah Lewis that tradition was about the land and about the people who had worked it and who were still working it. It was about the land, and the people, and their work.

And for her what was it all about? Perhaps stretching the tradition, perhaps building on it, perhaps just finding her place in it. As so many Negroes moved from the South, that was what they would have to do for themselves, find their places in new traditions and in the new worlds of city tenements and of city living in which they found themselves.

A sharp stinging in her finger where the pepper had found a small cut snapped her out of her daydream, and she quickly ran some water over it.

Miss Etta came out of the bedroom in a dark

blue housedress that buttoned up the front. "See what I mean about this girdle?" she said. "Some places it don't hold me in at all."

"Miss Etta, you still looking good!"

"Girl, I know that!" Miss Etta said. "Now come on and touch up my edges so I can break some hearts tonight."

The party was announced for eight o'clock sharp and started at exactly nine minutes past eleven, CP time. It would have started somewhat earlier, but Mr. Harrison couldn't find a needle for the Victrola.

Luvenia tried to stay in the kitchen and serve, but men who had come to the party kept asking her out to dance. She wasn't much of a dancer, but Miss Etta kept the party swinging with fast tunes, and the men, most of them glad they had a party to go to instead of lying up in their sweltering apartments on a hot Chicago night, just needed a girl in the vicinity.

"If you wa-wa-want to sneak on outta he-here to m-m-my house, it's okay with m-m-me." A grinning man who said that he worked as a cook was trying to hold her too close.

"My boyfriend wouldn't like it," she said.

The reaction was a quick "ohh" and a perceptible loosening of his grip.

The party lifted Luvenia more than she thought it would. There was something in the air, a feeling that everybody in the small apartment could sense, which held them all together.

Once, trying to catch a breath of fresh air, she
sat in the fire escape window and watched the
other dancers. Their black, brown, and high yellow bodies moved almost as if they were just
one large mass, one hard, vibrant body moving
to a driving beat that was at once apart from the
dancers and yet coming from them. As Luvenia
listened, they followed the hard brilliance of a
trumpet that shrieked from the turning record,
catching all the heat from the Chicago night. In
the distance the clatter from the overhead train
rattled its own raucous rhythm. The wail of an
ambulance sliced wildly through the darkness.
A nearby radio answered with an offering of a
tinny blues. It was all the black music of the
South Side.

Florenz and Katie have never seen anything
like this, Luvenia thought, and in all probability,
even if they had, they wouldn't have understood
it. The party—the food, the music, the dancing—was something that you had to come to at
the end of a day of bone-crushing work, of frus-
tration, of despair. And there had to be a knowing that for a few hours the party, the swinging
of arms and shoulders, the rolling of hips and
snapping of fingers, would be wonderful. But
more than that was the realization that it would
end, and life and work, love and heartache,
would go on.

"Okay, all y'all, listen to this!" Miss Etta had
put on a slow blues and had turned the volume
down just loud enough to be heard. Outside,

across the city, the first streak of light was barely visible between the buildings. "All the whiskey is gone. All the food is gone. And when this record is over I want all of y'all to be gone, too. Thank you for coming to our rent party for Miss Luvenia Lewis. Luvenia, thank the people!"

Luvenia looked at Miss Etta who showed a mouthful of teeth.

"Thank you, everybody," Luvenia said, still looking at Miss Etta. "I really appreciate you coming."

"And this girl can do up some hair!" Miss Etta said. "Soon as she gets her shop together we'll be letting you know."

"Go on, girl!"

Two men were asleep on the coats and had to be wakened. One woman said it was too early to break the party up, and Miss Etta said that she could stay and party by herself if she wanted to.

A few people stopped and told Luvenia how nice the party was and how much they had enjoyed themselves.

"You ever give another rent party, you be sure to let us know!" a young couple said. The man shook Luvenia's hand awkwardly.

As soon as the last person had left, Miss Etta took off her dress and wriggled out of the girdle. "I think everybody enjoyed themselves," she said. "What you think?"

"That you are the most wonderful friend in the world!" Luvenia said.

"Well, that is true," Miss Etta said. "Now I'm going to get me some serious sleep. We'll talk later."

Mornings in the black neighborhoods in Chicago started earlier than they did in the white neighborhoods. Black men had to deliver the goods that white shopkeepers would sell; black women had to get to white households to put in a full day's work. Some men and women had to go downtown to look for work with the army of whites that was also looking.

Luvenia walked home slowly, realizing for the first time how tired she was. She held the brown paper bag with the rent party money tightly as she walked. She was trying to remember how much the Madame Walker products were. She had glanced in the bag. There was at least fifteen dollars in bills and God only knew how much in change. She knew that if she could make as much doing hair and selling as she thought she could, things would be all right.

"Morning, sister!" An old man was pulling scrap metal through the street on a homemade wagon.

"Morning, brother!" Luvenia smiled at the man, and he tipped his hat.

"You got you a nice step to start off the new day," the man said. "Look like you ready!"

"I am," Luvenia called back to him. "I am!"

JANUARY 1964,
JOHNSON CITY,
SOUTH CAROLINA

THE LEWIS FAMILY, 1964

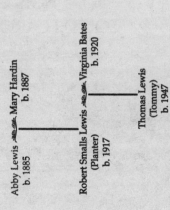

Abby Lewis ⚭ Mary Hardin
b. 1885   b. 1887

Robert Smalls Lewis ⚭ Virginia Bates
(Planter)   b. 1920
b. 1917

Thomas Lewis
(Tommy)
b. 1947

Tommy Lewis felt himself being pushed from behind as he tried to back toward the basket. The guard for Curry looked over the court as he brought the ball across the half-court line. Tommy saw the blade-thin guard glance at the scoreboard. The score was tied, forty-eight all, with two minutes to go, and Aiken, the Delaney player holding him, knew the ball would be coming to Tommy.

"You're not going to score, man." Aiken leaned heavily against Tommy.

Wilson, the big center for Curry, came out to set a pick.

The guard passed the ball in to Wilson and took it right back as he cut past the big man. Tommy lifted an elbow and placed it gently in the middle of Aiken's chest. Aiken quickly knocked the arm away.

Tommy brought the elbow up again, let Aiken knock it away again, then spun to his right, stopped short, and brought the same elbow hard into Aiken's side. Then, using the taller player's body for leverage, he brought his head and shoulders toward the basket, stopped short, stepped back from the reacting defensive player, and took the pass.

He went straight up, the ball resting on the fingertips of his right hand, his right wrist cocked, his eyes on the rim of the hoop. As he reached the top of his jump he felt Aiken's hand on his stomach and sensed the other player's leap. The ball arched slowly, just inches over Aiken's straining fingers, coming down in the center of the black iron rim, catching momentarily on the net, and falling through. Curry was up by two.

Delaney was the biggest black school in Johnson City and the heavy favorite to win the tournament. They brought the ball up court quickly, forced it inside to their big man, Hepplewhite, who turned and threw up a hook from too far away. He had often done that, thrown up the big hook, then rushed in like a mad man for the rebound.

Tommy slid over to the lane that he knew Hepplewhite would take to the ball just as the center came in for his follow-up. He felt the big man's elbow in the back of his head, winced slightly, and spread his legs. He could hold off Hepplewhite for a second or two, long enough for Curry to get the rebound.

Curry got the rebound and, with Hepplewhite and Aiken boxed in, got out on a quick break. Moments later the Curry Cougars were up by

four, and then six, and then the coach was tossing towels in the air as Curry had won its first
All-City tournament.

In the locker room, the team celebrated its win.
There were hugs all around, and Tommy's hand
was shaken a hundred times. He felt as good as
he had ever felt.

"Tommy, you did it!" Jimmy Manigault
grabbed Tommy's shoulders.

"No," Tommy said. "We did it! We won because we're the best team. One guy doesn't beat
Delaney!"

The original name of Delaney High had been
Calhoun, but when a new school was built, it
had taken the name of Calhoun, and the old
school, which had become predominantly black
two years after school integration, had been re-
named Martin R. Delaney High. They had won
the championship three years in a row, but this
year the top prize had gone to Curry and
Tommy.

Mandy McKinnon was waiting with Coach
Smith and a tall, wide-shouldered man with
sandy blond hair near the trophy case when
Tommy came out of the locker room.

"That Aiken looked pretty mad when the
game was over," Mandy said. Mandy was looking good. She wore a short, white skirt and a
sleeveless blouse.

"Yeah, he was mad," Tommy said. "Said the
referees didn't want them to win."

"If they hadn't run their mouths so much it

wouldn't have looked so bad," the coach said. "They were trying to talk themselves into a win."

They started toward the door. Most of the crowd from Curry had already left, and the students from Delaney were too down to even speak. The ones that he knew nodded toward Tommy.

"This is Leonard Chase." The coach indicated the man who was walking with them, and Tommy shook the offered hand. "He played for State."

"State?" Tommy looked at the tall white man. He stood like an athlete.

"Thought we could drop by my place for some iced tea," Chase said. "My wife doesn't cook much, but she makes some mean iced tea."

"You shouldn't say that about your wife," Mandy said.

The conversation went on about Chase's wife, and Tommy wondered what the man was about. Coach Smith had said that there were going to be college scouts at the game and that some of them might want to talk to him afterwards.

Mrs. Smith, the coach's wife, was just recovering from a heart attack, and he had to go home. But he congratulated Tommy again and told him that he would see him in the morning.

"The principal wants to call an assembly tomorrow so the whole school can thank the team for the honor it brought to the school."

"He's actually going to say something good about the basketball team?" Mandy asked.

"Miracles will happen," the coach said.

"I think half the world are people who are basketball fans and the other half hate the sport," Chase said.

"I can tell you which half our principal is in," Mandy said.

The Chase house was in the historic waterfront area. It wasn't as large as some of the homes, but it was just as elegant and better kept up than most. There were six thin white columns on the front porch, three on either side of the double doors. The doors opened onto a long, mirrored foyer, which led to a spiral staircase.

"One day I'm going to have one beer too many and come tumbling down those stairs," Chase said.

Mrs. Chase was a pretty woman with a small, almost puckish mouth that spread into a warm smile as she appeared from a room off the foyer. "Well, the news is all over Johnson City that Curry won tonight," she said, taking Mandy's jacket.

"We were lucky," Tommy said.

They went to the room Chase called his office and sat around on leather chairs as he told about his days playing high school ball.

"We had seventeen guys on the team and not one of them could play defense." Chase was still wearing his suit jacket and slowly loosened his tie. "We could play the worst team in the league and we'd win, but they would score fifty points against us."

"A lot of teams play like that," Tommy said. "Just run up and down the court and heave the ball. I don't mind that kind of game."

"Yes, but you have a nice all-around game," Chase went on. "A lot of the scouts at the game were looking at Aiken, the guy who was holding you. Only knock against him is that he's too old."

"To play college ball?" Mandy asked. She balanced a plate with cherry pie and ice cream on her lap.

"He's almost twenty," Chase said. "If it took him that long to get through high school, he might have trouble keeping up his grades in college."

"He might have been left back," Mrs. Chase said. "And college ball is a lot more demanding than high school basketball. You have to remember a lot more set plays."

"Did you play basketball in high school?" Mandy asked.

"In my day, young ladies didn't play basketball," Mrs. Chase said, putting on her best *Gone With the Wind* accent. "There was a girl's basketball team, I suppose, but it was for the type of girl who didn't mind per*spiring* in public."

"And Sally was not going to perspire in public or anyplace else if she could avoid it," Mr. Chase said. "But she wrote about sports for a while in college."

"Then I discovered gossip," Mrs. Chase said.

"I don't know if I like writing it more or just spreading it over the phone."

"Honey, I need a beer," Mr. Chase said. "Me and Tommy are going to run down to the kitchen and see if there's anything cold to drink. Why don't you show Mandy the sewing room. See if she has any ideas about how to fix it up. I mean she has to have a better idea than that art *rico* stuff you were thinking about."

"Mr. Leonard J. Chase, you just don't have a clue as to what looks good and what doesn't." Mrs. Chase's voice rose a level. "And it's not art *rico*, it's art *deco*. Come on, Mandy, let's leave these males."

Tommy watched as Mandy followed Mrs. Chase out of the room. Both women were pretty, Mrs. Chase in a more sophisticated way than Mandy. The smooth skin of her face seemed almost as if it were made of porcelain. Tommy thought her mouth was too small, but she was still pretty. Mandy's mouth was wide, and her smile was so warm it always made him smile in return. He often thought of the time she had sat in front of him and dared him not to smile. She kept looking at him and smiling and smiling. He had tried to think about a movie he had seen and about his math homework, but the only thing that came to his mind with clarity was the fact that he loved Mandy.

"You drink beer, Tommy?" Mr. Chase asked.

"No, sir," Tommy answered.

"I forgot about that. How old are you, anyway?"

"Sixteen last week."

"You know, I've wanted to talk to you for a while. I like the way you conduct yourself on the basketball court and the way you conduct yourself off the court, too. You don't find a lot of young people who really have their heads on straight these days."

"I know what you mean," Tommy answered.

"You got one more year left at Curry?"

"Right."

"The coach said your grades are really good." Mr. Chase took a cigar from the humidor on his desk and sniffed it. "You really could have a good future in front of you if you dealt with it right and maybe met the right people. What I'm thinking about is talking to some people about you. You mind if I do that?"

"What people?"

"You smoke?"

"No."

"Nasty habit to start," Mr. Chase said. "I used to smoke cigarettes even when I played ball. The game at State was slow, so it didn't hurt me that much."

"You ever think about playing pro ball?"

"I had a tryout with Cincinnati back in 1950." Mr. Chase nodded as he spoke. "I played with them twice in the preseason and did all right. Then they asked me to play on an industrial team that served as sort of a farm club for them. I figured my pride was hurt and if I couldn't play on the big team, I didn't want to play at all."

"I think I would have played on the industrial team," Tommy said. "They offered you a contract and everything?"

"And a five-hundred-dollar bonus," Chase responded. "Sometimes I think I blew it. I had a chance to do something exciting. But I had met Sally then, and we were pretty much committed to getting married, and her father had a nice place for me in the business. So here I am."

"You're still in good shape."

"For a forty-year-old," Mr. Chase answered. He lit the cigar, inhaled deeply on it, and then exhaled slowly, letting the smoke drift in a thin wisp toward the ceiling. "What I wanted to find out about tonight is what you thought about the possibility of skipping your last year at Curry?"

"You mean go to another high school?"

"No, I mean going right into college," Mr. Chase said. "I think you can handle the work. A lot of young people skip that last year of high school and get right into college. State's looking for some good people."

"State?" Tommy shifted uneasily in the chair. "I don't think they take Negroes."

"Well, let's face it, Tommy," Mr. Chase said as he turned in the swivel chair so that he faced Tommy squarely, "integration is here to stay. And it's about time if you ask me. Anyway, there's a lot of pressure to get Negroes into the schools. What I see is that there aren't that many

Negroes qualified for some of the colleges."

"Oh." Tommy was trying to put together what Mr. Chase was saying.

"Sort of a shock?"

"Yeah, sort of," Tommy said.

"Well, there has to be a start in everything," Mr. Chase said. "Just like Jackie Robinson was the start of Negroes in baseball, and Marian Anderson was the first Negro to sing, or at least I think she was the first, to sing in Carnegie Hall in New York."

"You want me to be the first Negro to go to State?"

"We want to put together a group of young people we can bring in quietly, without a lot of commotion. One of the things the other schools—the ones having trouble—did, was to drag their feet and push things to a confrontation. What we want to do is to get the right Negroes and get things prepared."

"You think I'd play ball for State?"

"Can't guarantee it," Mr. Chase said. "But it's probable. You've got outstanding skills and a good head on your shoulders. How does it sound to you?"

"Sounds good."

"It's not going to be easy. I won't feed you any lies. A lot of people aren't going to like Negroes going to school with whites, and that's just a fact that you and I have to live with. I don't see where it does that much harm on a college level. I'm not sure if integration is good on a grade school level. Nothing to do with race, either. You take a Negro family and maybe they don't read as much as a white family and their children are going to fall behind. By the time they reach high school, they're either still behind or they're caught up. Now, when they catch up, it means, far as I'm concerned, that they've really got something special. That's what I think about you."

"Thanks."

"Well, I want to get back to the girls. We'll talk in a week or so, but I want you to think about the idea of leaving Curry to start State in the fall. What it means on your part is that you finish this year with the same good grades you've been getting and you make sure you don't get into any trouble. On our part I think I can get you a full scholarship. And that stands if you make the team or if you don't make it. We can even get you some tutoring help if you need it. Still sound good?"

"Sounds great," Tommy said.

"Let's find the girls and complain about this room," Chase said, standing. "Even if you like it, we have to keep them on their toes."

Leonard Chase gave Tommy a big wink.

Tommy followed the tall man down the hallway toward the sewing room. He knew he was holding his breath. It was the same feeling that he had before the start of the game. He knew that going to State was going to be a big challenge, and he wasn't at all sure what the outcome would be. More important, though, was that it would be a challenge in which he wouldn't be at all sure who was on his team.

Tommy walked Mandy home, kissed her in the shadows of her porch, and then half ran, half walked to his own house. The idea of going to college even before he finished high school was exciting.

"I still don't see how you can go to college if you don't finish high school," his mother said. "Remember this, child. You are not white and you cannot be cutting corners like white folks do."

"So you think Mr. Chase don't know what he's talking about?" Tommy's father was in his bathrobe, his thin legs ahead of him on the hassock.

"I didn't say he didn't know what he was talking about," Virginia Lewis said. "All I'm saying is that he doesn't know who he's talking to. What happens if Tommy doesn't make it through his first year of college? Is he a college dropout or a high school dropout?"

"Once they let him into a college, he is a high school graduate automatic," Robert Lewis nodded, agreeing with his own wisdom. "How you going to be in college without graduating from high school? Tell me that, okay? How you going to do it? And he going to State, too?"

"Mr. Chase said that I won't have any trouble in college, Mama. That's why he selected me. He said he could look at my grades and know I was college material."

"Tommy, I think you're college material, too." Virginia Lewis lifted the coffeepot, determined that it was still half full, and put it back on the stove. "But what's tripping out his mouth without a care is worrying my ears something terrible."

"If Mr. Chase said that it was going to be all right, he knows what he's talking about." His father ended his remarks with a *humph!*

"Oh, you so full of your son tonight you can't even think straight." Tommy's mother looked over her glasses at her husband. "You should have seen your face when the game was over tonight. And when we were leaving, you were strutting around like a young rooster!"

"I am a young rooster!" his father said.

"Then you don't need me to wrap your knee up before you go to work tomorrow?"

"I might not," his father said, smiling.

"The coffee's hot. You want some?"

"Yeah, I'll take a cup," his father said. "Did the coach know about this?"

"I think he must have," Tommy said. "Maybe I should call him."

"Too late now," his mother said. "Call him in the morning. You want something to eat?"

"No, ma'am."

"What did that boy say to you after the game?" his father asked. "I know it wasn't anything good."

"You probably don't want to hear it, either," his mother said. "The way these children talk today."

"His father works down at the ice plant," Robert Lewis said. "He's got a bad mouth on him, too. I can't wait to go into the city tomorrow and see what they talking about down at the barbershop. I know he has some heavy lying to do about how they lost the game."

The telephone rang. Tommy was yawning when he picked up the receiver. It was the Reverend McKinnon's wife for his mother.

The conversation with Mr. Chase had come too soon after the game for Tommy to absorb it easily. His mother had been right. The idea of going to a white college wasn't something to take lightly, and neither was leaving high school ahead of time. Tommy took his shoes off and fell across his bed. After a good night's sleep, he thought, he would think about it all again and sort out the pieces. But he thought like his father did, that if Mr. Chase thought it was all right, it probably would be.

He was almost asleep, just vaguely aware that the telephone rang several more times. His mind was somewhere between the congratulations he fully expected in the morning and the surrender to sleep he knew was coming, when the knock came on the door. It opened before he could answer, the way it always did when it was his mother.

"Yes?"

"Skeeter Jackson just called. He got bit by a snake," she said. "He wants your father to take him over to the hospital. You want to go with him?"

"Skeeter got bit by a snake?" An image of the lanky white boy came to Tommy's mind. "Okay, I'll go with Daddy."

There were no hospitals on Curry and two in Johnson City. No one had ever said officially that Mercy Hospital, south of Calhoun Street, was the hospital for whites, or that Dow, north of Calhoun, was the hospital for Negroes, but everyone understood that to be the case. So when Robert Lewis pulled the old Nash away from Skeeter's house, everyone knew where he was headed.

"How you feel?" Tommy heard his father asking.

"Oh, man, the pain is something else!" Skeeter had stretched his legs out in the backseat. Even in the darkness of the car Tommy could see that the fifteen-year-old had lost the color in his face.

"Where are your parents?"

"They went to a revival up in North Carolina," Skeeter said. "Greensboro. I sure appreciate y'all coming over."

"What happened?" Tommy was twisted in the seat and looking back at Skeeter.

"I heard a rustling out back," Skeeter said. "I don't know how long I can stand this pain!"

"You want to stop and get a BC?" Robert Lewis asked.

"No, just get me to the hospital," Skeeter said.

"So you saw the snake in the back?" Tommy urged Skeeter on.

"I come from the game, and when I got back—"

"You saw the game?"

"Sure, you were really good," Skeeter said. "Man, I was looking at you and you looked like Oscar Robertson."

"I was smoking!" Tommy agreed.

"So when I got home I decided to shoot a few baskets." Skeeter inhaled through his nose. "Then I thought I heard something, and—you know how the grass in my backyard is long near the fence?"

"Should be," Robert Lewis said. "You haven't cut it since Skippy was a pup."

"Anyway, I looked over there and I saw the snake. I told you we had a couple of chickens being killed?"

"Go on," Tommy said. "Then what happened?"

"So I went in and got my daddy's shotgun. When I come out I didn't see the snake, so I went through the grass looking for him. That's when it bit me."

"It bit you after you shot it?" Mr. Lewis asked.

"No, sir, I didn't even have a chance to shoot it. It just jumped up and bit me."

"What happened to the shotgun?" Tommy asked.

"I dropped the thing when I felt that snake hit me," Skeeter said. "We get back from the hospital, we're going to go out and kill that thing. Cut it into about a thousand pieces."

"We?" Tommy looked at Skeeter. "You mean you let that snake—what kind of snake was it?"

"A rattler," Skeeter said.

"A rattler?" Robert Lewis looked over his shoulder at his young white passenger. "A rattler bite ain't nothing to fool around with."

"I know that, Mr. Lewis!" Skeeter's voice had just a hint of panic. "That's why I wish you would hurry on to the hospital. Then we can go back and kill the snake."

"Look here, Skeeter"—Tommy rubbed the end of his nose with his fingers—"You mean to tell me you got a rattlesnake with a shotgun in your backyard and you think I'm going to go mess with him?"

"Tommy, don't make me laugh or nothing!" Skeeter's voice was getting higher and higher. "If I get to laughing and carrying on, the blood's going to go faster, and the poison is headed right for my heart."

"He got the basketball, too?" Tommy asked.

"Mr. Lewis, he's making my blood run faster,"

Skeeter said. "If the poison gets to my heart, I'm going to die right in this car!"

The drive to Mercy Hospital took less than twenty minutes, and when they pulled up to the emergency door, Tommy thought that everything would be all right. Two ambulance drivers sat by the side of the building, playing checkers.

Tommy had to help carry Skeeter into the hospital. They put him on the gurney, and watched as two nurses in crisp white uniforms rolled him into the emergency room.

A male nurse came and told them they could wait on boxes outside the emergency entrance.

"That Skeeter can get himself into more messes than the law allows." Tommy's father shook his head. "I bet they won't let him go tonight. You see the way that ankle was swoll up?"

"You don't think he going to die or anything like that?" Tommy asked.

"Not from a rattlesnake," his father said. "They got that serum for rattlesnake bites right here in the hospital. Now you get bit by a coral snake then they got to send clear to Atlanta for the serum. If you're white they telephone for the serum and tell them to fly it down right quick. If you're black they send for it by mail and say if they see anybody coming this way and if it ain't too much trouble give them the serum to bring with them."

"Get out of here." Tommy liked his father's humor.

"So you think you a man, now," his father said.

"Born a man," Tommy said, knowing what his father would say.

"Get out of here!" his father said, slapping his knee. "You ain't no man yet! Boy, when I was your age, they used to say 'Planter, put some fertilizer on your lip and grow you a mustache because we need some men around here.'"

"Planter?"

"That's what they called me. Planter was a boat a cousin stole during the Civil War. They said when I was young I could steal a pea out the pod."

"You scared about me going to a white college?"

"A little," his father said. "Then again, scary times ain't news to a black man."

"I'm man enough to handle it," Tommy said.

"I don't know, maybe you are just about a man," his father said. "You're taking on the responsibility of a man. It's heavy going to a college, and if you go to a white college, it's even heavier. How you feel about going to a white college?"

"Feel good about it," Tommy said. His father looked serious. "How do you feel about it?"

"It's nice being around white folks," was the answer.

What was not said, what Tommy knew was on his father's mind, was that it could also be dangerous being around white folks.

"You see Reverend McKinnon at the game tonight?" Tommy asked.

"No. He's busy getting a march ready for Johnson City next week. You know they're still not hiring Negroes on King Street like they said they was."

"What kind of march?" Tommy asked.

"He was talking about a march for togetherness." Robert Lewis pushed his legs out in front of him. "He said it would be like a little march on Washington. He wrote to Dr. King's people, seeing if he could get him to come on down here."

"Martin Luther King, Jr.?"

"Yeah, you know Dr. King's daddy ain't from that far away from here."

"Where's he from?"

"Some little town in Georgia." The older man nodded and looked toward the soda machine that stood halfway in the shadows. It was hot, and the air was still. From inside the hospital the sound of a white gospel station gave movement to the still air.

"You think there's going to be trouble?" Tommy asked his father.

"No, I don't think so. Mostly folks around here see what's happening. You can't send all those colored boys over to Vietnam and then don't give them jobs when they get home. I don't expect no trouble. You young people are going to have a whole different world than we had in my day."

"Then you think it's okay me going to a white college?" Tommy asked.

"I think it's good," his father said. "We come a long way and we got a long way to go. You can't make much progress if you don't leave home, but you can sure mess yourself up if you don't remember where home is. What did Mr. Chase say?"

"He said I could do it," Tommy said. "He said I was the right guy to start Negroes going to Johnson City State."

A short, heavyset man, a stethoscope around his neck, came to the doorway. He smiled, nodded, and spoke in an accent that both Tommy and his father decided was either New York or some other place up North.

"You the people who brought the Jackson boy to the hospital?" the doctor asked.

"Yes, sir." Tommy's father stood up.

"Well, you can go in to see him for maybe two minutes," he said, smiling. "He'll be all right. We'll keep him overnight and let him go home in the morning."

Mercy Hospital had the smell of a strong antiseptic cleanser. Tommy thought that the smell was enough by itself to make you sick. On the way to Skeeter's room he let his mind wander to the boy's parents. His mother was all right, but his father never had much use for Negroes. He didn't even like Skeeter calling his father Mr. Lewis.

"He said if I call him anything I should call

'Uncle Lewis,' or 'Robert,' " Skeeter had said.

Skeeter's room was dark. The lamp on the white end table was barely bright enough to see his face. He looked okay. Not great, but okay.

"You look worse than a horse that's been rode all night and put away wet," Tommy's father said.

"Just about how I feel, too," Skeeter said.

The door opened and Tommy turned to see Skeeter's aunt come in. She was a short, fair-skinned woman with high cheekbones and a sprinkle of freckles around her nose.

"How you doing, boy?" she said, going to the side of the bed.

"Pretty good, Aunt Lillian," Skeeter answered, forcing a smile. "These are my friends, Mr. Lewis, and his son, Tommy. They brought me to the hospital."

"Ma'am." Tommy's father tipped his hat to the older woman.

"I appreciate it," she replied.

"Your leg hurt, Skeeter?" Tommy asked.

"Worse than anything," Skeeter answered. "That snake bit me something terrible. I can't believe how much it hurts. Got pain all up and down my leg."

"The doctor said you were going to be all right, honey," his aunt said.

"Got pains all in my leg," Skeeter said. "Hurts so bad I can't hardly think straight. But I'm sure glad you got me over here when you did."

"Well, you just get some rest, young man,"

Robert Lewis said. "You're going to feel a lot better in the morning."

"Mr. Lewis, how am I going to feel better in the morning when I know that snake is probably sitting in my living room right now, that shotgun across his lap, watching television?"

"You don't have to worry about that," Tommy said. "Ain't nothing good on television this time of night."

"So the way I heard it," Jennie Epps said as she sat on the floor in front of Mrs. Lewis looking through the Lewis family Bible, "when the Civil War broke out, everybody just ran off the plantation and joined up. That's what the Eppses did, anyway. That's what my grandfather told me. Now, this white teacher said hardly any blacks from Georgia fought in the Civil War."

"That's Miss Finney. She's got to be the oldest teacher on Curry Island," Tommy said. "She probably fought in the Civil War."

"And lost," Jennie said.

"You children shouldn't be talking about that teacher like that," Mrs. Lewis said.

"Ma, you know who she is?" Tommy was sitting sideways in the armchair. "She's that woman that said that black people should use Orange Beach just before the tide goes out so no white people would get polluted."

"She's no worse than anybody else on Curry," Mrs. Lewis said. "Segregation is segregation and that's all there is to it."

"I wonder if they going to let the students up at State know that Tommy is coming," Jennie said. "I wouldn't want nothing happening to the father of my children."

"Jennie, would you cut that out!" Tommy said. "People are going to start believing you."

"I believe me," Jennie said. "You think you going to marry that little—what's her name?— Pandy? Sound like one of them Pandy bears."

"Mandy!" Tommy said.

"Jennie, you are just about as forward as you want to be!" Mrs. Lewis said.

"Thank you, ma'am."

"She didn't mean it as a compliment, Jennie," Tommy said.

"Whose car is that outside?" Mrs. Lewis stretched her neck to look out of the window. "Looks like Reverend McKinnon."

"Who was Muhad?" Jennie asked. "You have Muhad at the top of the page."

"Sister Saran wrote that in before she passed on," Virginia Lewis said. "She said she didn't know exactly how to—go get the door for Reverend McKinnon—didn't know how to spell his name, but he come over right from Africa. 'Cept he didn't call it Africa. He called it Akubelan, or something like that."

Reverend McKinnon came in right behind Mandy McKinnon. The two girls exchanged looks and polite smiles as Mandy sat on the couch.

"Mandy, go in the kitchen and get your father a cold glass of iced tea," Jennie said. "How you doing today, Reverend McKinnon?"

"I'm okay." Reverend McKinnon wiped the band of sweat that had gathered under his hat. "You know them tomatoes I was raising, supposed to be winter tomatoes?"

"Yes?"

"The worms got to them something terrible!" Reverend McKinnon said, giving Tommy's knee a shove in the way of greeting. "I went out there to see if any of them were ready for the table. I took a look and saw that they were dark, and when I cut into one of them, the things had worms. You know I was mad."

"The Lord giveth and the Lord taketh away," Jennie said.

"The Lord wasn't talking about tomatoes," Tommy said.

"You spoke to the Lord?" Jennie asked. "He told you He wasn't talking about tomatoes. I mean *personally*? Well, do tell, Mr. Lewis!"

Mandy returned with two glasses of iced tea and gave one to Mrs. Lewis and the other to her father.

"Mandy, you must have been eating oysters again," Jennie said. "You getting them little pimples around the tip of your nose. Don't they bother you, girl?"

"Is Robert home?" Reverend McKinnon asked.

"No. His boss called him into work today," Mrs. Lewis said. "He's getting a lot of overtime these days."

"You didn't see the papers today, did you?" Reverend McKinnon's voice flattened out.

"No. It don't come till late. . . . What's wrong?"

"The Klan made an announcement that it's going to hold a demonstration next Wednesday morning," Reverend McKinnon said. "That's the same day we're going to have our march in the afternoon. Just an excuse for getting a lot of people into town and causing a lot of trouble."

"You speak to the sheriff?" Tommy asked.

"Yeah. He called this morning and asked me to call off our march," Reverend McKinnon said.

"I know you're not going to call it off, right?" Jennie looked up from the page she was reading.

"Can't call it off," Reverend McKinnon said. "We got to keep the march going because we want to send the story about it up to Birmingham. Only way we going to get Dr. King down here and get some real progress is to show him we're doing something and that the papers are paying attention. And if we don't get Dr. King down here, we're not going to get any progress in Johnson City."

"That's right," Jennie said.

"We need to get the march going and get it in the paper. Don't make much difference if the white papers don't carry it, long as the Negro papers play it up big."

"You speak to Mr. Diggs?"

"I didn't speak to him because he's such a fool," Reverend McKinnon said. "He's so busy trying to please the white folks, he can't even write a headline. He thinks he's a white man running that paper up in North Carolina, that Asheville paper. He even told me he wants to be a moderate. You understand that? A black man who thinks he's a moderate?"

"That's something," Mrs. Lewis said, using the tone that Tommy recognized as the one she used when she wasn't sure of what was going on.

"I need Robert to be up there among the leaders of the march," Reverend McKinnon said.

"The sheriff said that nobody of consequence was even going to be in the march," Jennie added.

" 'Just a bunch of people with nothing in the world to do.' " Reverend McKinnon used the sheriff's tone of voice.

"Right. But the Lewis family's been here and knows what is going on," Mandy said.

"Not only that," Reverend McKinnon said, "you have land around here, and that's what white folks understand. Can I count on you?"

"Sure. We'll be there," Mrs. Lewis said. "I'll tell Robert as soon as he gets home."

"I'm going to ask Sister Williams to have a dinner ready at the church when it's over,"

Reverend McKinnon said. "And we need some people to take care of any injuries. I spoke to Dr. Calloway in Johnson City, and he's going to set up a small aid station out here, and he said he'll bring a nurse."

"The Klan going to be real trouble?" Mrs. Lewis asked.

"Who knows?" Reverend McKinnon downed the rest of his iced tea. Tommy thought he looked worried when he stood up. "Sheriff Moser said they might, but you can't tell. And you can't let struggle turn you around. You just can't. What did Frederick Douglass say? There is no progress without struggle. When Robert gets home, you tell him to give me a call. We'll go over things together."

"We still going to march down Calhoun Street?" Jennie asked.

"Yeah. And we still didn't get the permit, so you can expect the sheriff and the dogs and anything else they want to use," Reverend McKinnon said. "I'm not just marching down Calhoun Street, I'm marching all the way to freedom."

"The doctor told you to keep off your feet," Mandy McKinnon said.

"Well, I'll walk the first few miles to freedom, and then I'll look around for a trolley headed in that direction," Reverend McKinnon said. "Anyway, these aren't the times to be talking about what one man needs."

"How about those white folks?" Tommy asked. "Some of them said they were going to march, too."

"You can't depend on them," Reverend McKinnon said. "They mean well in their hearts, but it's just not their fight."

When Tommy got to work at five-thirty, he was surprised to see that the Clark's Five-and-Dime was closed. It usually closed at six, and he wondered what had happened. He looked in and saw people in the back; he knocked on the glass door. It had been a hot day, and the few sprinkles of rain that hit his face felt good.

"C'mon in, Tommy." Miss Robbins was heavy and looked older than she probably was. "We got us a first-class mess in here."

"What happened?" Tommy stepped in past the white-haired woman.

"I don't know," she said, shaking her head. She had the keys on a chain fixed to the blue smock she wore. "Something with the plumbing."

Jed Sasser was on his knees behind the counter. Tommy looked down to see what he was doing and saw that he was trying to wrap tape around the bottom of a pipe. Jed looked up at Tommy.

"You know where the cutoff is?" he asked. "I tried three valves downstairs, and none of them was right."

Tommy looked under the counter sink, saw the valve nearly hidden by the back of the tub, and turned it to the right. The water stopped. "How come you didn't call the plumber?"

"Don't know where he is," Jed said, wiping his brow with the rag he had been using to try to stem the flow of water. "We ain't going to be able to open tomorrow unless we fix this tonight. You know how to get this pipe off?"

Tommy saw the box with the new pipe that somebody had bought. "I guess so," Tommy said.

"I'm glad that somebody knows something," Miss Robbins said. "I've been mopping for the last hour."

Miss Robbins mopped up most of the water that was still on the floor and then handed Tommy a newspaper. Tommy spread the paper on the still-wet floor and watched it change color. The headline on the paper read *Citizens Council to March*.

"It just started to leak?" Tommy asked as he adjusted the wrench to remove the nuts from the U-trap.

"It was stopped up," Jed said. "I tried to clear it out with a hanger and the metal was so thin, the hanger went right through."

Tommy took off the nuts and pulled off the

U-trap. He looked inside it and saw what looked like a rag. It was the one that was used to wipe off the top of the counter.

"With all the mess that's going on I sure didn't need this tonight," Miss Robbins said. "We had to close an hour early."

"What mess?" Tommy asked.

"The colored getting ready to march through town and that King coming down here," Miss Robbins said. "He's from Atlanta and he should stay in Atlanta. It's people like him who stirs up the coloreds."

"You take the average one of your black folks around here," Jed said. He was sitting on a high stool that normally stood on the other side of the counter. "He don't want race mixing any more than the average white man. But when they start bringing in them people from out of town, things get stirred up. When's the last time you had any problems between whites and coloreds?"

"Negroes can't get food in here," Tommy said.

"Whoa! They can get anything they want anytime they want it," Miss Robbins said. "And you've been working here long enough to know that. They just can't sit at the counter and eat it. Most coloreds don't want to eat here, anyway."

"You can eat in a colored store," Tommy said. He put the new pipe in place, saw that it fit, and began to hand-tighten the nuts.

"Now I don't want to eat in a colored store," Jed said. "And I don't see why a colored man or woman would want to eat in a white store. And that Reverend King—and I don't know if he's a real preacher or not—don't care where colored people eat. What he wants is race mixing. You hear that speech he made in Washington about little black boys and little white girls playing together?"

"Who's that other one they got up in New York? Malcolm X or something?" Miss Robbins said. "Now he don't want no race mixing."

"I don't trust no man that calls himself 'X,' " Jed said. "That man hates white people something terrible."

"You got any pipe compound?"

"What's that?" Jed asked.

"That's the stuff you put on the threads so the pipe won't leak," Tommy said. "If you ain't got any, you better get some from the hardware store."

"You take the truck and go on over and get some," Miss Robbins said. "I want to clean this mess up tonight."

Jed wiped his hands on a paper towel. "When we got our boys fighting in Vietnam and all them riots in New York, we don't need another problem," he said. "We sure don't need it here in Johnson City."

"Get some pipe string, too," Tommy said and, noticing the puzzled look on Jed's face, added that he should just ask someone in the hardware store for it.

Miss Robbins went to the door with Jed and locked it behind him.

Tommy looked at the floor he had been hired to sweep nightly and saw that it was fairly clean.

"What I think," Miss Robbins went on, "is that people should leave things the way they were and let people work out what they want to do without people from the outside coming in. Tommy, you certainly don't have any problems getting along and you never will, because you are a fine young boy. If everybody were like you, we'd all get along just fine."

"Yes, ma'am."

"The truth is that white people are a certain way, and coloreds are a certain way," Miss Robbins went on. "And Lord knows that doesn't mean that one race is better than the other. It just means that people are a certain way and get along with people who are like them. You take Jed and you. Jed is better at some things than you are, and you're better than Jed at some things. If you ask me, I'd rather have you working for me than him any day."

"If I had a big place, would you work for me?" Tommy asked.

"Sure I would!" Miss Robbins said. "You being colored would not bother me one bit as long as you paid a decent wage and had decent work. But I would not socialize with you because you are not the kind of person I would socialize with. Everybody has their preferences, and my preferences are for my own people. And don't you prefer to be around your own people?"

"Yes, ma'am."

Tommy found the push broom and started sweeping the floor. He saw Miss Robbins take the straw broom and start at the other end of the store. Miss Harriet Robbins did not own Clark's, but she had managed it for as long as Tommy had worked there part-time. She had always been fair and pretty tough on all the employees, but she never fired anyone who really needed a job and was respectful.

Mr. Robbins, it was rumored, had run off with a waitress a year after they had married and Miss Robbins had devoted herself to Clark's and the church, in that order. It was Miss Robbins who enforced the rule that Negroes could not eat at the counter. It wasn't any different in any white-owned store in Johnson City or in any other place in the South that Tommy had ever heard about.

He wondered what it would be like to go into a fancy restaurant in New York or Chicago and sit down at a table with a white couple sitting at the next table. It didn't sound like any big deal, he thought.

The only thing that really bothered Tommy was the drinking fountains. He didn't like to have to look all over town for a drinking fountain labeled "Colored." The other things, like voting or going to school with whites, he really didn't know about. He had seen pictures of life in Harlem, and it looked all right. A little fast, but still all right. And he liked the way the colored sailors from the North sounded. They didn't seem to have much sense, but they seemed to be really confident for people who didn't know much.

"Tommy!" Miss Robbins's voice broke through his thoughts. "I'm not working for you yet. Get that broom moving!"

Tommy hustled down the aisles, getting halfway through the sweeping before Jed got back.

When Miss Robbins had let Jed back in, he went to the counter and took out the pipe compound and plumbing thread and put them on the counter. Tommy got a knife to cut the string and started on the pipe again.

"You know what a friend of mine said?" Jed was leaning over from the waist as he spoke. "He said that he thought that Malcolm X and that Elijah guy were Satan worshipers!"

"Somebody told you that?"

"And he said that he never saw Martin Luther King actually preaching no service!"

"Did he ever go to a colored church?" Tommy asked.

"Hoot, no!" Jed said. "My friend is a *white* man!"

"Then if he never went to a colored church, how is he going to see a colored preacher?"

"Some people just know that kind of thing. They got it right up here." Jed tapped the side of his head with his finger. "Right up here!"

"Who brought you home, Tommy?" Virginia Lewis was sitting at the dining room table with Miss Mary, her mother-in-law. She was pasting pictures in the family album. There was a bowl of dumplings in the middle of the table and another bowl that was covered.

"Jed, from the store," Tommy said. "Daddy home?"

"He's in there watching *I Love Lucy*," Miss Mary said. "You want something to eat?"

"What you got?"

"I ain't got no menus, mister," Miss Mary said. "Now you want something to eat or not?"

"I can use a little something," Tommy said, sitting down.

"You can use a little washup," Miss Mary said.

"How come you're so late?" his mother asked.

"I had to change one of the pipes under the counter," Tommy said, washing his hands at the sink even though he didn't think they were dirty. "The plumbing in that store is so old, they must have got it used from Noah's ark."

"Watch your tongue, Tommy." Miss Mary peered over her rimless glasses. "The Good Book don't say a thing about thou shalt have a fast mouth."

"Yes, ma'am."

There were snap beans and oxtails on the back burner, the one where all the good food was cooked in the Lewis house, and dumplings on the front burner, and corn bread in the oven. Tommy knew his grandmother had done the cooking. The older woman was pouring lemonade as his father came into the dining room.

"Ricky should just get that woman a job in the band and they wouldn't have half the trouble they have," he said. Robert Lewis sat across from his wife and surveyed his son's plate. "You must have about two or three jobs to need all that food," he said.

"Hesh, Robert!" Miss Mary adjusted the lemonade in front of her grandson. "Tommy's still growing and needs a good plate."

"He's eating faster than we can grow the food. We're going to have to open the field next to Glory and raise corn just to keep him going."

"You want something?" Miss Mary asked.

"Any more snap beans in the pot?"

"There's a little," Miss Mary said, getting up to serve her son a plate of food.

"Tommy, what did that guy say on television last Saturday when we were watching?" Tommy's father asked, keeping his eyes on the plate Miss Mary was fixing. "Didn't he say that anytime you dream it meant something?"

"Now how could it mean something *any*time you dream?" his mother asked. "You can lay up in bed and just dream some foolishness that doesn't have a bit of meaning."

"What the man say, Tommy?"

"He said that sometimes we don't know the meaning of the dreams but they usually have some kind of meaning," Tommy said.

"Last night I dreamt two bunny rabbits were playing hopscotch in the school yard," his mother said. "Now what does that mean?"

"You didn't dream about no two rabbits playing no hopscotch," his father said.

"Man, you sleeping on one side of the bed and I'm sleeping on the other, so now how do you know what I'm dreaming?"

"I know you didn't dream about no two rabbits playing no hopscotch."

"You Almighty God now and you can tell what people dream?" Tommy saw his mother getting angry.

"He used to have a dream book when he was working in Johnson City." Miss Mary put the plate in front of her son. "That's when they were playing the numbers over there."

"Daddy, you played the numbers?" Tommy asked.

"I didn't play no numbers," his father mumbled.

"I guess that's why you didn't bless the food," Miss Mary said. "You knew you were getting ready to tell a lie."

"Tommy, bless the food." Robert Lewis put down his fork and bowed his head.

"Lord, we are thankful for the food we are now about to receive. Let us use it for Thy honor and the nourishment of our bodies, Amen."

"Hope the Lord can hear as fast as you can spit out the blessing," his grandmother said. "And don't drink that lemonade too fast, or you'll get cramps."

"Anyway, Sister Trevylian dreamt that her husband was put into jail for stealing chickens," Mr. Lewis continued. "Now the way I figure, that must mean something."

"He's probably stealing those hens," Tommy said. "Or maybe he's just stealing eggs."

"Okay, Thomas, that's enough." Miss Mary's tone of voice changed. "You shouldn't be signifying after you just finished blessing your food!"

"Signifying about what?" his mother asked, looking up from the album.

"He's talking about Brother Trevylian and the way that man carries on," Miss Mary said.

"With who?"

"I wouldn't know," Miss Mary said. "Old no-talking Bill Johnson said he saw him in Johnson City tipping around with Katie Lee's sister."

"Katie Lee's sister?" Virginia Lewis closed the family album. "I guess she's wearing those tight dresses for something but I can't believe she's tipping with Brother Trevylian."

"I thought we weren't supposed to be signifying," Tommy's father said, smiling.

"I'm not signifying. I'm telling what God loves, and that is the pure D truth," his wife said. "What is wrong with that man?"

The phone on the counter rang and Miss Mary answered it as Tommy's mother sat shaking her head. She opened the album again, and Tommy turned to see one of the pictures.

"That's your great-grandmother," Virginia said. "Don't she favor that colored girl who sings so pretty on the Mitch Miller show?"

"It's for you, Tommy," Miss Mary said. "Mr. Chase."

"I spoke to some of the trustees at the school, and they were really pleased that you were thinking about the offer to come to Johnson City State," Mr. Chase said.

"Oh, that's good."

"This summer, after school's out, the Committee on Academic Standing is going to meet and decide who's going to be admitted next semester. You'll have to submit an application and everything," Mr. Chase said. "What you can do is just run it by my office, and I'll take it in to the committee."

"Am I the only Negro that's applying?"

"No, that wouldn't be fair to you." The voice

on the telephone sounded either tired or slightly drunk. "We've got two young girls from Johnson City we're considering and a young man from Gadsden, Alabama. You know, we just have to show people there's a better way of doing things than going into the streets and making a lot of noise. You know what I mean?"

"Yes, sir," Tommy said. "Who are the girls from Johnson City?"

"A girl named . . . Just a minute." There was a pause, and Tommy could hear papers being shuffled. "A girl named Arlene Smith. I think she just moved to Johnson City from Columbia. And another girl named Denise Williams. You know them?"

"No," Tommy answered.

"Well, it doesn't really matter. They're good girls and good students. The only things that can stop it is if any of you kids get into trouble or if the governor runs into a political snag, but I don't think that's going to happen. Just make sure you don't get caught up in any demonstrations or anything," Mr. Chase said. "Your people need leaders, and it has to be leaders with education. That's why you keep getting people coming in from other places and interfering with local affairs. That King fellow is an educated man, and he's all right. But there's no way that he can understand what's going on around here like somebody who's lived around here all their life. Now if you have any trouble, you just give me a call. And don't worry about the money for the application. You just fill out the papers, okay?"

"Yes, sir."

Tommy put the receiver down and went back to the table. The dumplings were still hot, and he cut one in half with a fork and moved it around in the gravy.

"What did he want?" his father asked.

"Talking about me going to college next fall," Tommy said. "He said they're going to try to get four Negroes in if the governor says it's okay."

"College man!" his father said.

"You go to college, you going to come back here and farm?" Miss Mary asked.

"I'm going to learn so much I'll grow sweet potatoes that come with their own butter in them," Tommy answered.

"You grow sweet potatoes with their own butter?" His father looked at him. "That's got to be some college!"

"Yeah," Tommy said, thinking about the rest of Mr. Chase's conversation.

The pounding on his door seemed to shake the walls. Tommy forced his eyes open and looked at the clock on the small table next to his bed. Eleven-thirty.

"Who is it?"

"Jennie. You decent?"

"No. Go away!"

The door opened and Jennie stuck her head in. The girl was too tall, her eyes were too far apart, and she was too pushy.

"So what you doing?" Jennie sat on the end of the bed.

"I fell asleep," Tommy said, wiping the saliva from the corner of his mouth. "What are you doing over here so late?"

"My daddy is talking to your daddy about the march," Jennie said. "And I thought I would come up here and tell you who sent me a letter offering me a scholarship to attend their college."

"Who?"

"Guess."

"Go away."

"Wrong! Meharry!"

"Get out of here!" Tommy sat up. Jennie had always talked about being a doctor, and Meharry had the best black medical school in the country. "They offered you a scholarship?"

"What they said was that a scholarship was possible if I kept my grades up this coming year," Jennie said. "You know what that means? It means that when you get a cold or need your appendix out or have some other little medical emergency, I'll be able to take care of it right at home and you won't even have to go out to the hospital."

"You really think you're going to get lucky and marry me?"

"I really think you're going to get lucky and come to your senses, Mr. Thomas Lewis."

"Look, I got to get some sleep," Tommy said. "And I need to get out of my clothes, so why don't you go. I'll see you in school tomorrow."

"I'll go, but *please* don't start begging me for a kiss before I leave. I can't stand to see an almost grown man begging for my affections. Did you hear the bad news?"

"What bad news?"

"Dr. King's not coming to the march," Jennie said. "Reverend McKinnon got a letter from Reverend Abernathy. He sends his blessings, and stuff like that, but he can't come. Half the newspeople left already. Reverend McKinnon said that the only way we're going to get any coverage is if the White Citizens Council makes a big showing."

"He thinking of calling off the march?"

"Can't," Jennie said. "How often you coming to see me when I'm at Meharry?"

"How come he can't call it off?" Tommy asked. "If he doesn't think we're going to get press coverage, we might as well call it off."

"If the council marches in the morning and we don't march, then it's going to look like we were afraid," Jennie said. "You know who told me he was going to march with us?"

"I can't see what the march is going to do." Tommy sat up and swung his legs over the side of the bed. "People don't care if you march or not."

"Well, we got to do something," Jennie said. "Or just act like we belong on our knees, and I know that my mama's daughter don't belong on her knees. Anyway, Skeeter said he's going to march."

"He's out of the hospital?"

"And wouldn't let me see his snake bite," Jennie said. "I offered the fool a quarter if I could see it and find out how they treated it."

"What's he marching for?"

"You know how Skeeter is," Jennie said. "If he thinks something's right, he's going to go with it until you prove to him it's not right!"

"What time is the Citizens Council going to march?" Tommy asked.

"Sheriff Moser is trying to get them not to march," Jennie said. "But if they do march, it's going to be at ten. We're supposed to march at two, but Reverend McKinnon is saying we should march at twelve, maybe even eleven, to make sure we get some coverage."

"What are we trying to do?" Tommy looked at Jennie in the mirror. "Get jobs downtown or get in the newspaper?"

"The newspaper coverage makes it official," Jennie said. "When we get married I'm going to make sure we have an announcement in the colored newspapers and the white newspapers."

"Anybody ever tell you that you're sick?"

"You want to play doctor with me?"

Tommy lay back down and pulled a pillow over his head. He felt Jennie pat his side and then leave. Even from under the pillow, he knew she turned the lights out before leaving.

Jennifer was nice, and lots of guys liked her, but she just came on too strong for Tommy. He was glad that she had been accepted to Meharry, though. And if her grades at Curry High were any indication, he knew she would do well.

His mind drifted back to the march. Mr. Chase had said that he didn't want him to get into any demonstrations. It was the first time he realized that he did want to go to State. He had always thought about going to Avery or some other black school, but he knew if he went to State he'd have it made. More people knew State's reputation than had even heard of Avery. But

Jennie was right, too. Even if the march didn't accomplish anything, they would at least be saying that the Negroes on Curry and in Johnson City didn't like the way they were being treated, that it was time for a change. Maybe Miss Robbins was right. Maybe it was better to stay with your own.

Tommy closed the screen door quietly, and rolled his bicycle to the front gate of the Lewis home. The body of the black-and-red Schwinn was slightly rusty, and he had promised himself a hundred times that he would sand and paint it, but he never got around to what promised to be a boring job.

It was less than a mile to the Curry side of Tombee Bridge and four miles from the Tombee Bridge to downtown Johnson City. The early morning roads were nearly empty except for an occasional truck or horse and wagon taking food to the downtown market. Tommy passed two women pulling an enormous cart loaded over twelve feet high with sweet grass baskets. He remembered his grandmother talking to a white woman about how people in West Africa made the same kind of baskets. The white woman had known more than he or his grandmother did about the baskets, and he had felt ashamed of the fact.

"Don't worry me none," his grandmother had said. "All she got is book learning. You don't know nothing about them baskets until you have to spend all day pitching short grain rice in them. Then your arms and back get so tired they start telling you things that aren't in the books."

His grandmother didn't have a lot of respect for book learning. She respected schools, but always said that it didn't matter what you learned if you didn't learn not to be a fool.

Tommy stopped on Bay Street where he saw four men, three Negroes and one white, trying to load a large machine onto the back of a truck. The men were grunting, clinging desperately to the straps they were using to lift the machine. The white man and the shortest black man were nearest the truck and it was their job to get the machine onto the edge of the truck. The white man was big, with wide shoulders and a thick neck that showed the strain as he lifted. The black man on his end was nearly square, his face glistening with sweat and his teeth a brilliant white against his black skin.

The white man finally got one corner of the machine onto the truck, and the black man squatted, put his shoulder under the machine and lifted the front on. When they saw that the front was secure they moved the machine down, never taking their hands off it, until they got to the rear where they pushed the machine squarely onto the truck bed.

None of the men moved away from the back of the truck, they all leaned against it, and Tommy wondered how long they had been working at it. Then the white man reached into his pocket and pulled out some money and paid the Negroes. They touched their hands to their heads and nodded and then went off together.

That's what Johnson City was about, Tommy thought. Whites and Negroes worked together in the streets and in the market and had lunch together from brown paper sacks on the levee, but it was always the whites who paid the Negroes. And even though they mostly got along with the whites, it was only under special circumstances. They couldn't drink out of the same water fountains or eat in the same restaurants, but Negro women still took care of white children, and bathed and washed them, and sometimes even gave them breast milk.

"What you have to change is the laws," Reverend McKinnon had said. "You change the laws and let God worry about changing their hearts."

There was a coffee shop across from Cadet Park on Calhoun Street. Cadet Park was where the White Citizens Council was supposed to have its rally. Tommy leaned his bicycle against the wall of the coffee shop, went in and ordered a large container of lemonade, and went back out. In Cadet Park there were a number of white men. Two of them had on Klan robes and hoods. Tommy felt his mouth dry as he straddled his bicycle and watched them mill about. A car pulled up, and Tommy recognized it as Sheriff Moser's. The sheriff and a uniformed man that must have been his deputy got out of the car and went quickly to the men in the Klan outfits. There was a brief discussion, and the men began taking off their Klan getups.

Next Sheriff Moser stood back and called something to them. Some of the men crowded around him, clearly angry. Sheriff Moser crossed his arms over his chest and spread his legs. Tommy had seen him do that before. Once when they had a demonstration and Reverend McKinnon had tried to take a few of his church members into a white church, Sheriff Moser had stood in the door, his holster unbuttoned, in the same stance he was in now.

The men in Cadet Park backed off from the sheriff and held up their signs. Two had the word "niggers" on them, and he made them put those signs away. He was toning down the demonstration.

The men in the park marched around the edges of the field. Some of them could march; the others just went along the best they could, doing a little skip step now and again to get on the right foot. Then they stopped marching and just stood around.

Tommy finished the lemonade, even though it was too sweet, and went in to get another one.

He was just in the store a moment when two men came in behind him. They were white, and one of them opened his jacket so that Tommy could see the pistol stuck in his belt.

"They calling us everything under the sun and we can't call them niggers!" one of the white men said. "The more you ease up on them, the more they push up into your face!"

The other man started to answer, when the door opened again and another white man, older, with a broad, handsome face, announced that the television cameras had just arrived.

The whites left together and rushed across Calhoun Street to the park.

"Can I have a refill?" Tommy asked.

"You can't get a refill for free," the white clerk said sharply. "You got to pay for it."

"I didn't ask for a refill for free," Tommy said.

She gave him a look that she hadn't given him when he had first come in to buy the lemonade. She was getting caught up in the moment, the same as the white men who had run out looking for the cameras. She filled another cup and pushed it across the table. Tommy put down the fifteen cents and walked outside.

Across the street the White Citizens Council members were marching again. Some were talking to the television people.

Tommy moved his bike around the corner in front of an empty store. He put down the kickstand and watched the parade in the park. They went through a sloppy drill that was supposed to be military-style. Some well-dressed white men stopped their conversation and looked at them, then continued down King Street toward the college.

A dark-skinned Negro woman carrying two shopping bags stopped, leaned forward at the waist as if she could hear what was being said across the street, shook her head, and continued on her way.

"Kluxers!" she called back to Tommy.

The march ended an hour later when the television crews got bored and a few Negro kids started marching at the edge of the park. The deputy chased them away, giving one a kick when he didn't move fast enough.

Tommy rode down to the market and saw that most of the booths were already set up. The same women he had seen bringing in the sweet grass baskets were weaving new ones in the doorway, hoping for tourists. He hadn't eaten breakfast and looked around until he saw Virgil Clift, who sold fresh fruit.

"Hey, Virgil, how about a peach on credit?"

The black man was built well in his upper body, but he had one leg that had never grown. He looked over his peaches, found a large, ripe one, and threw it to him. "Don't forget what you owe me," he called.

Tommy took the peach and ate it as he rode. He rode down toward the waterfront, down in the neighborhood where no Negroes or poor whites lived. He went all the way to the docks and thought about what it must have been like during the Civil War when Union boats had shelled Johnson City. He knew what he didn't want to think about. That was the march.

When he finished college, he thought to himself, he would come back to Johnson City and make a difference. Maybe he would even be a lawyer, the first Negro lawyer to graduate from Johnson City State.

He took his time going back toward Calhoun where he had bought the lemonade, going down Magazine Street instead of King. When he reached the college, he could see the size of the crowd that had gathered. He stopped his bike a little past the five-and-dime and looked. He could see, through gaps in the crowd, the Negro marchers and could hear snatches of their singing. They were singing "O Freedom!"

The crowd that had gathered to watch was white. There were a few Negroes on the street who, like Tommy, looked at the march from a distance. He saw dark objects fly though the air. Somebody was throwing stones and bottles at the marchers.

But the music came to him. Drifting through the streets of Johnson City, lifting itself like an anthem of everything that Tommy had ever heard about being black.

O . . . Freedom! O . . . Freedom! O Freedom over me!

Tommy imagined Jennie singing, arm in arm with people she only knew by the color of their skin. He imagined Miss Mary singing, her gray head held high, her back straight as an arrow, her thin legs marching with the others.

And before I'd be a slave, I'll be buried in my grave,
And go home to my Lord and be free.

"Where were you?" Jennie had found him, had come up to him and called his name as he sat on the curb across from the market. "I thought something had happened to you."

"I don't know," Tommy said. "Maybe it did."

"Were you marching?"

"I saw it," Tommy said. "I wasn't in it."

"Yeah. I figured you must have been tied up or something," Jennie said. "I thought we should have had more signs. The television cameras played them up big. My cousin Ida said she saw the whole thing on television. She said she saw me but I don't know if she really did or not."

"I was checking on the Citizens Council march," Tommy said, swallowing hard. "I thought I needed to keep an eye on what they were going to do."

"Then you saw them throwing rocks and stuff," Jennie said. "It was worth it just to see Sheriff Moser chasing some of them for a change. You eat anything?"

"What we need—what black folks really need—is education, not demonstrations, anyway. That's what I think," Tommy continued. "You know what I mean?"

"What *don't* we need!" Jennie said. "They're having some food at your house since nobody got hurt. You want to go and get something to eat?"

"Hey, I'm asking you something," Tommy said.

"Tommy, I want to be a doctor so I don't have to answer questions like that. I can try to save Negro lives and to make Negroes healthier, and that's cool. You know what I mean? I need something that's, like, reach-out-and-touch-it realness."

"And what do I need?" Tommy asked.

"Tommy, you're a Lewis, and that means something," Jennie said. "What you need is to be a strong black man, like the Lewis men. Then, of course, you being a strong black man and everything, you need me to take care of you. I bet you can't even imagine yourself with that little ugly McKinnon girl, can you?"

"Hey, she's cute."

Jennie stood up. "Look, I can wait for the bus, if they're taking Negroes today, or I can sit on the back of your bicycle and watch you sweat and strain all the way back to Curry. And I can tell you how fine you look, only you probably won't be able to hear me, because I'll be in back of you and I'll be saying it soft and low."

"Why do you always have to say things like that?" Tommy asked. "It makes me feel . . . I don't know."

"No problem." Jennie Epps stood and lifted Tommy's bicycle. "You taking me home or do I have to wait for that stupid bus?"

"How come they're having the food at my house?" Tommy asked, throwing a leg over his bike.

"Reverend McKinnon said it was in case the Citizens Council figured us to be at the church. Since nobody was hurt that we know about, we moved it to your house."

Tommy arrived home at the same time that the white man was getting out of his car. He was carrying a black medical bag. Mary Lewis was standing in the doorway and signaled to him.

"Wait here," Tommy said to Jennie. He let his bike fall to one side and headed for his house, just vaguely aware that Jennie was right behind him.

Inside, the room was full of fresh cooking smells. Three matrons from the church, all dressed in white, were sitting near the window. Cleon Davis was sitting at the window, a shotgun cradled in his arms.

"What happened?" Tommy asked.

"Skeeter Jackson," one of the white-clad women said. "They caught him after the march and beat him up bad. Dr. Calloway thinks he may lose his eye. That's why he called that white doctor over."

"Where is he?"

"Upstairs in your room, I think." The answer was flat, dry.

"Anybody else hurt?" Jennie asked, looking toward Cleon Davis.

"No, but it don't hurt to be ready. You 'member they bombed that church after the march on Washington."

Tommy nodded and started upstairs. His mother was standing in the hallway with Mrs. Calloway. Tommy nodded to the bosomy woman even as his mother was reaching for him. She pulled her son to her and held him close.

"I didn't see you," she said. "Didn't know where you were. You okay?"

"I'm okay," he said. "How's Skeeter?"

His mother shrugged and released him.

The white doctor was looking at Skeeter's eye. Dr. Calloway was on the other side of the bed. From where he stood, Tommy could see that there was blood on the pillow. He suddenly felt tired, so tired that even standing was difficult. He stepped forward and held on to the bedpost. The white doctor turned and looked at him.

"It doesn't look like nerve damage," Dr. Calloway said.

"No, but there's a lot of bleeding into the retinal area. What we have to check for is possible retinal detachment. I don't think there's going to be permanent damage, maybe just a lot of floaters, but he won't lose vision. Can you get him over to me tomorrow?"

"Yes. I'll take him home tonight," Dr. Calloway said. "And I'll give his folks your number. I don't know if they'll want a Negro driving him around."

"He took a real beating." The white doctor was large, round-shouldered. "You report it to the police?"

"What for?" Dr. Calloway asked. "He was beaten for associating with Negroes. You think they're going to arrest somebody for that?"

"I'm reporting it," the white doctor, "because it's the way things should be."

"Better check with his parents first," Dr. Calloway said. "See if they want you to report it. They might not want the attention, and that's the difference between the way things should be and the way things are."

"You going to speak to them?"

"I owe it to them," Dr. Calloway said. "He was marching for us."

The white doctor reached out and shook hands with Dr. Calloway.

Tommy watched as he packed his bag, took one more look at Skeeter's form on the bed, and left.

Tommy went to Skeeter's bedside and knelt on one knee. The right side of Skeeter's face was swollen, the right eye was bulging and shut. The flesh around the eye was dark purple. His lower jaw seemed to jut out at a sharp angle, and there was dried blood in the corner of his mouth.

"His jaw was dislocated," Dr. Calloway said, "but that will heal. I'm just worried about the eye, which is why I called Dr. Grier."

Tommy put his hand on Skeeter's shoulder and squeezed it gently.

Skeeter opened his other eye, saw that it was Tommy, and took his hand.

"I'm glad I marched," he said, the words coming out slurred through his bruised lips.

There was a shuffling on the stairs, and Mrs. Calloway came into the room and announced that Skeeter's parents were there.

Skeeter Jackson's father, Grady Lee Jackson, had been an oysterman all of his life. Mr. Jackson was small, thin-lipped, and quiet. Tommy had never heard him say more than three or four words at a time. His face was expressionless; his hands, scarred from years of oyster shells, years of grit, and cold sea, ran quickly through the dirty-blond hair.

"He going to be all right?"

"He should go to Dr. Grier over in Shelby tomorrow to see about his eye," Dr. Calloway said. "I'll drive him over there if you want."

"You okay, son?"

"Doing pretty good, Dad," Skeeter said. His open eye glistened over with tears.

"I think you're doing pretty good, too," Grady Lee Jackson said.

Skeeter's mother went silently to the side of

the bed, stepped past Tommy, and touched her son gently, allowing her fingertips to caress the smooth face. Skeeter turned to her and forced a smile.

Tommy and Mr. Jackson helped Skeeter down the stairs, past the anxious black women who had gathered to eat and to be together. No one spoke as Skeeter eased himself into his family's car.

"If you want me to, I'll drop by later and see how he's doing, Mr. Jackson," Dr. Calloway said.

Skeeter's father nodded and slipped behind the wheel of the old Chevy he drove. Skeeter was sitting in the back with his head on his mother's shoulder. Jennie threw him a kiss.

"I'd appreciate it," the elder Jackson said.

"It just a shame the way they beat that boy," Sister Smith said. "They did that so we wouldn't get white support. That was supposed to send a message."

"What they was doing was just beating up a boy they could beat up," Sister Ward said. "That's all they want to do anyway, beat up somebody and make them feel smaller than they are. If they catch somebody off to themselves, then they beat them up. If it had been one of us, they might have killed us."

"The sheriff is going to have a press conference tomorrow," Sister Smith said.

"About Skeeter?" Jennie asked.

"Here comes Reverend McKinnon now!" Sister Ward said in a quick whisper.

When Reverend McKinnon and Mandy entered the large room, it quieted down quickly. He asked Tommy's mother how Skeeter was, and she told him about his eye. He said that they would all have to pray for Skeeter.

"Most of you have already heard that Sheriff Moser is holding a press conference tomorrow morning at ten o'clock," Reverend McKinnon said. "He's going to announce that there's going to be a meeting of black leaders and several businessmen in the downtown area to see if we can talk out our differences."

"Talk about *what*?" Miss Mary asked.

"I asked him that and I asked him which businesses, and he said he didn't want to make the names known publicly. Personally I wasn't sure if he was telling the truth or not. But he said that there was a lot of talk about firing a lot of people who work in Johnson City if we don't agree to the talking."

"Let them fire us," Miss Mary said. "I've been tired long enough to get used to that. I've been hungry enough times to get used to that. And I ain't got nothing worth taking. What else can they do to us?"

"Maybe we ought to listen to what they got to say," a man said. "Maybe we can get something out of it."

"What he wants to do," Dr. Calloway said, "is to have one of those press conferences that has everybody sitting around agreeing to meet after the press is gone."

"If he's t-talking 'bout t-taking our jobs, he's talking about t-t-taking away what little hope we got," a tall, black man stammered. "I know w-we live by every word of God, but we have families. And we need jobs."

"Who else is going to be at the press conference?" Jennie asked.

"James Caro from the Citizens Council," Reverend McKinnon said. "He's going to talk about how the Citizens Council was nonviolent—"

"How about Skeeter Jackson?!"

"What you know about Skeeter and what they're going to say about Skeeter is two different things," Reverend McKinnon said. "They're going to say Skeeter got into a fight with some people, and it didn't have anything to do with the march."

"Lord, Lord, Lord!" Miss Mary shook her head. "I got a scream in me so big this room ain't big enough to hold it."

"O Freedom! O Freedom! O Freedom over me!" It was Mandy who started the song.

Tommy looked away and let the music of the small choir that sang in his living room take control of his soul, and of his life. Jennie's words came to him. "You're a Lewis, and that means something," she had said. But that wasn't true and he knew it. Being a Lewis didn't mean a thing unless he gave it meaning.

The night passed with the men sitting in the parlors of Curry Island with their rifles ready and the women and children sleeping away from the first-floor windows. Everyone black was accounted for and either in his own home or gathered in the homes of friends, waiting to see if the White Citizens Council would react to the demonstration, or if some single white man, filled with liquor and hate, would ride by and fire a random shot into a black home or throw a stick of dynamite onto a porch as a friendly warning that Negroes should learn to stay in their place.

Tommy's mother had changed the sheets and pillowcases, taking the ones that had been stained with Skeeter's blood and putting them into the closet to be washed the next day, to be cleansed and hung out for the world to see that life would, indeed, go on.

Lying in the darkness Tommy first thought of what he would have done if he had been confronted as Skeeter had. He imagined himself fighting against his attackers, delivering blow for blow, beating them off, making them retreat from his strength. But even in the midnight imagination of his fury he could not beat them off successfully, for they would always come back, always come in the night or in an attack against somebody else. Medgar Evers had been shot down in front of his home in Mississippi for trying to register Negroes to vote. The little girls in the Sixteenth Street Church had been killed and their only crime was being Negro and therefore a target for those who would hate Negroes. What it was all about was violence. It was violence that was needed to keep things the way they were, blacks apart from whites, blacks forced perpetually to take the leftovers of white life. Whether those leftovers were clothes that a black woman brought home after a hard day's cleaning in some white home, clothes offered instead of a decent wage, or the leftover jobs after whites had taken the ones that provided them with at least a passable living in Johnson City.

And it was about an everyday violence that made being beaten up or killed a constant threat, that made the violence to the soul a constant threat as mothers had to take young children past "white only" parks and "white only" lunch counters or explain why Negro men were called "uncle" instead of "mister."

There was even violence in the little progress

that was made, violence that wrenched the heart and spirit as token Negroes were allowed to pass through doors once forbidden, exposing the armies of people left behind.

Tommy tried to put the day out of his mind, tried to make himself think of playing basketball, of riding his bike, even of what he would do the next day. But all that filled his mind was the image of Skeeter being beaten up, images of himself fighting in the streets and of his father sitting in the darkness of their living room, waiting for whatever would come from the bowels of the dark night.

What sleep came did so in fitful starts and ended in the early dawn with his mother's voice calling his father by the name he had been known by as a boy. "Planter! Planter!"

"Okay, baby." His father's voice was hoarse, yet comforting "Just fell asleep and dropped Peter."

Peter was the old single-barreled shotgun he had held in his lap as he sat listening to the radio.

Tommy looked at the window and saw that the sky was already streaked with light. He got up, slipped into his pants, and went out to the bathroom. By the time he had finished washing, the smell of coffee was already drifting up from the kitchen.

"You going in with Reverend McKinnon this morning?" His mother was speaking to his father. She had on the blue-flowered housecoat she had worn for as long as Tommy could remember.

"Bob Archer and Make Williams are going in with him," his father said. "You think I should go, too?"

"I don't think it's necessary," she said. "Sheriff Moser isn't going to let anything happen at a press conference. He's trying to keep things cool."

"I might go into town to see it," Tommy said.

"You have to go to school," his mother said.

"I'll get to school later," Tommy said. "I just want to see what he has to say. Maybe I'll write it up for the school newspaper."

His father yawned and cradled the cup of coffee his wife handed him in his large hands. The shotgun was in the corner. His mother was quiet, thoughtful, as she made breakfast for her husband. Tommy wondered how many nights of sleepless and fearful waiting they had shared in their lives.

When the thought came to him, he put it out of his mind at first. It wouldn't work, he thought. It would be too hard to pull off. And then he thought of himself sitting outside the market, waiting for the march to end instead of being in it, thought of himself trying not to think of what was happening as protesters threw rocks at the marchers, and knew that somehow he had to be involved.

He went to the storeroom, looked in the closet, and found the stained linen package on the shelf. He carefully unwrapped the heavy chain, saw again how it worked, and rewrapped it.

He put the package in a shopping bag and placed some old magazines over it.

"You be careful," his mother said.

"Yes, ma'am."

The press conference was held at the public library down the street from Cadet Park. There were only a handful of out-of-town reporters and two photographers. Reverend McKinnon was sitting behind a table with Sheriff Moser and a white man. There were more whites in the audience than Negroes. Mr. Diggs, who published Johnson City's only black newspaper, was there, and so were Make Williams and Bob Archer. They were both big men. Bob had even played two years of pro football.

A television camera had been set up on a tripod, and a balding man stood behind it, a container of coffee in his hand. He started peering through the viewfinder when Sheriff Moser started speaking.

"What I called everybody together for"— Sheriff Moser toyed with his keys as he spoke —"was to announce a new policy of not allowing any demonstrations of any nature within two miles of this library. This is to secure public safety. In the future, demonstrations and marches can be held away from the downtown area, in the less populated areas, but not on public property."

"Won't that just about stop all demonstrations in Johnson City?" a white reporter asked.

"I've made the rules clear to Reverend McKinnon here," the sheriff continued, "and Mr. Caro of the Citizens Council, and they both understand the rules and the necessity for them. As to future demonstrations, well, they can be held elsewhere. You press people got cars."

"What do you think of the rules, Mr. Caro?" a reporter asked.

"Well, I don't like them that much." Mr. Caro spoke in a slow drawl that Tommy knew was put on. "But I'll inform my people, and we'll try to do the right thing, as we always do, but we won't have other people trample on our rights, and that has to be understood."

"Sheriff, aren't you just making Negro protests illegal?" another reporter asked. "Isn't that what this is all about?"

"No, it's about public safety for Negroes as well as whites," the sheriff answered. "That's all we're trying to do. We're putting together a series of meetings between local businessmen and some prominent Negroes to see if we can talk out solutions to some of our problems instead of just jumping into protesting."

Tommy had the shopping bag on his lap and his left arm in the bag. He felt the shackle that he had locked to his wrist, making sure it was tight. He listened as Mr. Caro said something about how they didn't need disturbances at home while there was a threat of Communism coming from Cuba just a few hundred miles away.

"We don't know if some of these demonstrations aren't being inspired by the Cubans," he said. "They got their little Communist nation down there and some people see that as the way to live."

"It's not about Communism," Reverend McKinnon started to say.

"Just a moment! Just a moment!" Sheriff Moser said, "If you start making a speech here, then I'm going to construe it as a demonstration, which I just said was illegal!"

A reporter asked were there any injuries from the march of the previous day, and Sheriff Moser said that there were none to his knowledge.

When a photographer started putting away his camera, bored with the conference, Tommy stood up and walked quickly past the assembled chairs toward Sheriff Moser. When he pulled out the chain, Sheriff Moser leaned back in the chair and reached for his pistol.

"Watch it!" someone yelled.

Sheriff Moser had his gun out and pointed toward Tommy. Behind him there was the sound of scuffling and yelling.

"What the . . ." Sheriff Moser saw that what Tommy had brought out was not a gun and quickly put his away.

Sheriff Moser tried to take the chain off, realized that Tommy had locked it, and yanked it with all of his strength, jerking Tommy nearly across the table.

"What did he do?" A reporter came around to look.

"He chained himself to the sheriff."

"Why did you do that?" the reporter asked.

"This is an illegal demonstration!" Mr. Caro said.

"It's the chain used to bring the first of my family to Johnson City over two hundred years ago!" Tommy called out.

Sheriff Moser was looking at the lock and desperately banging it against the table to try to get it open. The chain was old, but it held as it had two hundred years earlier. Through all the banging and the twisting of Sheriff Moser's keys in the old lock, it held as Tommy hoped it would.

"Where are the keys to this thing, boy?" Sheriff Moser's face was twisted with anger.

"They didn't give us the keys," Tommy answered. "Just the chains."

It was nearly nine o'clock when Tommy was released from the Johnson City station house. Reverend McKinnon's car was out front, and his father's was close behind. There were two other cars that he didn't recognize; he could only see that the drivers were Negroes.

His grandmother was sitting next to his father, and Tommy slid into the backseat next to his mother.

She took his hands in her own and kissed them gently. Her face was wet with tears. His father reached over the backseat and patted his son's legs and then started the car. The small convoy started off slowly, careful to stay within the speed limit. Tommy saw his father check the rearview mirror, looking to see if they were being followed.

"Did you eat anything?" Tommy's grandmother asked.

"I'm not hungry," Tommy answered.

His mother was crying again, and he put his arm around her shoulder and held her close to him. She clutched his shirt, her hand shaking with emotion. When they had crossed the bridge from Johnson City to Curry Island, his mother seemed to relax. But his father was still vigilant, still checking the rearview mirror, watching any car that came too close to them. The muscles in his temple flexed and relaxed whenever Reverend McKinnon's car slowed ahead of them.

"You hurt anywhere?" his grandmother asked.

"No, I'm fine," he said.

They drove the rest of the way in silence, wrapped in their own thoughts. Tommy knew they were relieved just to see him alive and unhurt. He knew what they had been thinking, what fear they had felt. He had felt it, too.

At his house Reverend McKinnon and the others came in. They all hugged him. Mandy kissed him and said that she loved him. Her round face was tear-streaked.

"Mr. Chase called," his father said. "He said that he was afraid he was going to have to withdraw the scholarship offer. Guess you expected that."

"Yeah."

"Tommy, you did all right," Reverend McKinnon said. "It was in all the papers, and a friend of mine, Reverend Haskells over in Columbia, said that it was on television over there. You brought attention to our needs here, and we're all grateful."

"Amen!"

"Now I think we should all give thanks to the Lord for being merciful and bringing you through this day. Brother Archer, will you keep an eye on the road?"

Big Bob Archer kept an eye on the road through the front window while everyone else knelt in prayer.

"O heavenly Father, our child Tommy has passed from his childhood into his manhood this night." Reverend McKinnon's voice wavered as he spoke. "He has been with the lions and with the Philistines and he has come through, O Lord. . . ."

> When they couldn't get the
> chains off in the library they had
> hustled him out into the police
> car. Sheriff Moser was furious,
> cursing him. He had been embar-
> rassed in front of the press, in
> front of the whole town. The
> deputy had tried to punch him
> in the car, but the sheriff
> stopped him.

"Lord, let us look at this day, at this time of tribulation, and rejoice in the struggle to achieve righteousness for all Your children. For it is truly Thee who has created heaven and earth and each and every creature. And it is truly Thee who has told us in the Holy Bible that we are created in Thy holy image. . . ."

When the man from the hardware store had cut Sheriff Moser loose, they had put Tommy in a cell with a young white man who was coughing up blood in a handkerchief. Tommy had felt heroic, as if he had finally done something. When the deputy came, Tommy thought he might try to hurt him in some way. Instead he had just asked the white man how he felt having the honor of being in a cell with a Negro. The white man, the deputy called him Bobby Joe, said that he didn't like it one bit. Then the deputy took him out.

"Jesus, thank You for sending Tommy back to me tonight. Look down on him, Jesus, and let him see Your face and follow the ways of Your sweet love." Tommy's mother held his hand as she gave thanks.

When Bobby Joe was brought back to the cell, there was a pistol in his belt. The deputy locked the cell, and then turned out the corridor lights.

"You scared, nigger?" Bobby Joe had asked. He asked again, demanding an answer.

"Yes, I'm scared," Tommy had answered, the words coming out thick and indistinct.

He heard the metallic sound of the gun being cocked.

"Our Father who art in heaven," Tommy's father was the last to pray. ". . . Give us this day our daily bread. . . ."

Somewhere between the first clicking of the gun, somewhere between the pounding of his heart and the sound of the chain, still around his wrist, hitting against the steel-framed bed, Tommy had stopped being afraid and had waited for whatever was to come. He wanted to see his family again, to be with them, to hold them and love them. He did not want to die. But he had stopped being afraid. Later, when Sheriff Moser had come in and taken the gun away from Bobby Joe, he asked Tommy if he had learned anything. Tommy had wanted to stand up and look him defiantly in the eyes, but his legs wouldn't work, and he was so tired he could hardly even lift his head.

"You learn anything here tonight, boy?" The sheriff had
repeated the question.

"Yes, sir," he had said, knowing that it was inadequate,
knowing that he would have to
find better answers, if not for
the sheriff, then for himself.

". . . and forgive us our sins, as we forgive
those that sin against us. And lead us not into
temptation, but deliver us from evil. For Thine
is the kingdom, and the power, and the glory
forever. Amen."

"You got to be starved," his mother said. "I'm
fixing you a plate."

There were more hugs and a few wet kisses.
Across the room, Bob Archer looked away from
the window just long enough to give him a nod
and then turned his attention back to the road.

AUGUST 1994,
HARLEM, NEW YORK

THE LEWIS FAMILY, 1994

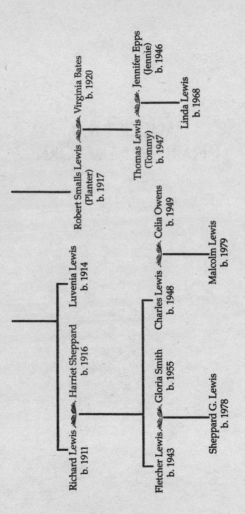

He was on the right side of the stage, just out of the circle of light that illuminated George and Deepak. Deepak rocked gently backward and forward as his fingers danced over his sitar. Behind him George was setting a counter rhythm on the snare drums. There was something strange, almost otherworldly, about the sound they were creating. Malcolm took a deep breath as he silently fingered the keys of the alto flute he held in his hand. His sound would have to be full, he knew, and the tones round and lush enough to bring real warmth to the music. As he lifted the flute to his lips there was another sound. He listened for a moment and then lowered the flute. Offstage there was a telephone ringing. He thought of ignoring it as he lifted his flute again, but the telephone continued ringing. He turned toward the audience, then felt something over his face. . . .

Malcolm Lewis pushed the pillow from his face and fought his way out of the sheets. He looked around frantically for the telephone, found it partway under the bed, and lifted the receiver.

"I'm leaving this afternoon for Curry," Luvenia Lewis spoke slowly, precisely. "I need to be at the airport at one-thirty, and I will be at your house at eleven-fifteen to talk to you. I won't be needing lunch."

"Yes, ma'am."

Malcolm repeated his "Yes, ma'am," once more, even though he had heard the telephone on the other end being hung up, then replaced his own receiver on its cradle. He shook his head twice, realized he was hanging off the low platform bed, and wriggled back onto the bed and into the comfortable nest he had made between the sheets.

It was too early to think. He would just lie in bed for an hour or so until his head cleared. Then he would plan his day. Maybe.

The light streamed through the windows of his room. He knew it was late, but all of him had not awakened yet. He took a deep breath, noted that his breath was terrible, and closed his eyes again. After a while he realized he had to go to the bathroom. He pushed the sheets away from his body, feeling how cool the room was, almost chilly. The cold air felt good against his skin. His parents and sister had already left for

the family reunion on Curry so he didn't have
to bother getting dressed. The bathroom light
was still on from the night before. He looked at
himself in the mirror. Not bad, he thought. A
little too round in the chin area, which made
him look younger than his fifteen years, but still
he was looking pretty good.

He used the toilet and then started back to the
bed. The digital clock on the end table read ten-
oh-seven. He fell across the bed and rolled himself into a warm position. It was the first day in
weeks that he hadn't been loading trucks at
Mahogany Beauty Products, the cosmetics factory his great-aunt owned. He thought he would
get up in an hour or so and then go downtown
for a late lunch in one of those little restaurants
near University Place.

Suddenly he sat straight up! What had Aunt
Luvenia said? He shook his head, trying to jerk
away the cobwebs from his mind. He went over
the conversation again. She was going to be at
the airport at one-thirty and at his house at
eleven-fifteen.

He checked the time again. He was still cool.
His room was a mess, but she wouldn't be coming into his room. Then he remembered what
the living room looked like. His band, String
Theory, had come over with some of their
friends and had brought pizzas and sodas.
George had made the popcorn, which had been
used in the popcorn fight.

Malcolm got up, went back to the bathroom,

and a moment later was in the shower. The shower was only warm, and he let it splash directly onto his face. The water felt good on his body, and he thought about splashing on some of his father's aftershave lotion even though he didn't shave.

Luvenia Lewis had never married, choosing instead to devote herself first to the beauty parlors she opened in Chicago and then to her nationwide beauty supply business. For years she had dominated beauty supplies for the black and Hispanic market. It was only recently, when the white-owned cosmetics companies started marketing products for black women, that the business had experienced any difficulty. Now she was branching out into real estate and travel services. Malcolm had been glad when she offered him a summer job and had asked him about his grades. She had often told him that if he kept his grades up and worked hard, she would see to it that he went to college. He hadn't known that when the old woman said that he should work hard, she meant that she would personally see to it that his back would be broken.

Out of the shower, he took the large terry cloth towel to the hallway and dried himself while he surveyed the living room. There was popcorn all over the rug and on the seat cushions. The pizza boxes were on the floor under the coffee table, and soda cans were piled at the side of every chair. It looked bad, but he thought he could handle it. It was only twenty to eleven.

He put on his shorts and went into the kitchen for orange juice while planning his cleanup strategy. That was when he saw the note he had written to himself and put under the magnet on the refrigerator door.

Jenn Che Po—amplified cello, 11 A.M.

He remembered the phone call. He had had to get everyone to quiet down while he answered it. The caller was soft-spoken. She said that she had seen his notice on the bulletin board at La Guardia High School. Was he still looking for someone who played an amplified stringed instrument? And could she come the next day to audition?

She had asked what kind of music they played and was clearly disappointed when he had said it was kind of a new thing. Then he had said it was sort of like postmodern funk, and she had asked how old he was. She told him she was fifteen and had been playing since she was six. She said her name was Jenn Che Po. He had asked her to spell it twice before he was sure that he had it right.

He vacuumed up the popcorn first because that looked the worst. There was more of it on the floor than he had thought, and he wondered if anybody had eaten any of the stuff. It had been a good crowd of kids, most of them from his school, all of them into good jams and reasonably together. He had wondered if they would all come to Harlem for the party, but they did.

He brought out a big garbage pail and started stuffing boxes and cans into it. His aunt probably didn't expect him to be too neat, but he didn't know what to expect from the girl who had answered his ad for a string player. Actually, he didn't think she would want to play with his band. She sounded a little sophisticated to play for nothing in a band that was just starting to find its way.

The telephone rang and he rushed to it.

"Hello?"

"Did the cello player come over yet?" It was Deepak.

"No. She's due in a few minutes."

"What do you think she's going to be like?"

"I don't know, man," Malcolm answered. "And I gotta get this place cleaned up before she gets here. I'll call you later."

"Aww, man!"

Deepak was a little miffed at his ending the call so soon, but Malcolm knew he needed to get the place cleaned up. He had finished picking up the worst of the garbage and had just put the vacuum cleaner away when the buzzer for the downstairs door rang. Malcolm answered it. It was Jenn. He buzzed her in and looked around the room. Not too bad, he thought.

He went to close the door of his room, saw his jeans on the chair, and realized he still wasn't dressed. He rushed into the room, put on his jeans, grabbed a dress shirt from the closet, and buttoned it furiously as he went to answer the front doorbell.

Jenn Che Po was small, almost fragile. She wore shades, which she immediately took off for a better look at Malcolm.

"You're tall," she said. "How tall are you?"

"Six-one," Malcolm said, pleased that she had mentioned his height. "Come in."

She entered, carrying her cello directly into the center of the living room. She turned to him with the suggestion of a smile on her face, but her eyes looked cautiously around the room. "Can you tell me more about what kind of group you're trying to put together?" she asked.

"I'm trying to get a group that's not set in its ideas," Malcolm said. "I don't want it to be labeled this or that and then get stuck in that mode so we can't be creative. You know what I mean?"

"No," she said firmly.

"Well, if you're playing grunge, then you're playing grunge, and everybody expects the same kind of thing from you all the time. But I want people with ideas that can change and grow. I have a really cool Indian guy who plays guitar and sitar. I have a Native American who plays bass guitar. Me and the drummer are black, and I have this white piano player from Astoria who can play anything from an old-fashioned stride to classical Coltrane and Mozart."

"What's race got to do with music?" she asked, glancing toward the door. "You want a band of different-*looking* people?"

"No. What I want to do is to be who I am and play from who I am," Malcolm said. "You know what I mean?"

"No."

"Well, I mean I want to play from a black point of view, but as an individual, not like I'm being forced into it. We on the same page yet?"

"That's cool," Jenn said as the doorbell rang again. "You have other people to try out?"

"No, it's probably my aunt," Malcolm said. "I work for her, and she wants to go over some things with me."

He buzzed in his aunt.

"What do you play?" Jenn asked.

"Sax and flute," Malcolm said.

Jenn lifted her cello, and Malcolm thought she was about to leave when the doorbell rang and he went to answer it.

Luvenia Lewis was around eighty years old, but her posture was as good as it had ever been, and her step nearly as firm. She glanced at Jenn and nodded.

"She's here to audition for the band," Malcolm said.

"Oh, I would love to hear you play," Luvenia extended her hand. "I'm Malcolm's great-aunt. I heard his group play once, and it was . . . interesting. What kind of music do you play?"

"I've been playing European classical in

school," Jenn said, glancing at Malcolm to see his reaction. "I think I want to try some other things, but I want to know what the other things are."

"I've got a tape you can take with you," Malcolm said.

"Put it on."

"I'm not sure how much time my aunt has—"

"Play the tape," the older woman said brusquely.

Malcolm found the tape on the edge of the coffee table, picking up a kernel of popped corn with his other hand. He put the tape into the player, and pushed the play button.

The tape had been of one of the young group's best sessions. The music had been composed by Deepak and had a slightly bluesy tinge to it with a strong up-tempo beat. Jenn listened to it as she stood in the middle of the floor with her head down, not moving.

Malcolm had heard the tape many times, and he was constantly surprised that they had pulled it off. The music was fresh and interesting. He had thought about trying to beg out of the re-union so that he could practice with the group every day, but he knew how disappointed his parents would have been. For as long as he could remember, he had been told that the only real strength was in family, and this week the family was going to be on Curry.

The piece on tape was nearly seven minutes long and slowed in tempo as it neared the end, with instruments dropping off like voices leaving a party until only the sound of a small drum remained.

"Can you play it again?" Jenn asked.

Malcolm looked toward his aunt, who nodded. He rewound the tape, and pushed the play button again.

"This isn't the only thing we play," he said.

Jenn listened for a while, then opened her cello case. She ran her fingers across the strings, adjusted two of them, and then picked up her bow and began playing with the tape.

She had heard the music once and not only knew it but could play with it!

When the tape had finished, she put the cello away. "When will you let me know if I've made the group?" she said.

"Uh." Malcolm rubbed the end of his nose. The young girl was good, and she knew it. "I have to go away for a week, but if you're interested, we're getting together on the second of September. A friend of mine is going to let us use his studio for rehearsals. If you leave your number."

"I'll send you a résumé," she said. She headed toward the door.

"Okay, well, it was nice meeting you," Malcolm said at the door.

"It was nice meeting you, too," she said. "The music's interesting."

When Jenn had left, Malcolm took a quick look

around the room to see if there was anything he should censor before his aunt saw it.

"That was a very confident young woman," his aunt said. "Had you met her before?"

"No, ma'am." Malcolm sat on the couch. "But she can play."

"I have to be going soon," his aunt said. She was looking in the dark cloth pocketbook she carried. She pulled out an envelope and handed it to him. "Here's the money for tickets for you and your cousin Shep. I expect you to be on Curry by Monday evening, which gives you two and a half days. If what I hear about Shep's problems are true, then I think you need to be very careful. Young men who take to drink are never reliable."

"Yeah . . ." Malcolm looked away from his aunt. He turned the envelope over in his hand. "Look, I'm going to try to get him down there. I think I can pull it off."

"It would be nice to have the *whole* family there." Luvenia lifted her head slightly and looked at Malcolm through the bottom of her bifocals. "But remember, as much as we hate to turn away from people, we sometimes have to avoid letting them hold us back. You think about that. If you have any trouble reaching Curry by Monday evening, you know the phone number down there. Don't you?"

"Yes, ma'am."

"Are you sixteen yet?"

"Fifteen."

"No matter," she said, smiling. "If you're smart enough to accommodate people of all . . . persuasions . . . and bring music from them, you're obviously smart enough to take care of yourself. I have a great deal of faith in what young people can do."

When Luvenia Lewis had left, when Malcolm had closed the door behind her, he began thinking about what he had wanted to say to her. Shep didn't have a drinking problem; he was using crack. What he wanted to tell his aunt was that the reason he could deal with a Chinese cello player was that he was able to find her, but that even if Shep were standing in front of him, he wouldn't have known where to find the boy.

The last time that Malcolm had seen Shep was when he had accidentally run into him in Marcus Garvey Park in Harlem. Malcolm had gone there with Billy Valentine and some other brothers from school to play basketball one Saturday morning. The guys who had invited them never showed up, and they spent an hour shooting baskets by themselves. They were on their way out of the park when Shep and two guys came into the park with a ball.

"These the guys?" one of Billy's friends had asked.

"No, man, these guys are winos, or something," Billy had replied.

Malcolm took a look at the guys. His heart sank when he saw that one of them was Shep.

"Yo, man, like, why don't you guys go on," he said. "One of these dudes is my cousin."

Sheppard G. Lewis was born on Curry on the twelfth of October, exactly six months before Malcolm, who had been born at a McDonald's restaurant on Bruckner Boulevard in the Bronx.

The two boys used to laugh about the circumstances of their births when they were younger. Malcolm's parents were on their way home from an antique show in Connecticut when Malcolm had come five weeks prematurely. Shep used to kid that his own parents had hoped for a Mercedes-Benz and had been surprised when he had shown up instead.

"Gee," he would say, rolling his head as he thought his father might have, "it's a baby!"

That was the reason, Shep would say when they spent the night at Malcolm's, that he was given the middle initial "G" when it really didn't stand for anything. Malcolm's mother explained later that Shep was bitter about his parents' divorce and used humor to cover it up.

But in the park, the last time the two cousins had met, Shep had lost his sense of humor. There was an uneasiness about him, and Malcolm thought that Shep was even glad when they parted.

Malcolm decided to start his search for Shep in the same park. It was dotted with small groups of men and women and a sprinkling of children. A bearded man, his pants tied around his waist with a rope, picked through the garbage for aluminum cans. A heavy woman, no more than twenty or so, ate fried chicken from a red-and-white paper bag. People who should have been off working in offices and factories were sitting around, idly passing the days. Days that should have been spent building their futures. Malcolm looked for the youngest people he could find and went up to them.

"Any of you know Shep Lewis?"

"Who you, the FBI?" a pretty girl with corn-rows and a nose ring asked.

"I'm his cousin," Malcolm said.

"In that case, we don't know him," the girl said. "If you were the FBI, we'd tell you."

Malcolm walked on as the trio cracked up. They hadn't been hostile, but still he felt uneasy. He walked up to three more groups of young people his own age, and none of them knew Shep. It was when he had walked away from the last group, two guys and two girls playing with a little black-and-white dog, that he realized he wasn't as anxious to find his cousin as he thought he had been. But that was all right. What had his father said? A real man does what he knows is right, not just what feels good.

He sat on the back rail of a bench and tried to figure out his next move. There was talk about this being a different kind of reunion, the last one to center around the farm. Malcolm heard his father say that moving away from farming had already changed the character of the family, and giving up farming altogether would put a real strain on it.

At past reunions, they had talked about the family history, about people being brought over from Africa, about the Civil War, and segregation, and all the struggles they had gone through over the years. Malcolm wondered if any of them knew anything about crack.

"Hey, you got two quarters?" The boy facing Malcolm was ten, eleven at the most, and didn't look in need of any handouts.

"Naw, man." Malcolm shook his head.

"Heard you were looking for Shep," the boy said. "He ain't got nothing. What you need?"

Malcolm looked at the boy and realized he was either a dealer or working with a dealer. "Don't need anything," he said. "Shep's my cousin. I'm just looking for him."

"Saw him a little while ago," the boy said. "He's selling tapes out in front of the Apollo. You know where that is?"

"Yeah, thanks." Malcolm stood.

"He favor you a lot," the kid said. "Tell him Mr. Brooks said hello."

"You Mr. Brooks?"

"Yeah." The kid swaggered away and Malcolm suppressed a smile.

The Apollo had once been a high-class Harlem theater, but now it was as seedy, as neglected, as the rest of the businesses along the once proud street.

"Integration is what did it," Malcolm's father used to say. "Before integration all the rich black folk had to live up here with the poor folk, so they took care of the neighborhood. Now the only people left in Harlem are people who can't afford to move."

You could buy anything on or just off 125th Street. Most of the street vendors sold cheap clothing, made in Taiwan or Korea, while others sold videotapes made by someone taking a video camera to the movies and running off copies in the basement or audiotapes made in much the same way. When Malcolm reached the Apollo, he found Shep sitting on a box next to a tray of tapes. There was a grocery shopping cart next to him with a radio/tape player in it.

"Yo, Shep, what's happening?"

"Hey . . ." There was a moment of hesitation as Shep searched Malcolm's face. "How's it going?"

"It's me, Malcolm Lewis." Malcolm extended his hand. "How's it going, cousin? See you in the tape business now."

"Jive gospel tapes," Shep said, standing. "Only time you sell gospel tapes is when there's a gospel show at the Apollo. Or sometimes when they have a revival meeting uptown. You can't make any money selling gospel, man. You need to sell something that's slamming, you know what I mean?"

"Yeah," Malcolm said. "Say, can we go someplace and talk?"

" 'Bout what?"

"We're supposed to be having a family reunion down on Curry," Malcolm said. "Aunt Luvenia gave me the money for you and me to go down together. Should be nice. Nothing but good eats. See all the cousins."

Shep turned away from Malcolm and rubbed the back of his neck. Malcolm thought the slightly older boy did look something like him, except Shep was thinner, his face less round. He was wearing a Grambling sweatshirt with the sleeves cut off and pants that were low and baggy, the way a lot of the hip-hop kids used to wear them. They were dirty, too, and so were his kicks, which looked like skips, but Malcolm didn't want to be caught checking them out.

"I got a lot of stuff to do," Shep said. "When is the reunion?"

"This weekend is going to start it off," Malcolm said. "Then they're going to stay for a business meeting. They're thinking about getting out of the farming business."

"Yo, they said that?"

"You got anything by the Wynans?" Two women came up to them. The heavier woman had asked the question.

"He ain't got nothing by the Wynans." Her companion wore braids that were much lighter than her own hair.

"I got CeCe Wynan by herself." Shep gave the second woman a dirty look. "And I got two or three tapes of the family."

"How much are they?" the first woman asked.

"They too much," Braids answered. "And half the time they don't play right when you buy them off the street."

Shep picked up the portable tape player and

held it up for Braids to see. "Anything you buy, you try," he said. "If it don't play, you don't pay."

"You going to be out here tomorrow?" the first woman asked.

"No, tomorrow I'm going to be on the moon," Shep answered. "So you better get your tapes today."

The woman gave Shep a look but bought a tape for three dollars and fifty cents. Shep looked at the money after the women were gone, then put a dollar in one pocket and the remaining two dollars and fifty cents in another pocket.

"I owe the tape guy some money," he said. "You listen to gospel?"

"Not much," Malcolm lied. The only time he ever heard real gospel music was when he was walking down 125th Street.

"Some of it's okay," Shep said. "You know anybody who needs some tapes, I can give them a discount."

"Yeah, I hear you. So you coming?"

"You got the money for the tickets, right?"

"Got it from Aunt Luvenia," Malcolm said. "All we got to do is to get out to the airport, find the plane, and we're on our way."

"So why don't you lay the money on me, and I'll meet you at the airport?"

Malcolm looked down the street. It was nearly four-thirty, and the street was jammed with people, all walking at their own pace, with their own rhythms. Some were hurrying, others merely strolling through the carnival atmosphere that was 125th.

"Look, Shep, this is about family," Malcolm said. "It's not about ripping off a few dollars."

"You saying I'm going to rip off the money?" Shep's voice raised. "That what you saying?"

"Hey, man, save your rap for somebody who wants to hear it," Malcolm said, looking directly into his cousin's eyes. "You know what they think of family. And you know they want everybody to show for the reunion. And yeah, up front, I do think you're going to blow."

"Later for you!" Shep put his tape player back into the shopping cart. "Maybe I'll show and maybe I won't. I know how to get there."

"You saying I'm wrong?" Malcolm asked.

"You're saying I'm wrong, ain't you?" Shep retorted.

Malcolm sucked his teeth and watched his cousin walk away. He felt like letting him go, and twice started to walk toward the subway at St. Nicholas. Then he took a breath and started after Shep.

"Look, show me where you live so I can find you again if I have to," Malcolm said. "And I'll give you the money so you can buy your own ticket."

"Hey, man, I'll take the money from you if I want to," Shep said, turning back to Malcolm.

Malcolm wiped his hands on the sides of his

pants and shook his head as if to say "no way."
He felt a small knot grow in the middle of his
stomach, one he had felt before. He had felt it
when somebody tried to take his game on the
basketball court, had walked up to him and told
him if he even tried to score he would get
punched out. He had felt it when he played,
when some other player or someone in the audience would say he couldn't play and didn't
know anything about music. He knew he could
play basketball, and he knew he could play his
horns, but the knot always came.

He didn't know if he could take Shep or not,
but he knew he would stand his ground.

"You ain't saying nothing now," Shep said.

"You ain't doing nothing, now, either,"
Malcolm said.

Shep fidgeted on one foot and looked around.
He then took the tray of tapes out of the shopping cart, covered it, and put it back into the
cart. "Come on," he said. "I'll take you to where
I live."

Malcolm exhaled. He didn't want to get into
a fight with his cousin. That's not what it was
supposed to be about. It was about hooking Shep
up with some blood, some roots.

From the street you couldn't tell that the
East Harlem Restoration Center was a men's
shelter. The guard at the door made Malcolm
sign a log book.

"You hungry?" he asked Malcolm.

"Hungry?" Malcolm looked at the big, brown-faced man. "No."

"You hungry they got emergency food on the second floor," the guard said.

"Thanks," Malcolm said, embarrassed that Shep had to live in a place where strangers asked if you had eaten.

"You sell any tapes?" the guard asked Shep. He seemed genuinely concerned.

"A few," Shep said. "Not enough."

"How come you're living here?" Malcolm asked when they had gone past the guard into a small dayroom.

"A tape got two sides to it," Shep said, sitting in a chair that looked like it belonged in a hospital waiting room. "One side is the main sounds and the other side is the sounds they just put on to fill out the tape. All this family stuff is the same way. One side of all this 'How great is the Lewis family' stuff is how all you uppity people are doing so good. The other side is the rest of us.

"All I hear is about keeping the family together and the whole Curry thing. When I got caught up in a trick bag and needed some help, you know, what I heard was what I should have been doing, and what cousin so-and-so was doing, and how I should be. Got so heavy I had to leave it alone, man."

"And come here?"

"And come somewhere!" Shep said. "I couldn't take it anymore."

"Look, if that's what it is," Malcolm said, sitting on the edge of a red Formica table, "that's not what it's supposed to be. And I don't think that people mean that kind of thing in their heart. I mean, that's not what I think I'm about. You know what I'm saying?"

"Yeah, well, you're okay," Shep said. "Least I see you sometimes. What you doing, anyway?"

"Keeping my head together. Trying to work up a new band," Malcolm answered. In the back of his mind it came to him that Shep had just blamed the family for his using crack. "I'm trying to hook up some new sounds. You still pounding skins?"

"Need some work on my timing." Shep held his hands out and hit some imaginary drums. "But, you know, I loved to play. I just got caught up in some other stuff."

"I got some tough dudes in the band and a Chinese girl who might join," Malcolm said.

"A Chinese girl?" Shep looked up at his cousin. "What she play?"

"Cello," Malcolm said. "Electric, man. It's amplified and it sounds good. She can play, too."

"I got to hear it," Shep said.

"Look, I'll make the reservations for the plane." Malcolm took the envelope from his pocket.

"Yo, put the money away!" Shep whispered and looked around the room. "They got stone vipers in here, man. You got to watch every move. Come on into the bathroom."

Malcolm followed as Shep wheeled his shopping cart into the bathroom. He gave Shep the portion of the money for his ticket and told him he'd call him the next day.

"You can come by my place, and we can leave from there," Malcolm said. "You remember where I live?"

"Why don't you come by here?" Shep said. "I don't dig those people up there on—what was it, 138th Street?"

"137th," Malcolm said. "If you want me to come here I will. Can I reach you by phone here?"

"Yeah, okay." Shep put the money Malcolm had given him into his sock. He fished through his pockets and found a card with his name on it and the name of the shelter. The other side of the card read MEDICAL EMERGENCY in large block letters. Shep's blood type was O positive.

"Peace, brother." Malcolm took Shep's hand and held it for a long moment.

"I guess I'll live through another family reunion," Shep said, grinning. "Talk to you tomorrow."

On the street Malcolm felt uneasy giving Shep the money, but he knew he would have felt bad, too, if he hadn't given it to him. He knew there was a good chance that his cousin would blow the money on crack overnight. Then again, there was a chance that he wouldn't.

Jenn Che Po called the next morning and said that she wanted to be part of his group and asked him if he had made up his mind about her.

"Sure," he answered. "Glad to have you. I'm really happy that you want to play with us."

"Do you have a name or anything?" The voice on the telephone seemed friendlier than the girl who had brought her cello to his apartment.

"We call it String Theory," he said.

"Okay, that's a good name," Jenn said, quickly. "You know, what you said about starting with being yourself, who you are, and then moving on?" Jenn asked.

"Yes?"

"Maybe I feel the same way," she said. "I know I didn't like what I was doing before. I think that it was just because I was trying so hard to be . . . I don't know . . ."

"Accepted?"

"Something like that," Jenn said. "Anyway, I'm glad to give you guys a try."

Jenn made sure that she knew when they

would meet again and said she would see him then.

Malcolm had never had a Chinese girlfriend, but that didn't stop him from thinking about her as he packed the small overnight bag his father had bought him for basketball games. He had to unpack the bag when he remembered his mother had told him to bring a suit. He went to his mother's closet, found the gray canvas case she had used when she and his father had gone to Bermuda, and packed that. His thoughts went to his mother. She was a strong woman. Sometimes she seemed even stronger than his father, but her focus was on the family, what he and his father were doing. She didn't know much about music, but she had always supported him. He folded the suit jacket carefully, then unfolded it and turned the arms inside out as he had seen in a magazine. That looked silly, so he turned the sleeves out again and just laid it as neatly as he could over the row of rolled underwear that he knew his mother would also check.

Malcolm didn't really have anything against a suit, he had explained to her, but he just didn't need one.

"Your father has six suits," his mother had countered. "And that's not counting his tuxedo."

His father, he had wanted to say, worked in an office, and suits were part of his job. He had decided not to continue the subject.

He finished packing and went on a search for

breakfast. There were cereal, eggs, cheese, and neatly labeled plastic containers of leftovers. He looked at some of the leftovers, decided that he didn't want any of them, took out the eggs and put them back, and settled on the cereal.

You hungry? the guard at the shelter had asked. Malcolm tried to push thoughts of Shep from his mind, knowing that he couldn't. On the dresser, propped up behind the miniature cut-glass perfume bottles his mother collected, were the old picture postcards his father had pulled out the weekend before they had left for the reunion. Malcolm picked one of them up. There was a picture of the Old Slave Mart Museum on one of them. On the other side was a brief note signed Mary saying that someone named Henry Epps had died. The card was dated October 1912.

The Lewis family reunions occurred every two years, and some of them were bigger than others. This was scheduled to be the biggest. Aunt Luvenia's firm, along with some Lewises from Johnson City, had put up the money to turn the Lewis property on Curry Island into a resort. Malcolm remembered the last reunion when he had played basketball with the other Lewis boys from around the country. There had been a lot of hand-shaking and hugs and stories that seemed to change according to who was doing the telling. In a way, Malcolm wasn't that pleased with going to the reunion. On the other hand, he knew that once he arrived, he would respond to the feelings of family and ritual as much as anyone else. The rituals, the traditions, were what connected him in a positive way with his own place as a black man. That's what he was, a black man with something to say and in need of a voice, sometimes even in need of a clear image of what a black man was supposed to be about.

He called the airline to check the reservations that his great-aunt had made for him, found out that the plane left at two-thirty from La Guardia, and hung up. He called the shelter and left a message for Shep with the deep voice that answered.

The radio came on exactly at nine the next morning, and Malcolm rolled quickly out of bed. He tried to remember what his mother had told him to be sure to do before he left. Bring a suit. Lock and check the doors. Put the perishable food from the bottom of the refrigerator into the freezer. Tell Mrs. Gates next door that he was leaving.

Malcolm left the door open while he was showering in case the telephone rang. By ten he was dressed and just waiting for the time to leave for the airport. He had a bowl of cereal and toast and then considered going out to play ball. Instead he decided to listen to some new reggae CDs he had bought.

The music was good, the rhythms vaguely interesting. He fantasized again about Jenn, gave himself a mental scolding about treating women as sexual objects, and then continued fantasizing about her.

At eleven-thirty he called the shelter, asked for Shep, and was told that he hadn't been there all night.

The sun was shining, the Harlem streets brilliant and busy. Malcolm walked down 125th Street, planning the trip to La Guardia Airport. They could take a cab from the shelter, he thought, and still have plenty of time to make the flight.

"Say, my brother." A tall, thin man leaned forward holding a newspaper. "You looking for a *Final Call* this morning?"

"No, thanks," Malcolm said, turning away from the man. He quickened his step as he headed toward the East Side.

The guard at the shelter recognized him and pushed the sign-in book toward him. Malcolm hadn't realized how big the man was.

"Is Sheppard Lewis in?"

"Yeah," the guard answered, looking away. "I guess so. Look in the back, near the exit sign."

Malcolm stood just inside the door for a long moment, letting his eyes adjust to the dimness. On the sides of the large room there were basketball backboards. One of them had a hand-drawn picture of an American flag painted behind the rim. Three of the beds were occupied. He could make out an older man on one of them. A pair of crutches were tied to the bottom rail with shoestrings. On another there was a figure beneath a dark blanket. It was small, perhaps even a child.

The exit glowed in the back, and from where he stood Malcolm could see the figure on the bed. It was partially covered by a sheet. Malcolm took a deep breath and walked as quietly as he could toward the sign. By the time he reached the rear of the large room, he could make out a scoreboard. It read HOME: 44 AWAY: 64.

"Shep!" Malcolm knelt near the edge of the cot. "Yo! Shep! Wake up!"

"Shut that noise up over there!" the old man on the other cot said.

Malcolm turned and saw that the old man hadn't moved. He turned back to Shep and shook his shoulder.

Shep sat up; then, realizing that someone was near him, he jerked around toward Malcolm. "What you doing?" he asked.

"Come on, man," Malcolm said as Shep looked for his clothes. "We got to get out to the airport."

"Hey, you got the tickets?"

"We're supposed to pick them up out there," Malcolm said. "You still have the money, right?"

Shep wiped his face with the sheet. "Where's my blanket?"

"You still have the money for the ticket, right?" Malcolm repeated.

"I got robbed," Shep said.

"Man . . ." Malcolm looked away.

"Hey, I didn't ask to get robbed."

"Yeah, so I guess you're just not going."

"Yeah." The small voice that seemed to come from somewhere deep within Shep seemed unreal. It was as if some other man-child, less man than child, was speaking from a great distance.

"Take care of yourself," Malcolm said.

His steps back to the front door were stiff, awkward. His legs refused to work as they should, refused to remember their usual smooth gait, their one-on-one quickness, their supple, slam-dunk strength.

The guard was drinking from the water cooler when Malcolm came out.

"You find him?"

"Yeah," Malcolm said. "He said he got robbed."

"Stuff happens," the guard said. "You can watch all night and all day, and if it's going to happen, it's going to happen. What you going to do? Give up and die?"

"How old you got to be to stay in there?"

"Supposed to be eighteen." The guard wiped his face with a handkerchief. "But we don't ask that many questions. The only youth house they got any room in is way out in Queens. You need a place to sleep tonight?"

"Uh-unh."

"Don't be ashamed," the guard said. "It's better than the subways."

"Yeah, I guess so," Malcolm said.

He turned and looked back into the dim room full of cots. Shep had lain back down again, the sheet over his head, his body curled toward the wall. The old man who had complained before was coughing into a handkerchief.

Malcolm leaned against the inside of the door.

There was a narrow, rectangular window between the door that led to the street and the painted cinder block walls. Through it Malcolm could see the gleam of shiny cars as they passed, colorful blurs on their way to somewhere else. Occasionally a walker would pass, infinitely slower than the cars, passing more time than distance.

Malcolm turned and walked back through the darkness to where Shep lay.

"Yo, Shep, come on, man." He put his hand on the boy's shoulder, surprised at how thin it was. "We can take a bus."

"I don't think I can make it," came the muffled reply. "Why don't you go on? I don't feel so good."

"You can try, Shep," Malcolm said. "We're people, man. I'm here to help you. Don't turn me away."

"I don't know." Shep still spoke into the bedclothes.

"Look, you got to either try or . . ." Malcolm searched for the words. "Give up and die."

For a long time Shep didn't respond. His shoulder, angled beneath the coarse blanket, moved ever so slightly with his breathing. Malcolm put his hand on his cousin's shoulder. *What was all the hugging and handshakes about down on Curry if he couldn't reach out to Shep in the shelter?*

Shep first sat up and then swung his legs over the side of the bed. He moved slowly, making small, tentative movements with his hands, as if he didn't know what to do with them or had somehow forgotten how to use them. He already had his pants on, and he looked under his bedclothes, inside the fitted cover, for his shirt, socks, and shoes.

They were still there, and he told Malcolm to watch them as he went to the bathroom. The bathroom was out the front door and down the hall.

Malcolm sat on the cot waiting for Shep. He felt the pockets of the shirt. There were some coins in one of them and something hard. Malcolm looked at the door, then took the hard object out of Shep's pocket. It was the box for a gospel tape. He opened it and saw that it contained a tape and a crumpled five-dollar bill. He replaced it and put it all on the end of the bed as Shep came through the door.

"You eat anything?" Shep asked.

"Yeah."

"You think we can make it down South?"

"Sure," Malcolm answered. "Why not?"

There was dried saliva on the side of Shep's face, but Malcolm didn't mention it. He just wanted to get him downtown and on a bus. He could sleep on the bus, if that's what he needed, and they would be at least on their way.

Malcolm had seen crackheads before, had

seen the desperation in their eyes, the wolf-hungry look, the nervous hands always touching their faces.

He tried not to look at Shep as they went into the subway toward the number 3 train. Shep took out a pair of shades and put them on.

Shep needed something to drink, and they stopped for sodas and hot dogs in the Port Authority bus station on 41st Street. A squat, blond man standing near the magazine stand was calling out first in English and then in what sounded like Spanish that he was leaving for Jersey City in ten minutes.

There was a Greyhound office on the first floor of the Port Authority building, and Malcolm asked about a bus to Johnson City. The woman selling tickets said that they had a bus that left at ten that night.

"Anything sooner?"

"Not on Greyhound," the woman said. "You can go over to Trailways and take the bus to Miami. That stops at Johnson City." The black woman looked from Malcolm to Shep and back to Malcolm again. "If you hurry down there you can get it. It's going to leave in twenty minutes, but it only gets to Johnson City about an hour before our bus because it makes so many stops along the way."

"We'll take it," Malcolm said.

The woman directed them to the window to buy tickets and told them they'd better hurry. They found the window, bought two tickets to

Johnson City, and then rushed to the third floor of the busy bus terminal just in time to get the bus.

As Malcolm thought he would, Shep fell asleep quickly. The miles went by steadily and they were halfway through New Jersey, slowed by the late afternoon traffic, before Shep woke.

"Well, we're on our way," Malcolm said. "How you doing?"

"This bus got a bathroom?"

"Yeah. It's in the back," Malcolm said.

Shep got up, squeezed by Malcolm, and went back toward the bathroom. He disappeared into the bathroom, and Malcolm went back to looking out the window. There was a sign that read Princeton Junction, and Malcolm wondered if it referred to Princeton University. He stretched his legs out as much as he could. It wasn't comfortable, but it was better than nothing. He thought of calling ahead so that someone would meet them at the bus terminal, but he remembered that the bus fare for the two of them had taken a lot of his money and they still needed to eat on the way.

Shep stayed in the bathroom a long time, and Malcolm began to worry. He wondered if Shep had any crack with him. An image of the boy taking out a plastic crack vial from his sock came to him.

When Shep did return, he looked all right. Then he sat down and threw up on the side of the seat under the window.

The bus driver heard the commotion made by the passengers around Shep and Malcolm. He looked up in the rearview mirror several times and glanced back in their direction.

"Guy back here is sick!" a tall, thin man with a gold tooth called out.

The driver looked back several times, then slowed the bus while looking into the mirror. A few minutes later he pulled the bus over onto the shoulder of the road.

"You okay?" Malcolm asked in a whisper.

Shep took several deep breaths and leaned his head back against his seat. His eyes were open and staring and a line of perspiration on his upper lip captured the overhead light. He looked terrible.

The driver took one look at the vomit, and went toward the back of the bus.

"Shep, you all right?" Malcolm asked again.

Shep nodded that he was.

The bus driver came back, his face twisted

with disgust, and motioned for them to leave the seat.

Malcolm got out and moved to the back of the bus. Shep followed him. The bus driver sprayed the dirtied area from a can and wiped it with a large sponge. He wiped it down afterward with a large cloth and then sprayed it again, this time leaving it wet.

"There's a restroom in the back!" the driver said. "You didn't see it?"

"He just got sick," Malcolm said. "He didn't mean it."

The bus driver scowled and mumbled under his breath. He brushed past Shep and Malcolm and returned the cleaning materials to the restroom.

Shep quickly fell into an uneasy sleep and leaned on a pillow against the window. What Malcolm thought, what stampeded through his mind, was that he wanted to be away from Shep. He did not need Shep or even, at this point, like him. The smell of vomit was still in the air, and the rocking of the bus almost made Malcolm ill several times. Outside the bus, the roadside scenery raced by, boring in its sameness. Even the occasional buildings and houses they passed were just the raw, ugly edges of towns.

A passenger had moved away from the seat in front of them and was sitting near the driver. He made no effort to conceal that he was talking about Shep and Malcolm. The bus driver looked back at them several times.

Malcolm forced his mind to String Theory, his group. For a while he couldn't think of the name of the Chinese girl, then remembered it was Jenn. He thought about her playing. She seemed to understand the music so well, so easily. He wondered if it was too simple. He thought of adding counterpoint, melody lines that would allow Jenn to play against the main melody instead of with it.

Shep's breathing, which had been raspy and deep, seemed to settle into a constant pattern. He made small murmuring noises in his sleep, and Malcolm thought he must have been dreaming.

The first rest stop was at a diner outside of Alexandria, Virginia.

"Thirty minutes!" the driver called out.

Malcolm thought of letting Shep sleep through, but he wanted something to eat and thought that his cousin might be better off if he ate something when he wasn't being bumped around by the bus.

He waited until the bus was nearly empty. Then he woke Shep and told him they were going to have a rest stop. Shep nodded, stretched, and stood.

"Where are we?"

"Virginia," Malcolm said.

"Already?"

"How you feeling?"

"Better," Shep said. "Sorry about throwing up, man."

"Yo, it happens," Malcolm said.

The rest stop was not much more than a diner with a jukebox and a small pool table. Malcolm noticed that the waitress had put lipstick on her bottom lip but not on the top one. She was busy, taking orders for all of the customers and calling them into the kitchen as fast as she could.

"They ain't got nothing on the menu to eat," Shep said.

"Tuna fish," Malcolm said. "You like tuna fish?"

"I hate tuna fish," Shep answered. "You die and go to hell, all they give you to eat down there is tuna fish."

"How about cheese sandwiches?" Malcolm asked, glad to see that Shep was willing to joke. "We can get some cheese sandwiches and some cookies."

"Yeah, that's okay."

They ordered the cheese sandwiches and saw the waitress place them in a microwave oven.

From the jukebox came the hard-driving sound of Bonnie Raitt and John Lee Hooker sassing and sashaying their way through "I'm in the Mood."

"You like that?" Shep asked.

"I like it a lot," Malcolm said. "But I don't see myself playing it."

The waitress served them the sandwiches still wrapped in cellophane with a red-and-white label that read "American Cheese."

"Why don't I think this is going to be a great sandwich?" Malcolm asked.

They ate the cheese sandwiches, which cost three dollars each, and Shep felt sick again. He went to the restroom and Malcolm wondered if he was still using crack and was just using the fact that he had been sick on the bus to get away from him.

He really didn't know what someone using crack would look like as they used it. He knew what people who used crack looked like when they hung out on the streets, looking for their connection, or some way to make money. They looked empty, like bad photos of what humans should look like. He remembered reading about the sixties when the Nation of Islam, the Black Nationalist group, talked about "fishing for the dead." That's how the crack users looked to Malcolm, like dead people running through the streets, looking for their lives in small plastic vials.

The bus driver, who had been sitting at the counter, left the diner, followed by some of the passengers. Some of the other passengers had already returned to the bus. Malcolm went into the restroom after Shep.

Shep was leaning against the wall near one of the basins, catching handfuls of water and dripping it on his face and neck.

"What's wrong, man?"

"I think I got a cold," Shep said.

"You using?"

"Using what?"

"Anything," Malcolm answered.

"What you mean . . . 'anything'?" Shep looked away from his cousin. "No," he said, "not now."

"Then what's the matter with you?"

"Coming down," Shep said. "Trying to slide down. You know, reaching for all the hard changes without blowing the beat. You down with that?"

"Yeah," Malcolm answered. He was uneasy with Shep. If being black meant reaching out to people as difficult to reach as Shep, then it was going to be harder than he thought. "We got to get out to the bus. They're ready to go."

"Right."

Shep turned on the cold water tap, cupped his hands beneath it, and gathered cold water, which he splashed on his face. He took a deep breath, looked straight ahead for a moment, and then jerked his head away and went past Malcolm out of the restroom. Malcolm looked to see what he had turned away from. It had been Shep's own image in the cracked mirror.

It was gone. Not there. Disappeared. Where the bus had been, next to a covered waiting area, there was nothing. Malcolm's first reaction was to run back into the diner and tell them. He took two running steps toward the diner, then one slower step, and then he stopped.

Malcolm looked up to the sky. It was a cloudless night. Stars gathered in clusters he never remembered seeing in the city. Behind him Shep was cursing, saying what he would do to the driver if he ever saw him again.

"We can sue them suckers!" Shep was saying.

Malcolm wondered if the bus driver would realize that they weren't on board and come back. He knew better. They were young and black, and Shep had thrown up on the bus. The driver didn't want them on board. He would say, if the case ever came up in court, that Malcolm and Shep had just missed the bus.

"Come on." Malcolm headed toward the diner.

They ordered pound cake and sodas and sat in the upholstered booth. The waitress served them without speaking, putting the cake in the middle of the table and pushing the bill toward Malcolm. Malcolm looked at the bill and gave the woman a ten-dollar bill.

"How late you open?" he asked.

"We don't close," the woman said. "You miss the bus?"

"Yeah."

The woman shook her head and walked away. She leaned on the far side of the counter, turning the pages of a newspaper.

Malcolm and Shep sat, Shep finishing his cake, Malcolm pushing his around the plate.

"We can take turns sleeping," Shep said. "I can watch for you and you can watch for me."

"I'm not sleepy," Malcolm said. "There's probably another bus coming here tonight. We can get that somewhere. They owe us a ride."

"They owe us more than that," Shep said. "We come all the way down here, and then they just snatch the whole thing from us."

"They didn't snatch it from me," Malcolm said. "Maybe we can hitchhike."

"Ain't nobody going to pick us up," Shep said. "Especially two of us."

"Maybe, but we have two choices," Malcolm said. "We either give up, or we keep trying. I don't give up that easy."

"You ride a white horse?"

"No, you the only one riding horses," Malcolm said.

"What's that supposed to mean?"

Malcolm looked away without answering. He was close to crying, close to breaking down and wanting to go home.

At the counter the waitress was making slow, lazy movements with a rag as she cleaned off the counter. She was talking to some truckers who had just come in. One of them jerked a thumb toward Shep and Malcolm.

The trucker that turned on his stool to face them was white-haired and wide-shouldered. His face, under the visor of a baseball cap, was deeply lined. He looked directly at Malcolm and Shep, sizing them up. Malcolm looked back at him defiantly.

"What's up?" Shep asked. He had sensed Malcolm's uneasiness.

"Nothing," Malcolm said.

The trucker slid off the stool and came toward

him, a slight swagger to his walk.

"You boys miss the bus?"

"The driver left us," Malcolm said.

"I'm headed toward Panama City with a load of cow hides. If you want to come along, there's some room in the back," the man said.

"Where's Panama City?"

"Florida," the trucker said. "Where you boys headed?"

"Curry Island, near Johnson City. You know where that is?"

"I don't go into the city, but I skirt it. I can drop you off about a mile or so from Johnson," the trucker said. "Like I said, you got to ride in the back. I'll be going in fifteen minutes. You want to ride, be ready."

They watched him go back to the counter and sit down. The waitress had brought him what looked like a hamburger and a small paper cup of cole slaw.

"I don't trust that sucker," Shep said. "He could be a skinhead or something, or a serial killer."

"Yeah," Malcolm said. "And he could get us to Johnson City. How you feel? You still sick?"

"I'm okay."

"Then we go with him."

"I ain't going," Shep said.

"If I got to kick your butt, you're going," Malcolm said. "We're not in Harlem now, man. It's just you and me out here, blood to the bone.

We got to either do it or let it do us. What you going to do?"

"Nothing," Shep answered. "I'm not doing nothing."

"That's what you're about, right?" Malcolm stood. "Folding up like some sissy."

Malcolm saw that he had hurt Shep. He could see the pain in his eyes, in the way his face twisted as he searched for an answer. He saw the hurt, and then he turned away. He didn't want to deal with it, just with getting to Johnson City. He went to the trucker and said that he'd like to ride with him.

"You got it, sport," the trucker said.

Two of the other truckers looked Malcolm over, letting their eyes say that they didn't approve of him.

Malcolm was surprised how cool it had become. He pulled his jacket around him and turned the collar up. When Shep moved next to him he felt good. Maybe they would make it after all.

The truck was huge and, in a strange way, beautiful. The body was white and clean. The cab was mostly silver, chrome, and glass. On the front of the cab, in red, white, and blue letters, was the slogan "GOD, AMERICA, AND ME!"

There was a dog in the cab. Its huge head came from what looked like a solid block of fur. The trucker had brought a hamburger out to the dog and put it on the ground in front of the truck. The dog sniffed it and then wolfed it down in two bites.

"He's a chow chow," the trucker said. "His name is Dirty Harry. What you think about that name?"

"Okay, if you like it," Malcolm said.

"I'm Bernie Hatfield. You fellows have names?"

"Malcolm Lewis." Malcolm nodded.

"Shep Lewis. We're cousins," Shep said.

"Let's get rolling!"

The hides took up over half of the twenty-four-foot trailer. There was an eight-foot space between the last box and the rear doors. On the floor, neatly folded, was a small pile of burlap and quilting.

They climbed into the back of the truck, located the ventilators that Bernie showed them, and settled in.

They felt the truck begin to move. In the darkness Malcolm felt Shep reach over toward him and feel along his chest.

"What do you want?" he asked.

"Where's your hand?" Shep asked.

"Why?"

Malcolm found Shep's arm, then his hand. He felt the hand in his and held it tightly as the truck lurched onto the highway.

The smell of the hides was terrible and seemed to suck the air out of the back of the truck. There were times, like when they passed street lamps or signs, when flashes of light briefly illuminated the truck's interior. It was at these times when Malcolm saw Shep working at making it, trying to ignore the violent jerking of the truck, lifting his head to catch what fresh air he could. He looked strong even though he had been ill a short time before. Sometimes just the front of his face would be visible for a few seconds, and Malcolm would have to guess what he was doing with the rest of his body.

At the end of the first hour, the heat had become nearly unbearable, the gulps of air more difficult to find in the darkness and less satisfying.

The pain came from within, from the knowledge that it did not have to be this way, Malcolm thought. He could have made his way to the airport, found the luxury of a scheduled plane, and never have known the desperation that was overtaking him. There was a struggle within Malcolm, a struggle between what he thought was right, what his mind said was right—that he should be with his cousin, his fellow black man, his fellow human being—and the feeling that he could do without the misery and without the risks that he was facing because of Shep. Shep was an anchor that made moving on hard.

Malcolm thought about praying, and he wondered if God would notice that it was not religious feeling but a feeling of panic that prompted his prayers.

"What do you think of this guy?" Malcolm spoke softly in the darkness. He shifted his position slightly, trying to spare his hip the agony of pressure against the bed of the truck.

"I don't think anything about him," Shep answered softly.

Malcolm thought about the man. He seemed sure of himself, traveling the highways of America with his rig. He probably had a family, maybe even a son their age, a boy playing basketball for some high school team in Florida. His accent wasn't southern, maybe he was from the Midwest. Maybe he just had girls who didn't know anything about drugs, or Harlem, or trying to bring somebody addicted to crack to a family reunion.

The Lord is my shepherd. . . .

First it was the darkness, then the jolting ride, and then the fear that filled him even as he denied it. Then it was the breathing. He heard Shep gasping for air in the darkness, heard his breath offer a rasping rhythm that echoed his own. Malcolm sucked in the air and still his lungs cried for more. He pushed himself up and to his knees and crawled toward the back doors. He ran his hands along the door and felt the hard metal lining of the trailer. He crawled back to the quilting, stretched out, and lay as still as he could, his eyes closed.

When they stopped and there was light through the grating, Malcolm could see particles of dust floating in the air, as if suspended on the stifling heat that seemed to come from the hides and perhaps from him and Shep. The stench of the hides was crushing. It seemed to fill him up, to take his breath away.

Lying against each other in the darkness, they fought for precious air. Malcolm sucked in as much air as he could, listening to it hiss past his parched lips. Next to him, Shep moaned.

"You okay?" Malcolm asked.

"Yeah."

No, Malcolm thought. Shep wasn't okay. He still had crack dreams, still had the memory of it in his arms, in his chest. He was still chained to the weight of it even though the truck was hurtling through the night. The chains could rattle, but they weren't broken.

Malcolm thought of water, of iced tea. The thoughts quickly faded, and then he thought of nothing but trying to get more air. He rolled over and got to his knees again, looking up into the darkness, looking for light. He was isolated in the fear that tingled along the surface of his skin.

"Malcolm?" Shep called to him.

Malcolm didn't answer. He looked for the grating, finally saw it, and then climbed to his feet, nearly falling twice. He reached the grating and put his mouth over it, sucking in the air, filling his lungs.

"Malcolm!" Shep was on his feet. He tried to pull Malcolm from the grating.

Malcolm pushed him away hard, then kicked at him and put his face back to the grating, sucking in the cool air until his lungs were filled. Then he sank back down to the bed of the truck.

He felt Shep climb over him and heard the sucking noise as he struggled for breath at the grating.

Malcolm knew that it wasn't only the lack of air, it was the smell and the awful feeling of being imprisoned that made the fight for a breath of air seem like a fight for life.

"Man, it's hard to breathe in here!" Shep was saying.

"Yeah," Malcolm said.

"Where are you?"

"Over here," Malcolm said. "I'm sitting over here."

Shep crawled to him and lay back against the baled skins.

"Next time we go anywhere," Shep said. "I'm busting out the limo."

"How did you blow the money?" Malcolm asked.

"You know," Shep said. "The pipe."

For the next few hours, Malcolm Lewis kept his face close to the grating, thinking of nothing but filling his lungs for the next minute of life, hoping that when he needed it, he would be stronger than Shep.

Somewhere in the darkness, Shep's demons caught up with him. He started screaming and beating against the walls of the truck. Malcolm tried to comfort him, but Shep fought him off, pushing him away from the grating. Malcolm knew it was the need for drugs that created the nightmare that drove Shep. Malcolm first tried to calm him, then fought him off, then moved away into a corner against the hides until Shep's screaming had subsided to a fearful whimpering, until his cousin had fallen into a rasping sleep.

Malcolm calmed down and sat against the side of the truck. There was a rail there, and he occasionally used it to lift himself to his feet and go to the grating. But he had already survived Shep's rage, his wild fighting, his tortured frenzy. He, Malcolm, was exploring what it meant to be black. Shep was giving him another definition.

When the truck stopped on the shoulder of the road at the edge of Johnson City and the door was opened, Bernie, the truck driver, held Dirty Harry by the collar. In his other hand he held a large flashlight.

"We're here," he said, shining the light into the truck. "What the hell were you guys doing back here?"

"He had a bad dream," Malcolm said, nodding toward Shep.

"Guess he did," Bernie said. Dirty Harry was at his side. The dog shook himself, his head seeming to swivel on his neck.

Malcolm dug his nails into Shep's arm. He was grateful to hear Shep curse, then ask what was going on.

"We're stopped," Malcolm said.

Malcolm stood and pulled Shep to his feet.

"C'mon!" The truck driver took a step backwards as he called to them. "I got to keep rolling!"

Malcolm was off the truck first, and Shep followed right behind him. They walked a few steps from the truck as Bernie slammed the doors of his rig shut.

"Thanks!" Malcolm called to the man who was already headed for the cab, the dog by his side. A second later, Malcolm heard the air brakes being released, the red rear lights increased in intensity, and the truck pulled away. It was cold.

"Where we at?" Shep asked.

"I don't know," Malcolm said. "Here comes a car. Maybe we can get a lift."

"I don't want no more lifts," Shep said. "I'm freezing. I thought it was supposed to be warm down here?"

"We lost my bag on the bus," Malcolm said. "And we need to get some directions."

Malcolm waved his arm to flag down what turned out to be a small pickup truck.

The pickup rolled past them and stopped, and a man looked out of the window. Malcolm started toward the truck only to watch it pull slowly away. Malcolm stopped and the truck stopped.

"You need help?" the man called back. "You want me to give the sheriff a call and tell him you're out here?"

"How far are we from Johnson City?"

" 'Bout ten minutes by car," the man called out. "You know people in Johnson City?"

"On Curry," Malcolm said.

"Well, there's a telephone booth about a mile up the road," the man said, nodding ahead of him. "You can get you some help there."

"A mile?"

" 'Bout a mile," the man said, his window already closing.

Malcolm took a deep breath. The trucker had brought them to Johnson City after all. He started walking up the road without turning toward Shep. Shep walked behind him for a quarter of a mile, then ran after him.

"Hey, Malcolm, wait up!"

Malcolm didn't answer or look at Shep when he caught up with him.

"I'm sorry," Shep said. "I didn't mean to put you through all this, man."

"Yeah, but you did," Malcolm said. "You put me through it just like you putting everybody else through it. I'm just the one here right now, that's all."

"Hey, we're still blood, right?"

"Yeah, but when you were needing to catch a breath in the truck, you were ready to kill me for it," Malcolm said. He stepped to the side of the road as a car hummed past. In the distance, there was the sound of thunder, and the wind picked up, sending warm, welcome gusts of air their way.

"That wind feels good," Malcolm said. "Smells good, too."

"Never thought I'd be thankful for fresh air."

"It's free out here," Malcolm said. "Being in that truck was torture. The air out here is free, and it's clean, and right now it's about the sweetest stuff in the world. You hip to that?"

"Yeah."

It was well over a mile along the highway into Johnson City. Malcolm didn't recognize anything they passed. He didn't even see a phone booth. By the time they reached the city, there was more traffic. Trucks loaded with fruits and vegetables passed them and turned down a small street and they decided that the street probably led to the market. When they got to the market, they asked about a bus going to Curry Island. The round-faced black man that answered them had a high voice, and they had to have him repeat the answer three times before they understood him.

"He's from the old part of Curry," Malcolm said as they walked down High Street toward where the man had indicated the bus stopped.

"Sounds like he's from under the island," Shep said.

"They speak something close to African," Malcolm said. "It's not exactly African but there's a lot of African words in it."

"Still sounds like he's from under the island," Shep said.

He grinned, but Malcolm didn't like it a bit. He wanted to say something about who did Shep think he was, making fun of somebody on Curry that he didn't know a thing about?

The bus didn't come for an hour. When it came and they got on, it wound its way all over Johnson City before crossing the bridge to Curry. Malcolm had the address and became more and more excited as they walked the last half mile. When they reached the Lewis place, the sky had already turned from a soft gray to a brilliant blue. Shep didn't seem to be doing that well. He was sweating and wiping at the corners of his mouth. Malcolm asked him if he was going to be all right, and Shep said that he would be. Malcolm asked for his father and was told that he was in the small house out back.

"With a whole bunch of people." The woman who told him was making bread. "You handsome boys took the train to Johnson City?"

"Hitchhiked," Malcolm said, glancing in Shep's direction. "Just for the heck of it."

"You wouldn't catch me doing any hitchhiking," the woman said. "Anyway, everybody is going to be up in about fifteen minutes. They're bringing in the last crop."

"Last crop of what?" Shep asked.

"Sweet potatoes." The woman took a large bowl of dough from the countertop, inspected it carefully, and started shaping individual rolls. "They're supposed to be starting the developing soon as the weather breaks. You know they're making a resort out of this place."

"Aunt Luvenia told me," Malcolm said.

"Well, they're not going to do it over the sweet potatoes," the woman said. "So I hope you boys are ready to do some serious picking. Y'all know who I am? Don't lie, now."

"No, ma'am."

"I'm Jennie. I was married to Tommy Lewis. You know Tommy was killed in Vietnam?"

"Yes, ma'am."

"Planter is here, too," Jennie said. "That's Tommy's father. He can't talk about his son. Gets him all choked up. Sometimes when he sees his granddaughter — she was born a month after Tommy died — you can just feel the pain in the man. Other than that, he's just a lot of hard work and hard family."

"Yes, ma'am."

"And you don't have to 'ma'am' me like I'm ninety," Jennie said. "You can call me Jennie."

"Yes, ma'am," Malcolm said, "I mean Jennie."

Shep found a bed that wasn't being used on the first floor, and Malcolm slept on the pullout couch in the den next to a child he hadn't remembered seeing before. He dreamt of being back in New York and then being in Hollywood, which, in his dream, seemed only a few blocks away. He had just reached the part in his dream when String Theory was being offered a huge contract when he felt someone shaking him. It was his father.

"I see you finally got down here." Charles Lewis was wearing a pair of overalls that were two sizes too large for him.

Malcolm sat up and saw that the little boy he had been sleeping with was gone. "What time is it?" he asked.

"Time to get to work," his father answered with a cheeriness that sounded like trouble.

"That's what everybody is doing down here?" Malcolm asked. "Working?"

"Getting in the last crop. All the city folks are paired off with the people who know what they're doing so we don't mess up too much. Let's go."

"Looks like you're enjoying yourself," Malcolm said. He was surprised to see that he still had his clothes on.

He was stiff as he got up. "Lost my suitcase on the way down here," he said.

"Get you a new one," his father said. "Shep come down with you?"

"Sure. He's sleeping somewhere."

There were greetings being handed out in the hallway, and he found himself shaking hands with people he didn't know and whose names he forgot almost as soon as he heard them.

"Don't he favor Richard?" a short, light-skinned woman asked a big man in overalls.

"Yeah, he does a little," the man said, offering

his hand. "I'm Tony Epps," he said. "We're in from Chicago."

"Pleased to meet you," Malcolm said.

He shook two more hands and was told that he "favored" four other people before his turn came up to use the bathroom. He looked at himself in the mirror. His eyes were bloodshot and puffy. He stuck his tongue out, the way he normally did when he felt bad in the morning. It looked okay, although in truth he wasn't sure how it would look if it wasn't okay.

He had just finished washing and was drying himself with a towel he had taken from a stack when there was a banging on the door. He quickly put on his shirt and opened it.

"Sorry," he said.

"You Malcolm?" The man who stood in the doorway looked to be about seventy, perhaps even older. He was dark with hair that was more white than gray. His eyes were bright and eager, and he was smiling.

"Yeah."

"Well, I am Planter Lewis, your great-uncle or something like that," the man said. "I was named after the boat that Robert Smalls stole away from the Confederate army and took to the Union. Now ain't that something?"

"It sure is."

"Anyway, I'm a Lewis the same as you, and you and me are going to be working together this day."

"Oh, okay," Malcolm answered.

"You have your breakfast yet?"

"Not hungry," Malcolm answered.

"Not hungry? People from New York don't get hungry, I guess." Planter grinned and patted Malcolm on the shoulder. "You come on now and follow me."

They went around the back of the house and found a pile of burlap bags. The man grabbed a stack, threw them over his shoulder, and started for the fields. Malcolm had to walk quickly to keep up with him. When he stopped at the gate, Malcolm stopped with him, thought for a second, and then opened the gate for the older man.

"Where your sacks?" the man asked, laughing. "What you going to do, put the sweet potatoes in your pockets?"

Malcolm went back and got as many sacks as Planter had and threw them across his shoulder.

"See this field?" Planter shielded his eyes as he looked out over the field. "There's six just like this one, but this was the first one the Lewises had. That's why they call it the Glory Field. There's been a Lewis in this field as long as anybody knowed anything about this part of the world. We were here before most of the white people were here."

Malcolm did a quick count. There were already eight other people in the field. He wanted to ask how many people there were doing the picking, but decided not to.

Planter explained how they were going to

bring in the potatoes. They would pull up the potatoes by the stems that grew above ground, cut off the sweet potatoes, and put them in the sack.

"Now we ain't growing dirt, so don't fill the bag with a lot of dirt and stones," Planter said.

The hoe that they used was light for the first hour, then began to get heavier as his arms began to ache. Every time he looked over at Planter in the next row, the old man would look at him and laugh. Malcolm didn't mind. The work was hard, and the old man didn't expect him to keep up, but he would.

"What you do up in New York?" Planter called to him. "You pick sweet potatoes up there?"

Planter started laughing before Malcolm could answer. Somehow his laugh made Malcolm laugh. "I go to school," Malcolm said. "And I have a small band."

"Small band?" Planter stopped and straightened up. "What you play?"

"Saxophone and flute," Malcolm said.

"You got to play for us in church this Sunday," Planter said.

It seemed to Malcolm that all the pickers were headed in the same direction and that he and Planter were just about keeping up with the others. The next team of pickers were women, and one of them was pregnant.

"She's pregnant," Malcolm said.

"She lives on this farm," Planter said. "She'll

pick you to death. Pick sweet potatoes all day and make sweet potato pies on her break. You think you can pick with her?"

"No, I guess not," Malcolm said.

"So what kind of music you play?"

"Sort of a new sound," Malcolm said. "It's sort of like a cross between jazz and classical and maybe the blues."

"Can you dance to it?"

"Not really."

"It got words you can sing to it?"

Malcolm shook his head.

"Then I know just what you playing," Planter said. "You playing that three-figure music."

"What is three-figure music?"

"You got to figure out what you listening to," Planter said. "Then you got to figure out why you listening to it, and last you got to figure out why you ain't listening to something else!"

"It's not that bad," Malcolm said.

"Don't let me talk you down," Planter said. "Everybody got to find their own way. When I was your age I played funny music, too. Used to play an albino pig. Every time I squeezed that pig she would send out a note. Hardest thing to do was to keep her in tune."

Planter threw back his head and laughed a deep, hearty laugh.

"Planter, don't you be deviling that boy!" a woman called from across the field.

It took another hour before Malcolm noticed that he wasn't straightening up as much as he was when he started. That was just about the time when Planter's jokes stopped being funny.

"They didn't do this on the last family reunion," Malcolm said as he tied a sack of sweet potatoes.

"Why you only fill the sack halfway?" Planter asked.

Malcolm opened the sack and dragged it further down the row.

"This the last time this place going to be a farm," Planter said. "I know you hate that because you was thinking you were going to come down here and be a regular sweet potato man, wasn't you?"

"I don't think so," Malcolm said.

"Here come Luvenia." Planter pointed to Malcolm's great-aunt. "She probably coming out here to find out why you ain't working."

Malcolm looked up at Planter, saw the big grin on the black man's face, and shook his head. He knew what was supposed to happen. He was supposed to get back to the house that evening so tired he couldn't stand up, and then Planter would continue his jokes. Malcolm decided that he wouldn't let that happen.

"How you doing, Malcolm?" Luvenia Lewis asked.

"Nothing to it, Aunt Luvenia," he answered.

"You didn't fly down here?"

"No, ma'am. Had a little trouble getting Shep here," he said. "But we made it."

"I'm really surprised," she said. "I didn't think

you could get him down here at all. Well, keep working, but don't let Planter kill you. He'll work you to death if he can."

"I ain't working him," Planter called out. "He's working me!"

Malcolm took his watch off at nine-thirty. He had already been working for two and a half hours. They had been two and a half straight hours, except for the time his mother and a young girl came around to everybody with lemonade. His mother looked at him with that special pride that mothers had when their children were doing well, and he gave her the dirtiest look he could.

"He's having fun," Planter called out to Malcolm's mother. "Ain't you having fun, Malcolm?"

"Yeah."

Malcolm's mother moved on to the next pickers and Malcolm turned his attention to the next patch of sweet potatoes.

"Just think how it must've been working out here before we got our freedom," Planter said. "Working out here all day for nothing but the right to get up and do it the next day. Ain't that something?"

Malcolm looked at Planter and saw that he was still grinning. "Must have been hard," he said.

"Yeah, but how hard was it?" Planter said. He tied up a bag of sweet potatoes and brought them over to the row where Malcolm stood leaning on his hoes. "That's what you got to think on," Planter went on. "It was hard, but how hard was it?"

"I can't even think about that right now." Malcolm searched for the words.

"Well, the way I figure, it must have been past flesh hard. It had to go past bone hard. It had to go deep down inside. *Deep* down inside. Down there where the soul is."

"I think so," Malcolm said.

"Since we all had the same experience," Planter lifted a bag of sweet potatoes, turned it so that it fit, and placed it neatly on the pile, "we were the same people. Now ain't that a good thing?"

"That's good," Malcolm said. The back of his shoulder burned with fatigue.

"Then what happened?"

"What happened, Planter?"

"Well." Planter pulled out a handkerchief and wiped the back of his neck. "Well, what happened was that freedom come, and it was like cold water to a thirsty soul. Tell me you know what I mean."

"I know what you mean," Malcolm answered.

"Then sweet potatoes came!" Planter said. "And they gonna stay here forever if you don't get them out the ground, boy!"

"I'm working." Malcolm clenched his teeth and bent over the hoe again.

"You know, last year I went down to a sale they had in Johnson City," Planter said. He

leaned into the rake, his angular body comple-
menting its dark angle. "It was supposed to be
a sale of stuff the sheriff had. He had a set of
slave chains. Everybody round here knew where
they came from. They came from the Lewis family. They been in our family since the first one
of us put his feet in this soil.

"We knowed the sheriff's office had them, but
we never thought we could get them back."

"What happened after you bought them?"

"Hey! Who's telling this story?"

"You are, Planter." Malcolm couldn't stop the
smile that came to his face.

"Passed down from generation to generation,"
Planter said. "Then, during the civil rights time,
we lost them. The sheriff got hold of them, and
he held them. They brought them out for sale,
long with some stolen radios, a shotgun, and
some other stolen stuff that nobody claimed.
They were trying to raise money for a gym for
the police department. That was a good cause."

"You recognized the chains?"

"Yeah, I recognized them. But I had to pay
dear to get them. You know what they called
them?"

"What?"

"Black memo—Lord what did they call them
things?" Planter pushed his hat to the back of
his head. "Black something or the other—memorabilia or something."

"Memorabilia?" Malcolm asked. "That's like

things that remind people of historical events?"

"Yeah, I guess that was it," Planter said. "Anyway, they had a bidding for it, and I had to give two hundred and nine dollars to get them."

"But you got them," Malcolm said. "A black person should have them."

"A black person? Those shackles didn't rob us of being black, son, they robbed us of being human. Who should own them is a human being." Planter shielded his eyes from the sun. " 'Course it would've helped if the human being had a little more money than I had."

Planter turned away and went back to picking the sweet potatoes. Malcolm asked him if they had other memorabilia for sale, but he didn't answer, and Malcolm figured he didn't want to.

They broke for a lunch that was bigger than the dinners Malcolm had in New York. Someone said that they would probably be finished by the next afternoon, and how good it was to be able to bring in a good crop.

Malcolm saw Shep at the end of the table and a woman with an enormous bosom telling him that he should eat more. Malcolm smiled at his cousin and was happy to see him smile back.

There were at least twenty-five children running around, and they didn't seem to care that they had never seen each other before as they played endless games and had endless fights, which nobody seemed to mind. Some of the kids were dark, some were light, but to the grown-ups the only thing that mattered was that they were all part of the Lewis family.

Most of the conversation around the table was people finding out how they were related and talking about what they were doing. Some people spoke of the resort, and it seemed that three of the families that still lived on Curry were going to work at the resort, and three other families were going to move to Curry to help. Other people were going to do some work in promotion in other parts of the country.

It was a silly thing to do, to start laughing just when the lunch dishes were being cleared, but Malcolm couldn't help himself. His father asked him why he was laughing, and he tried to stop, saying that it was nothing, but Planter wouldn't have any of it.

"I can't be working with no fools out there," Planter said, pouring himself another glass of lemonade from the tall pitcher. "What you laughing at?"

"I can just look around and see who the farm people are and who the city people are," Malcolm said. "I don't see anybody from the city hopping up to get ready to go back out into the field."

"Child, you can say that again," a dark-skinned woman wearing brand-new jeans said.

"Oh, when you get used to it, it's real good," a man said. "You bring in your crops, and you can see what you did for the year. Man, that's a good feeling."

Several of the city people exchanged glances, figuring out just who they all were. It was Planter who jumped up and said that he thought he heard a sweet potato calling his name, as he put on his hat to go back out to the field.

By the time that the bell rang calling them in for dinner, Malcolm was in serious pain. His arms were so tired that he could hardly lift the sacks of sweet potatoes, even just to put them in a row for the truck to pick up. He looked at Planter, saw the smile on the big man's face, and looked away. A moment later he felt Planter's arm around his shoulder.

"A man's name is what he makes it," Planter said. "Malcolm is a good, strong name. You made it that way, the same way you're making Lewis a good, strong name."

"I'm trying," Malcolm said. "I'm trying."

They had sandwiches for dinner and a small salad. For dessert they had peach cobbler and ice cream. After dinner some of the Lewises, the ones who weren't too tired to think, sat around to talk. Malcolm took a quick shower and sat on the back porch and listened as the older people talked. They talked sense, and family, stringing memories together into a kind of music they wouldn't all remember, but would all understand. As soon as it was dark, he found the bed he had the night before. The young boy was already there.

"Tell me a story?" the boy asked.

"I don't know any stories," Malcolm said.

"If you don't tell me a story then you stink!" the boy said.

"Yo, man, what's your name?"

"Stephen Vernon Lewis, the second," the boy announced proudly.

"Look, Stephen, you tell me a story first, then I'll tell you one, all right?"

"I don't know any stories," the boy said. "I'm just a kid."

"Then you stink."

"If I tell you one, then will you tell me one?"

"Right." Malcolm eased out of his pants.

"Okay. There was this king named Mufaro." Stephen crossed his legs as he started the story. "And he had two beautiful daughters. . . ."

The next thing Malcolm knew was the dream in which he was fighting against the heavy-weight champion of the world and being beaten while going through his pockets looking for the key to get out of the ring.

The morning came too soon, and none of his parts worked.

"C'mon, partner." Planter's grinning face was over his. "You going to eat some breakfast this morning?"

"It can't be morning already," Malcolm said.

"It's morning, young brother," Planter said. "And the sweet potatoes is calling. I think they singing a song just for you. Hey, you're a musician. You ever play a sweet potato song?"

Malcolm lifted his head, looked at the window, and saw that it was indeed morning. He had to look twice to see if something was holding his arm down when he tried to get up. He hurt. He ached. He threw his legs over the side of the bed, slipped into his pants, and forced himself out of the room.

The rows of sweet potatoes seemed longer than they had been the day before, and his feet burned in his sneakers.

"We gonna be finished tomorrow for sure," Planter was saying. "If it don't rain."

Malcolm looked up at the sky. There wasn't a cloud in sight. He took a breath and bent over the hoe again.

It was an hour into the morning when he heard the low screech and the sound of women's voices off to his right. He looked over and saw that someone had fallen down. Malcolm glanced at Planter and saw the old man looking intently, his eyes narrowed as the women and some of the men rushed to the side of the woman who was pregnant. Malcolm looked as they gathered around her, then saw her talking and the women helping her up. One man lifted her and carried her toward the house. She looked over his shoulder and waved toward Planter.

"She going to be all right?" Malcolm asked.

"She's just fine," Planter said. "Ready to bring a vessel of hope into the world."

"Yeah," Malcolm said. "I guess so."

"Even the sweet potatoes like that," Planter said.

"I ever tell you I hated sweet potatoes?" Malcolm asked.

"Do tell, young brother." Planter grinned. "Do tell!"

It was at dinner that Malcolm found out that Jennie, the woman he had first met when they reached Curry, was a doctor. It was she who had taken care of the pregnant woman and had gone with her to the hospital in Johnson City.

"It's a girl!" Luvenia Lewis said. "And to tell you the truth, I hope that none of you knot-head boys get to be president before she gets a chance!"

"I'm going to be the first president who was a cowboy, an astronaut, and a president," said one little long-headed boy at the end of the table.

"All that?" Malcolm said, without looking up.

"Right," the boy answered. "And not a stink!"

Malcolm looked up and saw the boy he was sleeping with. He made a mental note to pinch him in his sleep when he went to bed that night.

There was a half-acre left to go the next day when Planter, who was telling Malcolm the difference between long- and short-grain rice, suddenly stopped and straightened up. Malcolm, bent over, looked up and saw Shep on his hands and knees between the rows. He was throwing up. Jennie Lewis went to him, and Malcolm put his hoe down.

"Wait a minute, son," Planter said. He put a big hand on Malcolm's shoulder.

Jennie got down on her knees next to Shep and put her arm around his shoulder. She was talking to him, whispering in his ear.

"Planter, he's got a problem," Malcolm said.

"We got those problems down here the same as you got them in New York," he said. "We know what they are."

Malcolm looked at the other people in the field. They had all stopped working and were looking toward Jennie and Shep.

"What's she doing?" Malcolm asked.

"Trying to get him to stand up," Planter

said. "Trying to get him to take that first step on his own."

The shadows were short. Malcolm's shadow was less than half his size. Malcolm looked at Shep, then away. The sky was clear. In the distance a jet liner left a long, white vapor trail that spread as the plane moved away.

"Planter, I think he needs help," Malcolm said.

"Yeah, he do," Planter said. "And his help starts from within himself."

The first move was just Shep pushing himself up off his hands, so that he knelt on his knees. Jennie was kneeling with him. Shep's shoulders lifted and fell, as if he were taking a deep breath, and then he stood.

"All right, brother!" a man called out. "All right!"

A woman came to him with a cup of water, and he drank it. Then Jennie went back and brought him his hoe.

Malcolm was glad that Shep had got back on his feet. He wanted with all of his heart for Shep to make it through just this one reunion, maybe just this one day, maybe just one more row of sweet potatoes. Malcolm looked around and saw that the work had picked up again. They were all glad to see Shep on his feet.

For the rest of the afternoon, Malcolm's hoe got heavier by the minute. Planter never stopped talking, but by three o'clock Malcolm was too tired to listen to him. To their right Jennie worked next to Shep. He didn't look good, and he wasn't getting up many sweet potatoes, but he kept his hoe moving.

It was four thirty in the afternoon when the last bag of sweet potatoes was loaded onto the trucks, and they brought their tools in from the fields. There were more hugs and some quiet talk.

They were proud of themselves, the Lewis family. Malcolm could see it in the way they walked, in the way some of them looked back at the fields, in the way they looked at each other. He was proud of himself, too. Every ache in his body said that he had done something, that he had helped to move them all to a different place. He looked around for Shep, but Jennie had taken him inside to lie down for a while.

Planter found him. "You're all right, boy," he said. "Yes, you're just about all right!"

He went to see Shep before he turned in. He was sitting up, sipping soup. Jennie was still with him. She was talking about how skinny he was.

"He's not fat enough to season greens!"

"How you feeling?" Malcolm asked.

"I'm kicking," Shep said. "Kicking slow, though."

"If I ever see a sweet potato back in Harlem, I'm going to mug it," Malcolm said.

Shep smiled.

That night the little boy found someone else

to sleep with, and Malcolm lay alone in the bed. He thought of Shep and all the people watching him in the field, hoping that he would have the strength to keep going. Knowing that he was part of their strength, and that they would be his, if he let them.

He thought of the woman Jennie, who was a doctor, and wondered what she had gone through to become a doctor. How strong had she been? How strong was Planter? Planter with his white hair and his grin and his kidding. What had he lived through?

The next day belonged to Luvenia Lewis. She introduced a man from the bank who explained how they were making shares in the resort they were going to build.

"In a very real way," the brown-skinned, balding man said, "you are at the beginning of what I feel will be a great adventure. I think you can look forward to something really great."

"We can look forward, and we can look back, too," Luvenia said.

"Amen to that," Planter said.

"Amen," the long-headed boy said.

Malcolm gave him a look and the boy stuck out his tongue and mouthed the words "you stink!"

EPILOGUE

Deepak Singh rocked slowly, his brown hands hardly moving over the small *tabla* between his legs, the slow rhythm seeming more an extension of his heartbeat than the result of his playing. They were at Brown University, and the student crowd had purchased close to two hundred tickets, and they had given away almost a hundred, just in case. It was the first time that String Theory had played a major college, and it had gone well, very well.

Malcolm liked his sound, liked the way the richness of the low flute seemed to fill the auditorium, seemed to caress the young audience.

He looked out to his audience as he played, saw that they were mostly white, but that there were Asians and African Americans and Latinos and Indians as well. It was a good crowd, a warm crowd. They had already played well, and there was the nagging feeling deep in his gut that he shouldn't push it, that he should back off, leave well enough alone, and enjoy the moment.

He closed his eyes and thought of the group,

of Deepak playing his heart out, of Daoud and George and all of them, and of Jenn, sitting on the small stool next to her cello, waiting to come in. She was a challenge, a challenge that always brought out the best in him. They had practiced together the whole week, with her memorizing his compositions, adding touches of Chinese classical music that created an almost unbearable tension. Somehow they all seemed to understand that the music, their music, was about who they were and the search for who they wanted to be.

The music had to mean something for all of them, each according to his or her needs. For Malcolm it meant remembering an old man he had met on Curry Island.

His mother had called him and told him the bad news that Planter had died.

He had flown to Curry for the funeral, had sat in the third car, too far from Planter's body, too far from the grin and from the strength of the man. After the funeral, he had gone to the Lewis place and had seen the surveyors lining up their poles where the old slave quarters had been. There were going to be tennis courts behind the hotel. Planter would have liked that, thinking about those courts and the people that had walked on that ground. He would have liked the one field they hadn't touched and wouldn't touch.

Around the Glory Field they had built a stone walk with live oaks on either side. In the field itself they planted azaleas. It was a small field, and Aunt Luvenia had said the architects didn't put up too much of a fight when the family didn't want to change the field into a miniature golf course.

In the days after the funeral, Malcolm was making the rounds of the colleges. He had decided to major in history, this despite his mother's insistence that he *looked* like a doctor. He didn't know what he wanted to do with String Theory. The group was better than he thought it ever could be, but they were going to different colleges. They had talked about playing together summers or at least getting together now and then just to jam. Then they were invited to play at two colleges, Oberlin and Brown, and they were all reluctant to give up what they had created.

A week after the funeral, on the day before String Theory was supposed to leave New York by train for Brown, Aunt Luvenia called him and asked if he had received the package.

"What package?"

"Planter's granddaughter sent you something," his aunt had said. "She sent me a picture of him, and I guess she sent you one, too."

The thought of having a picture of Planter made Malcolm smile. He hoped that it would be one of him grinning as only he could, the straw hat pushed far back on his head, the look in his eye that said he knew things that only a man named after a boat stolen in the Civil War could.

But when the package came, it wasn't a picture. Malcolm knew by the weight and by the shape of it what it was. It was the shackles.

They had been passed from generation to generation, and now Planter had entrusted them to him. In the quiet of his room, on a day in which the rain beat with a fury against his Harlem window, he lifted the shackles, felt their weight, ran his fingers along the smoothness of the well-worn iron. He had even thought about putting them around his ankles, but knew that it would never be the same. It wasn't his to experience, only his to know about, to imagine how hard it had been. The weight of the shackles gave substance to all the people who had worn them, and who had triumphed in spite of them. They gave weight, even, to those who had been broken by them, or by the invisible shackles they had found along their way.

Malcolm played. It was a hard song of sunrise to sunset. A song of pain. A song with echoes of an African past that had landed centuries ago on the shores of Curry Island and that was still alive.

Malcolm thought of his parents and of the man, Henry Epps, whose death was mentioned on the postcard. He thought of Shep and was glad that he had taken his cousin down to Curry, down to the Glory Field. For Shep, if ever so distant, was a part of that field. Shep was, and so was he.

Behind him Jenn was doing wonderful things

with the melody. Deepak allowed the rhythm to reflect his own quickened pulse. They looked at Malcolm, and when he turned to them, the glad lightness of his heart evident in his eyes, they each reached deeper in themselves to find him.

Malcolm played with Planter in his mind and in his heart. Somehow the old man had known that he would bridge the gap between them, even as he had somehow known that the shackles would be safe with the sweet potato picker he had met briefly in the Glory Field. It had been a good harvest.

About the Author

WALTER DEAN MYERS is the author of over 50 acclaimed works of fiction, nonfiction, and poetry. He wrote the award-winning novels *Somewhere in the Darkness* and *Fallen Angels*. His nonfiction books include *Malcolm X: By Any Means Necessary* and *Now Is Your Time*, a history of African Americans.

A native of Harlem, Mr. Myers now lives with his family in Jersey City, New Jersey.